DADDY'S

CONCUBINES

– AND ME!

To Al & Colleen,

Enjoyed meeting you on our

Mexico trip! Bessie Y. Reid

by

BESSIE YANG REID 楊

佩

怡
3/23/02

As Told To

ALLAN L. REID

(Her Honorable Husband)

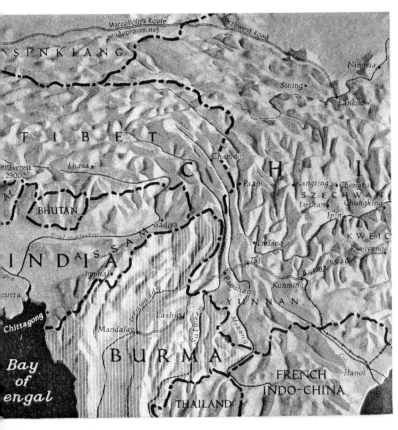

Map by National Geographic Cartographic Division

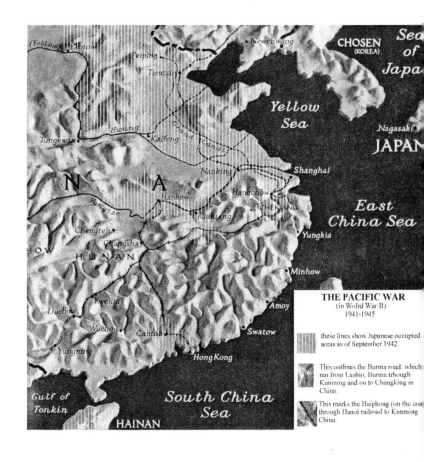

THE PACIFIC WAR
(in Wolrd War II)
1941-1945

these lines show Japanese occupied areas as of September 1942.

This outlines the Burma road, which ran from Lashio, Burma trhough Kunming and on to Chungking in China.

This marks the Haiphong (on the coa through Hanoi railroad to Kunming China.

ISBN: 1-58721-272-2

The author gratefully acknowledges the capable professional assistance of these
three 1st Books Library staff members in the physical preparation of this
attractive book: Joseph Kerschbaum, Production Representative, Jamie White,
Production, and Tony Potts, Cover Design.

1stBooks - rev. 6/28/00

SOME SPECIAL FEATURES
OF THIS BOOK

The basic reason for writing this historically and culturally accurate personal memoir book, and why its publication will be of real and lasting literary and historical value, is noted in second and third paragraphs from the top on page 74.

An explanation of why "Daddy" is used both in the title and frequently throughout the book is to be found in second paragraph from the top on page 99.

Today's illicit infusion of hard drugs into the U.S. and Canada is still minor compared to the British pushing of opium onto China and her people during the 18th century. In 1906 the Chinese government made a supreme effort to get rid of the curse of national opium addiction. They were so successful that by 1917 the opium problem in China had ceased to be a major concern! How did they do it? Can North Americans learn from their success, and apply China's methods to solve their own drug problem? Read about it on page 113.

Far too few North Americans, of any age, know much about China's considerable contribution to the Allied victory in World War II. Fighting virtually alone, with little material assistance from the outside world, China kept over one million veteran Japanese combat troops tied down throughout that war. Had these troops been free to invade Australia or India, the eventual outcome of hostilities in the Far East and Southeast Asia might have been far different. "CONCUBINES" explains China's significant military contribution during 1941-45.

The little known full story of how the 15,000 or so Jewish refugees from Europe who fled to Shanghai during 1937-39 were welcomed and later fared in that city's Jewish Ghetto, is briefly but interestingly described on pages 194-196. Jewish readers will welcome this informative material.

DEDICATED TO

My Father

T.Y. Yang
(The Old Rogue)

and

My Mother

Alice Yuen Yang
(A Victim of Custom and Tradition)

CONTENTS

A NOTE TO READERS

Events in these pages take place between August 13, 1937 when Japanese troops overran Shanghai, China, through the end of World War II in 1945 to February 19, 1949, three months before that city was taken over by the Communists.

While most of these events are centered in Shanghai, others take place in different parts of China and Southeast Asia.

Prior to January 1, 1979, Latin alphabet standardization of Chinese personal and place names was based on the long established Wade-Giles system. All such words appearing throughout these pages follow that traditional system.

Effective that date a new, simplified, standardized romanization system called Pinyin was prescribed by the Peoples Republic of China for use in English speaking countries. Many (but not all) of the traditional Wade-Giles spellings and pronunciations were changed, some considerably, some slightly, under this new system.

To help avoid reader confusion, transliterations in the more contemporary Pinyin follow in parenthesis when a Chinese name or place is first introduced – if required! As a further aid, an alphabetical Romanized Chinese Name and Place Index of these appears at the end of the book.

Allan L. Reid

Chapter 1

"Hurry, hurry," shouted Daddy excitedly from just inside the doorway of our house. "We will all have to go to the new house together now! The Japanese soldiers will soon be here. Everyone into the car!"

As if to accent the urgency of his words that hot humid morning of August 13, 1937 in Shanghai – the sound of artillery firing in the distance seemed to intensify, and dirty gray-black smoke filled the sky above the city to the east and south of us where Japanese warplanes could clearly be seen whirling, dipping, and bombing without aerial opposition as they had since before dawn.

"I said hurry – everyone into the car now," Daddy nervously shouted again above the din, as he gave the last of the group to exit the house a not-so-helpful rough shove.

That someone happened to be Ah Foo, our matronly, middle-aged Yang family cook, whose full wig, as she lurched for-

1

ward, slipped to one side exposing half of her totally bald shiny head. As she stumbled to regain her posture; the caged green and yellow parrot she was carrying in one hand let out a series of wild shrieks and flapped its wings in panic. As its feathers flew in every direction, a big wok filled with kitchen utensils slipped from under her other arm and its contents spilled haphazardly across the front steps. The two family maids who had gone out just ahead of her dropped their loads and scrambled to help pick them up.

The car itself, a slightly battered black 1934 Chevrolet four door sedan, parked just inside the driveway to our home near Christ the King Church off Rue Bourgeat in the French Concession district of the city, was the center of even more confusion. Behind it, Rue Bourgeat was filled with a rapidly moving, jostling procession of humanity – civilians with huge bundles and armed and unarmed Chinese soldiers – all rushing westward. Intermingled with them were assorted motor vehicles, bicycles, horse and hand-drawn wagons and carts.

"No, no, it's our mother's place to sit in the front seat" shrilled my fourteen year old brother Ping Liang (Paul) from inside the car, as two of Number Two Concubine Ching's four boys tried to grab that choice space of female rank of honor for their mother.

"And grandmother should sit up front too, "my sixteen year old sister Sou Sie (Suzie) chimed in firmly, as the little seventy year old lady hobbled frantically and painfully toward them on her tiny, claw-like bound feet, supported on one side by my twenty three year old oldest brother Guo Liang (no English name), and on the other by my ten year old sister Pei Cheung (Betty). I remember clearly the paintears that filled her eyes; but, sick with fear, she uttered not a sound.

My frail and sickly mother, and Number One Concubine Silver Lotus stood patiently to one side, along with me, as Suzie and Number Two Concubine's other two boys crowded into the back seat with their bundles and personal possessions.

At age seven, as the youngest child and a girl at that, I was by every count the least important member of the Yang family, I

2

held firmly to mother's hand clutching my new two month old Shih-tzu puppy Mong-Fu (Ferocious Tiger), tightly under my other arm and, with him, just trembled nervously in place waiting to see what would happen next.

"What do we do now Father?" asked Guo Liang, we can't all fit into the car!" Daddy who had just herded everyone down the driveway stood dumbfounded at the logistical impasse that suddenly demanded his resolving. All eyes were on him as he did a quick headcount. Everyone was present and accounted for, but obviously seventeen humans counting himself, to say nothing of all the bundles, one excited parrot and a small trembling puppy weren't going to fit.

But something had to be done – and fast – because sounds of shooting were now coming closer from what seemed to be only two blocks south on Avenue Joffre. The mob on that broad avenue headed west toward Chung San Road and open country had suddenly thinned and those left were now dropping their bundles and running.

It wouldn't have taken much brains to figure out that all of us couldn't fit at once into one small car, and my father hadn't planned on this situation at all. Actually, it was an unfortunate combination of events that had now come to a head at exactly ten A.M. on that Saturday morning that were – very shortly – to give him and the rest of us the greatest scare of our collective lives, and his greatest ever loss of face in front of us – his family and other household members.

It had all started innocently enough, with his decision to move all of us in shifts from our current house to our newly built home some six miles away on Peach Blossom Lane, a quiet residential street near Chiao Tung and Futan (Fudan) Universities not far from the intersection of Avenues Joffre and Haig at the edge of the French Concession. Filled with pride, authoritative and lordly in command, his idea was to get us all over there by early afternoon. Most of our furniture had preceded us that day before.

In his "moving plan," different elements of his household were to be shifted at different intervals so as to avoid confusion and mingling with each other. His idea was to drive mother, grandmother, and some of us younger Yang children over first, then Number One Concubine and the rest of us Yang children, then Number Two Concubine and her four boys, then Ah Foo, the two maids and all the household bundles. Four trips would do it – and since the God of Good Luck had always been with him, he undoubtedly assumed that all would go smoothly as planned.

He certainly didn't doubt his ability to manage any sort of family or household problem, for his supreme authority over this large household group rested on a cunningly devised system of "divide, keep segments weak, set all policy, and hold tight to the family purse strings." Up to this point in time he had enjoyed complete success in solving all such problems.

But Daddy's control, the way he ruled his mixedbag family and household and exercised his authority, was based on exerting the force of His Majestic Presence on one "weak link" at a time. In spite of his supreme power over all of us, his task of commanding order out of often real and always possible chaos hadn't always been easy, in spite of his relative success to date.

As his own number of children and servants had grown over the years, and Mother had become increasingly ill with tuberculosis, his problems of control had steadily mounted. They began to get more complex when, shortly before my birth, he brought Number One Concubine Silver Lotus into the house and installed her on the second floor. Old Chinese custom permitted this, but the act also posed some practical organizational and managerial problems. For instance, old Chinese custom also dictated that he do the proper thing and not affront my mother by having her and the concubine meet at any time if at all possible.

Living up to this for instance old Chinese custom became even more complicated after Number Two Concubine Ching and her four boys (none of whom could claim my father as theirs) moved in the previous year. His problem then became that of trying to keep the three household segments; our Yang family,

Number One Concubine, and Number Two Concubine and her family from running into each other within our home.

This problem was simply unsolvable due to the fact that there were far too many living souls in much too small a house.

This situation had led to his building the new and much larger home, and to his decision that we would move there this specific day.

Other more important decisions had been taken elsewhere however, bringing on another event that greatly changed that day, our lives and Daddy's family moving schedule. The history books now call that day "Bloody Saturday", and before it was over, not many miles away from us in other parts of the city, thousands of helpless Chinese men, and women and children were slaughtered by merciless Japanese ground troops and by cruel Japanese bombing of the largely undefended old Chinese settlement areas of Native City and Nantao among others.

I had heard my father and others in our family and household talk apprehensively of the fierce fighting that had broken out between Japanese troops and Chinese forces in Peking (Beijing) a few weeks earlier on July 7. This outbreak, known to history as the Battle of Marco Polo Bridge, commenced the full-scale hostilities between China and Japan known as The Second Sino-Japanese war (1937-45), that lasted until the end of World War II.

The significance of that battle was not to dawn on most Shanghai residents until our family moving day, however. In the early morning hours of that Saturday, the marines of what was known as the Imperial Japanese Naval Landing Party swarmed out of their Hongkew Barracks, north of Soochow (Suzhou) Creek. They had only two miles to cover to reach the main Shanghai business district, and as the day wore on consolidated that hold on the entire city and outlying areas. Their troops, planes and ships on the river crushed all resistance and spread death and destruction quickly throughout our city.

Daddy had gotten an inkling of what was going to happen the evening before when, through business friends, he learned that the Japanese had announced that their troops would be moving into our section of the city early the next day. Not unlike the Japanese commander of those troops he immediately began laying his final plans and issuing orders for our move based on this new situation.

It was probably easier, for the Japanese commander to issue orders and to move his several thousand troops quickly than for my father to issue the orders and to supervise the logistics of collecting and moving our assorted family and household group.

For one thing, the Japanese commander could assemble his key staff officers together and give them their marching orders at one time. If not carried out as ordered he could have the offending officers executed on the spot. This led to their paying very careful attention to what he said, and to their making certain that his orders were carried out to the letter – without argument or question.

Daddy's command system was more complicated. It involved issuing orders separately to the three major women in his life, to mother (who supervised grandmother, us Yang children, and Ah Foo and the two maids), to Number Two Concubine who was responsible for her four boys, and to Number One Concubine.

He had to issue his orders to each separately and individually, for under old Chinese custom everyone had to save face by not meeting together at the same time and place. This system worked well enough in peacetime, when time meant little and Father was in complete control of internal and external events. But now, for the first time, his separate crisis situation orders, excitedly issued in the midst of considerable confusion had not been clearly understood by all concerned.

This had led to mixed up execution of his orders early in the morning of this day of our move. So much so that the four separate trip plans had early on disintegrated into mass household confusion bordering on near hysteria! As pressures and tensions had mounted throughout the early morning he had acted and sounded like a War Lord of old as, with the sounds of war in the background, he barked conflicting orders excitedly throughout one minor household crisis after another.

Confronted by this newest problem, he wavered in indecision. As he did so, custom, shouts, shoving, tears, cries, screeches and a few small barks from my puppy intermingled about our family Chevy as age, courtesy, rank, and what have you claimed their due for what was obviously to be impossible seating arrangements. Father's sense of order, and his authority seemed to wilt for the moment in face of the tensions among his now panic-struck household group. As we all tried unsuccessfully to crowd into the car amidst pushing and hysterical arguments, we almost forgot about all the external excitement and commotion.

Suddenly, all seemed much quieter out on Rue Bourgeat, which was now nearly empty of human or vehicular traffic. All we could see was a handful of Tonkinese (natives of French Indochina) police and French Foreign Legionnaires, who were stationed in the French Concession, at their guard post half a block down the street. They stood motionless – watching the last few panic stricken civilians, intermixed with a few Chinese soldiers, surge past them headed west at full run.

Then, except for those at the guardhouse, the street was suddenly deserted, and an almost complete silence fell upon the scene. It was like being in the eye of a storm.

And an eye in the storm it was! For, surging up our street from its nearby intersection with Avenue Joffre, headed directly toward us at a dog trot, came two entire infantry companies of Japanese marines. With Rising Sun flags flying, long bayonets fixed, in full battle dress, led by three tanks, they looked quite fierce and determined. Fortunately, no shots had been fired by the fleeing Chinese soldiers, none were being fired yet by the rapidly advancing Japanese, and the nearby French Legionnaires and Tonkinese police obviously weren't about to start any shooting themselves. Our group about the car simply stood or sat quietly, staring wide-eyed and literally frozen with fear!

7

Then the wave of Japanese marines was upon us, around us; and one creaking, clanking tank was headed right at us!

I'll never forget that tank. It was a dinky little two-man thing with big spiky treads and a stubby cannon with what seemed to be a two-foot gaping mouth pointed right at me and my puppy, which I almost crushed as I clutched it tightly to my chest.

It had a horrible loud and snarling motor, and kept lurching from one tread to the other as it navigated half-blindly up the street toward us. It ground to a full stop in front of the entrance to our driveway. A round steel door on top of the turret suddenly opened, plopped backwards with a loud clank, and a perspiring leather helmeted Japanese face with bloodshot eyes over a bushy beard popped out and shouted unintelligibly at us. All this happened seemingly in a split second of time; leaving a picture of the event, etched so deeply by fear into my young mind, that I will never forget it. Then it rumbled off in its pursuit, leaving us dumb, speechless, and gagging in a cloud of acrid black exhaust fumes.

Suddenly, we were all snapped to alert attention by another single picture event – for an immaculate Japanese officer, with long Samurai sword dangling down to the bottom of his highly polished boots, was suddenly beside us shouting at Daddy. He was gesturing furiously, first at our family car, and then to a motionless Japanese command car half a block back down the street.

Fractured, shouted, tormented, mixed words of Japanese, Chinese and English passed quickly between them; and my father's face alternately flushed red with anger and white with fear as the officer insolently made his wishes plain. He was taking over our Chevy to replace his broken down military vehicle, and was taking over NOW, and no back talk, or Father's family would lose one father on the spot – beheaded!

What else could Daddy do except force a sickly smile, bow low in an act of obeisance and say "of course, Sir, take it, and thank you Sir!" The officer hastily scribbled a few words on a piece of paper and rudely thrust it at him; bad humoredly saying that it was a receipt and that our family would eventually get our car back upon presenting it, "once order was restored," to Japanese Military Headquarters at Hongkew Barracks.

Daddy's face blanched white with humiliation at the arrogant way the officer had spoken to him, and from the inward shame of his "kowtowing" – the showing of submissive deference in return – in front of us.

Then, while we all watched silently, helplessly, powerlessly; that Japanese officer plus three other officers and their driver, piled into our Chevy and, with Samurai sword hilts sticking out of every window, roared off after the tank and bayonet-waving, Banzai-shouting infantry troops. The commandeering of our car had taken only a few minutes.

Relative calm reigned over our immediate area once again, broken mainly by commands and sounds of a Japanese marine machine gun squad setting up on the corner across from and facing the nearby small group of French Legionnaires and their Tonkinese police comrades. These French speaking individuals nervously lighted cigarettes, whispered for awhile among themselves and then quietly drifted off in pairs to their own headquarters and barracks.

Our Yang household group and pets were suddenly all alone, facing the empty neighborhood shops and homes across the street, dumbly staring at the Japanese marines and their machine gun. They (and IT) ominously quiet but nonthreateningly stared back. The immediate crisis was over.

As always is the case after crisis events such as that we just gone through, life must go on, and our move was still the goal. Daddy, once again in command of himself and us, quietly directed Guo Liang to get the little wagon from behind the house that Ah Foo used when buying food at the marketplace. He nestled grandmother in it amidst some pillows with her pathetic tiny, crippled feet sticking forward out over the shaft. He then directed Paul to leave the parrot and my puppy with some nearby neighbors who were still cowering with fear within their home, and had the rest of us put all nonessential bundles and possessions back into the house.

9

Then, carrying what we could, we all set off in a straggling group past the Japanese machine gun squad, to join the mainstream of other refugees, on the long six mile hike to Peach Blossom Lane and our new home.

Daddy said little as he led us on our way, stopping now and then to issue orders, and to see to it that the boys helped the older, younger, and weaker among us. His own special burden was his mother, my grandmother, whom he pulled along by means of a rope looped over his shoulder and tied to the shaft of the little wooden wagon.

As we trudged slowly along we uneasily eyed the other refugees, the smoke in the distance, and the warplanes overhead. And we listened with apprehension and wonderment to the sporadic sound of gunfire and bombs in the distance. While the smoke was thicker over the wharf and godown area along the Whangpoo (Huangpu) River several miles east of us, and nearby Native City, the firing seemed to be less intense than earlier in the morning, and there were fewer planes in the sky. We felt lucky that there hadn't yet been any bombing or serious fighting in our part of the city, although frequent sounds of nearby scattered rifle or machine gun fire all about us marked the early route of our passage.

By 2:00 P.M. both the spirit and energy of our little group had wilted to practically nothing under the hot sun. Daddy ordered a rest halt under some streetside trees, and had us take off our shoes and socks so he could check blisters on our sore and aching feet.

As we spread our sticky toes to let some air in between them to cool the burning sensation, a sidewalk vendor suddenly appeared from nowhere and set up a little cart-stand across the street to sell cool sour plum juice.

"Oh, Daddy, can we have some," I begged him beseechingly, "I am so thirsty!" Betty, Paul and Concubine Ching's boys added their pleas to mine, so Father sent the boys over to get tall glassfuls for all of us.

I usually got a tummy ache from sour plum juice and really didn't like it for that reason. But now, as I poured it down my parched throat, I felt as though I had never tasted anything so delicious and refreshing.

As we drank, Daddy went around amongst us putting some dashes of salt from the salt shaker that Ah Foo had been carrying into our glasses of sour plum juice. He told us that the salt would help us perspire more easily and thus help keep us cooler.

When all had finished their drink, after a few more moments of rest, he ordered us to our feet where all except Mother shouldered our loads and painfully shuffled off once more. She helped him resettle Grandmother in her little wagon. He then once again looped the wagon's dragrope over his by now raw red shoulder and wearily moved out, pulling it behind him, shouting at the Yang boys to help their mother with her bundles, and for all of us to stay close together.

We were by now almost halfway to our new home, and after traversing many back streets, were moving slowly up a stretch of Avenue Joffre which ran westward from the famous Bund (Zhongshan Road) riverfront street area of the city. Here it was a rather wide avenue lined with several large stores, churches, and office buildings. No Japanese soldiers were in sight, but tall bearded, red-turbaned British led Sikh policemen (from India) directed the heavy vehicular and human traffic that filled the avenue.

It was quite a west-moving scene! Electric tramcars, buses, and cars were packed to overflowing with people. Men, women, and children were pulling small wagons or carts or pushing large wheelbarrows piled high with tremendous loads, and coolies rushed along staggering under the weight of bales or baskets suspended from each end of long shoulder poles. Large two-wheeled trucking carts, each pulled by six or eight sweating coolies leaning deeply forward into their pull ropes, jostled for space with rickshaws, bicycles, and those on foot.

In colorful contrast to the attractive window displays of some larger avenue store fronts, were the narrow cross streets with their forest of brightly colored banners, on which was painted in large gold characters the description of goods carried within the small shops they represented or announcements of

11

bargains. At various crowded corners, enterprising street vendors with portable kitchens suspended from shoulder poles were offering their wares to those who stopped briefly for a quick hot bite of food.

Some blocks past the American School area, we turned into a not-so-crowded secondary street that would lead to Peach Blossom Lane. Although the afternoon heat was humid and stultifying, and we were all very tired, we felt fortunate to be away from the really frightening mob that had packed Avenue Joffre. This quieter street was pleasant and tree lined, and since the shooting and explosions sounded less intense and further away than they had earlier, we felt more relaxed. We also gained new strength from the thought that we would soon reach the relative safety and security of our new home.

Suddenly, the sky above seemed filled with a loud off-stroke, tinny, washing machine sounding noise; and a small, greenish colored, open cockpit Japanese army light observation plane skimmed overhead almost at tree top level.

"Find some cover, duck, get behind a tree or doorway, it may machine gun us!" shouted Daddy, as he jerked the little wagon off the street to get behind a nearby round concrete sign-post. As grandmother hung grimly to the sides of the wagon to keep from toppling off, the rest of us dropped our bundles and dove for whatever close-at-hand cover we could find. Once again Ah Foo's wok and its contents flew into the air and clattered off in all direction, but she clapped her wig on firmly with one hand as she scrambled behind a large two-wheeled cart parked nearby. I flopped down flat on the pavement beside Daddy and Grandmother, bumping my nose in the process. As it bled profusely, I pressed close to the earth face down.

The plane banked so sharply it almost stood on its wing and zoomed back toward us. As it started its turn the afternoon sun rays suddenly hit the huge red insignia-balls painted on the upper wingtip and the fuselage side nearest us, and they seemed to grow larger, redder, and very evil looking as the sun rays flitted across them during the brief period of the turn.

The plane's wheels actually touched the top of one tree as it came rapidly back toward us. As it passed overhead, one wing dipped slightly. Peering up at it from under my arm, which I had thrown over my forehead, I could clearly see the pilot's face behind his goggles sweeping up with a cool and arrogant stare.

As we, and the other people on the street, flattened ourselves and cowered in fear, it banked steeply once again over us, then whined off westward into the setting sun. It was all over in a few minutes, but our collective group nerves were so shattered that all the women and younger children, including me, were sobbing in fear as we picked ourselves up.

Daddy's face was white with shock, his eyes were burning black, and his teeth were clenched tight in anger as he slowly rose and shook a trembling fist toward the departing plane. I was standing close beside him and was stunned at his expression – I had never seen him look like that before.

What thoughts passed through the mind of my proud, irascible, stubborn, normally self-confident father during those moments? Although I was too young and frightened to know or really care at the moment, I did wonder.

And in later years, after the long, memory-searing period of Japanese military occupation of our city, of being forced to study hated Japanese at school, after suffering repeated periods of food shortages, fear and despair; then wartime victory; young womanhood, and study and eventual residence abroad – as I often relived those moments – I finally came to understand the depth of humiliation, anger, frustration, and fear of the unknown his look had reflected.

That strong, distressed look on his face as the plane sped away personified the collective feelings and plight of poor, powerless, crushed China herself at that particular moment of time and history.

For my father, the hectic events of the day, capped by this most recent heart stopping experience, was but the latest of a series of acts by foreigners, Japanese especially, that had dogged him and the other 400 million people of once mighty and proud China since his very birth.

Born in 1889, his early childhood memories revolved around the chaos and internal revolution resulting from the practical and spirit-shattering defeat of China by Japan in the First Sino-Japanese war (1894-1895). That victory by Japan, a nation which had taken so much of its own heritage from old China, or the Middle Kingdom as it was known, had brought about the most rapid, dramatic changes in China's civilization of the past two thousand years.

Throughout the forty eight turbulent years of his life, as centuries of old family and religious ties and customs crumbled, he had struggled successfully against great odds to achieve his present high level executive position in Shanghai with Standard Vacuum Oil Company in China (called Stanvac), a big American company.

During those hard years he had risen from university lecturer to railroad building engineer to his current high status. Now, with several children of his own to raise and educate and a large household to support – as if in full circle, the Japanese had struck again – harder and more personally so far as he was concerned. Was there to be no end to it? What would the future hold?

He had known for some time that hard-line Japanese militarists aimed to drive the Europeans and Americans out of China and East Asia and exploit the area for themselves. They had started local wars in North China, especially in Manchuria, which they actually occupied, as early as 1931. All they needed to start full-scale war was an excuse, and the incident which they provoked, at Marco Polo Bridge in Peking the previous month had sparked the necessary crisis.

It was now clear to him that the day's events, which had so engulfed our household, were the beginning of a full-scale Japanese invasion of China, perhaps the most serious external threat his country had ever faced.

His distraught look and raised clenched fist had reflected the deep personal humiliation and disgrace he felt by having to "kowtow" publicly in front of his family and household during the morning's commandeering of the family car. It had reflected his anger, not only at the Japanese and other foreigners who had run roughshod over and humiliated China all though out his life, but at China's inept rulers who had allowed it to happen. And, it had reflected frustration at both China's and his personal inability to do anything about it.

But Daddy was a practical man! Composing himself, he once again set about organizing our group for the onward journey. Bundles were picked up and reassembled, and first aid given to those of us who had suffered minor scratches, cuts, or bruises during our scramble for cover to get away from the plane.

Grandmother, who was remarkably sprightly after all the hectic activity and events of the day, took charge of the first aid department. Since we didn't have any bandages or medicines anyhow, and my bleeding nose, suffered in my dive for safety, appeared to be the most serious problem, the adults in our group gladly deferred to her as they went about the more important business of collecting our scattered possessions.

It was only natural that she take over since in nearly every Chinese family one older female was the traditional repository of home-nursing and first aid ideas passed along verbally through countless generations. While this trial and error store of information was based more on a combination of the traditional empirical belief that all knowledge is derived from experience and faith healing than science, it often worked. In our situation it was all we had to fall back on.

"Hold your right arm high in the air," she commanded. Dutifully, I obeyed. Since the bleeding was from my left nostril, her centuries old home remedy to arrest it consisted of holding my opposite arm high over my head. The bleeding still continued.

"As soon as we get to the house I'll soak a piece of cotton in some tea and push it into your nostril," she said. "Until then," she added, "walk along holding your right arm high over your head, and push hard with a finger on your left hand between your upper lip and nose." As I stood there reaching, pushing, and still bleeding slowly, two of my brothers added my bundles to theirs. Grandmother then quickly turned her attention to tying bits of cloth around minor cuts and scratches on the arms and legs of three others of our group who required her attention. Soon we resumed our trek.

Suddenly, almost abruptly it seemed, after so many hours, our straggling, bone weary group turned into Peach Blossom Lane and in the lengthening evening shadows saw our new home. My nineteen-year-old brother Chia Liang (James) who had been guarding it alone since the previous day eagerly greeted us. The home looked huge, dark, and very strange to me, but I was too tired to care. All I wanted to do was have a little something to eat and climb into bed and sleep. Tomorrow, I thought, just had to be a better day.

After a quick meal of hot noodles and vegetables prepared by Ah Foo, the family and household moved to their respective quarters and settled in as best they could under the circumstances. This was done quickly since night was close at hand and a power failure had just plunged all of Shanghai into darkness.

Daddy had slipped out of the house and was sitting silently alone on the back verandah, wrapped in his thoughts. His face, reflected in the glow of the still-burning western part of the city, didn't look lordly and authoritative at all – just emotionally drained, physically exhausted, and sleepy like mine.

I know how tired he was, because as I stopped for a moment en route to my second floor room, and peeked through a window at him, I could hardly see through my own half-closed, sleepy eyes.

Chapter 2

SETTLING IN (SORT OF) AT PEACH BLOSSOM LANE

The remaining four months of 1937 and the early ones of 1938 following that August "Bloody Saturday" in Shanghai, saw quite a lot of moving to new locations throughout China and "settling in for the duration" by both big and small players in the exploding wartime drama.

For the Japanese, the rapid seizure of cosmopolitan Shanghai, gateway port city of the Yangtze River main artery that led into the heartland interior of China, was a major victory. With a population of three and a half million, it was the largest commercial and banking center on the East Asian mainland, as well as a major manufacturing center.

Among its inhabitants were many thousands of foreigners from nearly every nation on earth. Most of these lived in the International Settlement, the concession section of the city, run jointly (in theory) by several foreign powers, but actually controlled by the British. Nearly all the others lived in the separate French Concession. Over a third of the native Chinese population lived in these two foreign concession sections, the rest in other all-Chinese areas. As was intended, all these people were impressed by, and either filled with trepidation or actual fear, as a result of the stunning conquest.

Quickly fanning out from Shanghai, Japanese forces soon seized the key cities of Peking to the north and Soochow (Suzhou) to the southeast. Without delay they then drove on and captured, on December 12, 1937, the capital of Nanking (Nanjing). There, the generals deliberately turned their soldiers loose on the hapless civilian population to loot, pillage, burn, torture, rape, sodomize, hack to pieces (and eat if they wished) women, old men, children and babies without restraint.

This orgy of bestiality, known to history as the "Rape of Nanking" resulted in the death of, by most eye witness accounts, more than 200,000 civilians. Well over 20,000 women and girls of all ages were savagely raped; many of those then disemboweled and nailed alive to walls after having their breasts hacked off. Countless groups of people were bound together in bundles and either shot or set afire, and hundreds of individuals were tied to posts alive and used for bayonet practice.

This rapid "One-Two loss" of the great metropolis of Shanghai and the capital of Nanking nearly broke the back of large scale organized Chinese resistance. Had the Japanese continued pressing their attack against the demoralized and disorganized Chinese army, they probably could have won the war then and there. Instead they waited – a big mistake! They waited because they felt that Generalissimo Chiang Kai-shek, head of the National Government of the Republic of China, had no option but to surrender now on their humiliating terms.

But, surprise, surprise – a miracle happened! The Chinese government, given time to catch its breath, reestablished itself in the Yangtze upriver port city of Hankow (Hankou) some 680 miles inland from Shanghai. A new wave of unity and patriotic spirit swept all of unoccupied China. War Lords from the south and southwest and Communists from the north, all bitter enemies for years swiftly joined with the central government in

18

Hankow to lay common plans for continued national resistance to the Japanese invaders. The war would go on!

Among the smaller players, hundreds of frightened foreigners, stunned by the savage brutality of the Japanese troops in Nanking, moved out of Shanghai to wherever they had come from and countless thousands of uprooted, homeless Chinese refugees moved to anywhere they could find shelter, and settled in as best they could.

Last, but not least among the smaller players in the drama was, of course, our Yang family household (now including a newly hired third maid) of nineteen assorted souls, busily trying to settle into our new Peach Blossom "mansion".

My puppy was now safely back with me, as was Ah Foo's parrot; both having been retrieved two days after our "Bloody Saturday" move by two of my older brothers. Even the family Chevy was back with us, released by the Japanese marines a month or so following its being requisitioned.

Truly, our imposing new abode could only be described as a mansion; a three-story western style home with modern amenities that reflected the "show off" wealthy Chinese family lifestyle that my father was trying to emulate (in his own "cost conscious" way). He was so secretive about his business affairs, and so financially tight-fisted with his family and household that we never knew whether he was really wealthy, or just well off. We did know, through experience, of his firm belief that one way to save money was to "cut costs" in every way possible.

As a result of his putting this philosophy into practice, our new mansion was, for many reasons, a most unusual edifice. First, in order to save money, it had been conceived and designed by him without architectural consultation, and erected over a six-month period without benefit of an overall job foreman. He did all the subcontracting himself, beating each individual contractor down to the ground in price, and physically supervising the work of each so far as his own time permitted.

During the last several weeks of the construction period; from mid-June when school let out until our moving date, to pennypinch even more, he made my two older brothers, and the oldest son of Concubine Number Two ride over on bicycles to take turn standing guard from 7 a.m. to 10 p.m. so that construction materials would not be stolen. This represented a twelve mile daily round trip for each of them, plus their seven and a half hour guard stint. During the night a paid watchman stood guard.

The result, in spite of certain flaws, which will shortly be enumerated, proved to be quite a monument to its creator and builder. Standing three stories tall, covering most of a huge lot, it actually represented three quite large self-contained apartments or flats, each with an identical floorplan, stacked one atop the other. Each contained a large central parlor (a living/dining room), three bedrooms, kitchen, full main bath, maid's room and bath, corridors and stairwells. The parlor alone on each floor, to give some idea of the spacious size of the place, were 22' by 28' in dimension, and all the other rooms were proportionately roomy.

Especially when viewed from the not too distant intersection of Avenues Joffre and Haig, covered with light green-flecked with yellow stucco, flanked by a huge iron driveway gate on the left front side, it was quite imposing. As imposing as, and looking somewhat like -- on a much smaller scale, an urban main railway passenger terminal! This was due in part to the fact that while my father was a civil engineer by profession, his only practical engineering and architectural design experience had been garnered during his several years building railways and their associated buildings.

Fronting directly onto Peach Blossom Lane, with only a wide sidewalk in between, it represented a wealthy man's home; one of the largest and most imposing mansions in an area of fine mansions, apartments, schools, churches and shops. It created in onlooker's eyes just the sort of grand first impression that my egotistical, status-seeking father had hoped for.

This outside impression however, concealed quite a few flaws, some of which were rather basic. Somewhat like a main railway station, for example, it had three front entrances; the

20

iron gate driveway on the left, the main one in the middle where guests entered, and a third on the right for our servants and tradesmen. Due to its fronting position onto the lane however, it had only one small open ground space area between the guest and servant/tradesmen entrance. Thus it was not at all uncommon for tradesmen, garbagemen, night-soil collectors, and important visitors to literally rub shoulders as they crossed each other's path at the same time in this small area when entering and departing those two entrances on their respective business.

Inside, the walls and ceilings were all of smooth grayish colored cement, the strongest and cheapest building material Daddy could find. It was almost impossible to drive spikes into this hard cement to hang pictures or anything, so our interior walls were generally mausoleum-bare. If paint was applied it soaked right through the cement, so natural gloomy gray remained the basis of our interior decor, like it or not.

His biggest engineering failure however, was with the vital water system. While we had our own well in the backyard, with water generally so cold that it served to cool watermelons and as our only household refrigerator, we used piped in city water for drinking (after boiling) and other purposes. The problem was, that while he had rigged up a pump to force this city water throughout our household faucets and into our modern, western-styled bathrooms, it frequently failed to generate enough pressure to fill the pipe system. During its periods of frequent failure, the maids had to carry buckets of water into the two in use household kitchens and all bathrooms when needed.

Besides this, whether the pumping system worked or not, there was no central hot water system, and bath water always had to either be heated in the kitchen, or purchased from a local public bath house, and then quickly carried by the maids to be poured into the big imported English bathtubs in the family bathrooms. These tubs were so large, and there were so many of us to take baths at different times, that the maids grumblingly used every slow-down strategy they could devise during the tub filling process. To their delight, our patience would usually wear thin and we would jump into what rapidly cooling shallow water there was for a quick scrub. As a result, we seldom got to enjoy a good, deep, hot soak in our highly prized, modern bathtubs.

Even more, during periods of pump failure, the maids hated the task of lugging down to the front entrance the big round, red-painted, wooden pots used as emergency bathroom toilet facilities. Grandmother, who had difficulty walking, always kept one in her room. This had to be put out for pickup by the night-soil collector every morning, so his horse-drawn, square, smelly cart with a round hole in its top was always just outside our kitchen around breakfast time.

One maid emptying Grandmother's pot alone each morning was bad enough, but during pump-failure periods three maids would be scrambling and complaining to quickly empty two pots each. During such times, I often skipped breakfast and, holding my breath, would rush right off to school or play – often just ahead of the night-soil collector, who, when he had collected a cart-full from the neighborhood, would sally forth to sell it to farmers on the outskirts of the city.

Father's floorplan for our mansion had cunningly provided that his legal wife and most of his blood family, his Number One Concubine, and his Number Two Concubine; were each ensconced separately in separate apartments on different floors. A big, enclosed center stairwell gave him ready access to each with only minimum possibilities of meeting occupants of the different levels on his constant day and night moving and living back and forth. Later on we shall see how he managed, or failed to manage, successfully, his three separate lives under the same roof.

During the first weeks after we moved into our new mansion, before school started in mid-September, Betty and I teamed up frequently to explore our new neighborhood together. We found it to be far busier and more interesting than our old neighborhood had been.

Peach Blossom Lane itself was the first local area we checked out. It was a short, narrow, dead end cul-de-sac lane with eleven mansions, (counting ours); five facing five with another at the end; housing a mixed lot of Chinese, White Russian,

22

European and Portuguese families. While our mansion was by far the largest of these, they were all substantial residences. We soon got to know many of these neighbors, especially the several younger ones of our own age group.

The mansion right next to and half the size of ours, whose front joined our big iron driveway gate, and whose wall formed part of the driveway, soon became our favorite neighborhood visiting place. It was the residence of Father Nicholas, a roly-poly, jolly, gregarious priest whose big Russian Orthodox church was located a few blocks away. Residing with him was a family of relatives which included two daughters a few years older than ourselves.

While we had known some foreigners in our old neighborhood, we had never associated with them nor been into their homes. Thus we were delighted to find these White Russians to be interesting, warm, and friendly foreign neighbors who were always delighted to have us drop in on them for frequent visits.

Since other Russian Orthodox priests often visited or stayed with them, we loved the excitement of their bushy beards, long flowing black robes, and the long strands of black beads they wore about their necks. Most of them loved young people, and had many interesting stories to tell about their life in Russia before the Bolsheviks seized power, and how they and the thousands of other White Russians in Shanghai had fled to China as refugees after World War I in 1918.

We loved their huge always steaming brass samovar, in which they prepared endless cups of hot tea, the mysterious painted icons on their walls and the gaily colored little boxes on their table tops. And we especially loved to visit Father Nicholas' aviary on their second floor verandah, where he kept many different species of birds.

To make things even better, their Chinese male family cook Ah Liu, who came from Shantung (Shandong) province, also took a great liking to us, and made us feel welcome in his kitchen at any time. We didn't take him up this as often as he would have liked however, for he cooked Russian style and to our young noses the odor of that was sometimes horrible.

23

He had a big black mole on the left side of his chin from which grew one very long black hair. He refused to cut it, and we loved to admire and pull it gently – to his great delight. Our Yang family cook Ah Foo was also soon quite taken with him, and the two cooks soon became great friends, visiting together most often in our Yang family kitchen however, for even more than we younger Yangs, she hated the smell of his foreign-style cooking.

In the other direction from our mansion, there were many exciting things to do and see, especially along broad, busy, tree-lined Avenue Joffre. There were many intermixed small shops and homes there, and two blocks away there was a big open market area consisting of several narrow lanes where vendors set up stands each morning to sell fresh meat, live chickens, flowers, vegetables, and many other things. We accompanied Ah Foo or Concubine Number One there often when they made their daily morning shopping trips, and constantly enjoyed the often thrilling and strange sights and smells of this marketplace area.

Peddlers and vendors came and went constantly up and down our lane from this avenue, shouting their different slogans and chants. While they never bothered us at our doorway, we enjoyed watching them sell their wares. Some were cobblers, others were knife sharpeners, others sold food. Most carried their wares and equipment at each end of long shoulder poles.

In the afternoon, for snacks, some of the hot food vendors sold delicious chunks of hard preserved tofu (bean curd) which they first fried on a little portable charcoal stove, then dipped in hot pepper sauce before serving piping hot (in more ways than one) on the spot. In the evening, since people stayed up late, other vendors would cook on the spot and serve little snack bowls of hot wonton, (a meat-filled dumpling in soup), or noodles mixed with chicken and vegetables.

Our favorite among these street vendors, were those who carried liquid candy mixes in two cabinets, one at each end of the pole. They would blow the mix through a hollow bamboo stick, like a glassblower, into all sorts of colorful inflated shapes. These would then be affixed to one end of long thin bamboo sticks and stuck, like bright balloons, atop the cabinets for sale. The end result was a hard candy hollow outer shell with nothing but air inside, which could be licked, or shattered into pieces for sucking. While this candy didn't taste especially good, it was fascinating to watch it being blown into so many colorful artistic, assorted shapes.

Our few fun-filled, end of summer days of freedom came to a sudden end with the start of school in early September. Since all schools were privately owned, and tuition had to be paid in advance before start of each of the school year's two semesters, Daddy himself had to take us to be enrolled. This was no simple task, for we all were at different grade levels.

Suzie, Betty and I were all entered into different grade levels at McTyeire Number One, Main School, on Bubbling Well Road, some distance from our home. This was a well-known American Methodist Protestant church sponsored school offering grades one through twelve. While boys and girls attended class together in grades one through four, from fifth grade on students were all girls. It was a westernized institution that catered to children of wealthy parents.

School administrators, all teachers at lower grade levels and most at higher levels were Chinese women, although some high school level teachers of specialized courses such as Advanced English and Music, were Americans. The students at McTyeire were all Chinese or Eurasians; American, British and other foreign citizen children attended their own national schools, such as The American School or the German School.

Since Betty and I had previously attended a branch of McTyeire in our old neighborhood, and Suzie had been attending the Main Branch for the past three years, our enrollment went fairly smoothly. Paul, however had to be enrolled at an entirely different school (Nan Yang Model School) and James, a second year student at Shanghai University, had to be enrolled there. Since the boys enrollment represented visits to two entirely different campuses, it took him more time to throw his weight around and impress the school authorities there with his importance than it did at ours.

While Father hated to part with the advance tuition payment for any of his children's education, especially for his daughters, he loved playing the role of wealthy big shot before the various school principals. Part of that role-playing consisted of making us girls feel as awkward and insignificant as possible in front of these dignitaries. Paul and James of course, being sons, were praised to the hilt by Father at their enrollment sessions.

While, dickering with the McTyeire Principal over his proposed desired tuition discount for enrolling three daughters, he suddenly sensed a quick way to save a whole year's tuition by getting me double promoted. Discovering that English was a daily required one hour course from fourth grade on, he glossed over the fact that I had only completed second grade, and swiftly insisted that because of my past good grades and knowledge of English I should skip third grade and be promoted directly into the fourth grade. His rationale was that since he and Mother were already teaching me English at home, and since I was the daughter of an obviously successful executive (him) with prestigious Stanvac, I could easily handle fourth grade material.

When the principal protested that school rules strictly prohibited that sort of thing. Daddy ordered Suzie, Betty and me to step outside the room. A few minutes later he came out and told me, "you will be entering fourth grade!"

Years later, when older and wiser, I suspected that he had most likely threatened the Principal that he would withdraw all three of his daughters from McTyeire, an act that would cause her personally to lose considerable face. As we shall see, this "promotion" later turned out to be "monetarily costly" as well as a really dumb idea!

As soon as he got us Yangs enrolled, Father had to go through the process of enrolling the four boys of Concubine Number Two in different (and much cheaper); private schools than ours. Two had to be placed in an elementary school. If he hated to part with money for educating his own blood children, he hated it even more when it came to paying for theirs. But by taking their mother (a widow) as his concubine, he was obligated by tradition (but not by law) to finance their education as though they were his own. This didn't necessarily mean equal "quality" school for them as for us Yangs, however!

There was usually quite a commotion in front of our mansion early every schoolday morning as the eight assorted four through twelve grade school attendees in our household piled into different waiting rickshaws that were to take us to our various schools.

Since none of our schools were within walking distance, Daddy had contracted with some local rickshawmen to take us back and forth each day. While return times in the afternoon were different, depending on the distance involved and the time classes ended at our different types of schools, we all departed about the same time each morning. Betty and I shared one rickshaw, as did Concubine Number Two's two younger sons, but the other four students went solo. Six rickshaws, and their shouting coolie pullers, trying to load up and get out just ahead of the daily incoming night-soil cart, didn't exactly set the stage for a day of scholarly endeavor for any of us!

Once school started, Betty began spending most of her afternoon and evening hours with school chums and neighborhood friends of her age and grade level. Since she didn't always like to have her younger sister around at such time, and there weren't too many girls of my own age living on Peach Blossom Lane, and none of them went to my school, I more or less had to amuse myself.

This was no real problem, for there were plenty of interesting things to do around our always-bustling mansion. I would take turns, for example, visiting with Mother who kept busy knitting sweaters and socks for everyone, and with Grandmother, who, during daily late afternoon soaks of her poor, swollen bound feet, embroidered satin slippers.

Sometimes I would massage Grandmother's feet for her after these soaks, as she described how her mother had started tightly binding her toes back and under with long strips of cloth each day, from age three on, to stunt their growth. "The pain was so excruciating," she would frequently sob, "and the pain keeps getting worse as I get older."

This binding continued all throughout her childhood years. As her body grew, her tightly bound feet could only develop into hunched insteps, with a deep crease in the soles just before the start of the heel. Now they looked deformed!

The barbaric custom started hundreds of years ago," she told me, "because some Emperor's favorite concubine had delicate small feet that everyone envied. In time, small feet, achieved through this painful binding process, became a female status symbol. The Chinese ideal of feminine beauty became that of a frail, fragile willowy woman with tiny bound feet – carried about in a sedan chair!"

"Even now I have to bind my feet each day in order to give them support," she complained, "but am unable to walk on them more than a short distance at a time. My only consolation is to make my pretty slippers!" She held up her latest beautifully embroidered pair for me to see – they were of small, child's size, with very pointed toes.

Mother sometimes joined us during these afternoon "soaks," and told how she was spared bound feet because her father, who had studied for seven years in America as a boy, wouldn't stand for it. "But nearly all my contemporary female relatives and girlfriends had to endure foot binding," she said. "It was not until the early 1900's that the custom went out of favor in China and was eventually made illegal by government decree."

On weekends especially, I liked to visit our first floor kitchen and watch our cook, and the maids at work since something interesting was nearly always going on there.

Since we had no heating system in our mansion, except for a big wood or coal-burning stove in the parlor of each of the three floors, the kitchens were the only really warm rooms in the house. During colder weather this warmth was an added attraction for all household occupants to visit their kitchens. Our first floor main kitchen especially, as were the other main kitchens in the neighboring mansions, was thus always a bustling center of activity and talk from dawn till nearly midnight.

For our Yang family, as the war raged on, the last days of December of that year ended on a rather downbeat note. That came from Guo Liang's asking Father's permission to depart for the interior and join the resistance movement. He, like the other suddenly very patriotic adults in our family, and among our relatives and friends, was deeply angered by the savage Japanese bombing of unarmed civilians in Shanghai and the later atrocious "Rape of Nanking."

Having just graduated in June from Kwon Hua University in Shanghai with a degree in Chemical Engineering, he had been looking for a good job when "Bloody Saturday" occurred. Now, being of military age, he was afraid of being drafted into some local occupation force military organization or into unwanted factory work if he remained in Shanghai.

"I want to go into the interior and help the war effort in some way," he said. Father, agreed, on the condition that he seek a civilian position with the central government rather than joining the military. Daddy then promptly called an evening meeting of all the Yang family members (except Betty and myself) to announce his decision. Betty and I were considered too young and loose-lipped to be told, and were sent to sit out the meeting in our bedroom. Paul, of course, told us all about it later.

Assembling the invited family members in our second floor parlor, Father had Guo Liang and James check carefully to see that there were no eavesdroppers. Then, in a low voice he imparted the news. Except for a gasp from Mother, and worried looks all around, the momentous announcement was greeted in silence. The war once again had suddenly come close to home.

Said Father, "sometime soon Guo Liang will slip out of the house, and may not be heard from for an indefinite period". He stressed that it was safer for all in the room to know nothing;

that if any of them were ever questioned, from either inside or outside our household, that they were merely to say that Number One Son had gone out to visit friends one evening and simply disappeared; and that no one in the family knew of his whereabouts. "Since we really don't know where he is going, nor does he at this point," said Father, "we will all be telling the same truthful story."

Mother and Grandmother threw their arms around Guo Liang and cried their soft farewells. Suzie did the same. Then James and Paul shook his hand and wished him well. Father presented him with an oilskin wrapped packet of money, and after reminding him of his special responsibility as Number One Son to always honor the family and its ancestors, threw his arms around his shoulders and wished him a safe journey.

Everyone in the family was unusually subdued for the rest of that evening. From the next day on however, life resumed its normal tempo to aid the cover-up.

Chapter 3

WAR BETWEEN THE CONCUBINES
OVERSHADOWS REAL WAR

Grim foreboding of possible big troubles to come had first overcome Grandmother the afternoon of Chinese New Year's Eve Day, which had fallen earlier that 1937 year. That is the special day when, each year, family members come together to share a sumptuous meal, give out "lucky money" in red envelopes to children and often stay up all night to welcome in the next day's start of the New Year. She and the rest of our Yang family were all together in the living room of our old house.

The happy festivities and laughter of that day came to a sudden and baleful halt when Father announced casually, while handing over a gold embossed envelope of" lucky money" to me, "Oh, by the way, a new second concubine will be moving in with us next week! I know you will all make her and her four children feel welcome!"

Then, in the sudden utter silence of our crowded living room, he turned to Mother, and said "You can tell Ah Foo to set out the food now for our New Year's Eve banquet!"

Mother, with a stunned look on her face, saying not a word, quietly stood and started walking toward the kitchen, as her husband and head of the household had ordered.Grandmother was even more shocked than Mother, and instantly alarmed since she knew that family ancestors had not been consulted in advance about this matter. She knew so because she was the one who handled contacts with our ancestors, either direct via her bedroom Buddhist alter or through local mediums, on behalf of the entire family. This was her "big thing", chiefly because no one else in our household, except the cook and maids, really believed in ancestor worship.

Like all Chinese of her age, she had been brought up in the belief that ancestral worship was the central core of all belief and that any unworthy action, such as that seemingly now being committed by her son, represented a grave offense against our family's ancestors. Ancestor worship, in her mind, involved not only actual worship but constantly doing everything possible both directly and indirectly, to help make spirits of the departed content.

As soon as possible after the painfully quiet and depressing family banquet that followed my father's announcement, she caught him alone in the corridor to speak her fears.

In an agitated voice she half-shouted, "How can you possibly do such a thing as bring a second concubine, and one with four children at that, into our home without getting prior approval of our ancestors? You as my oldest living son, have known since you were a child in Ningpo (Ningbo) that our ancestors are far wiser and more experienced than you in such matters. And you know that you should never, ever embark on any important new venture that might affect the fortunes of our household without consulting them. We may all suffer big troubles because of your failure to secure their advance approval!"

"I met her in Soochow three months ago when I was there on a business trip," he replied. "She's an intelligent, attractive thirty-five year old widow who has been doing quite well selling insurance."

"But why did you have to announce it to all of us the way you did, on this special family day of the New Year?" questioned Grandmother.

"She agreed to become my concubine just the other day," he replied, "and I had to act today because her name is Ching, which as you know, means Gold. That is a very lucky name that I must quickly bring to the attention of the God of Wealth."

"What has that to do with shocking everyone a while ago, just before our family banquet?" she queried.

"Time is so short!" He continued. As you're well aware the upcoming third day of the New Year's Festivities is the most auspicious day of the year to pay homage to the God of Wealth. Announcing the news to you and the others this evening is a very good omen. I couldn't be more pleased!" With that, he turned on his heel and walked away.

Grandmother was left only with her fear and foreboding. She knew that while he was often superstitious about ancestor ghosts, that he did not really believe in ancestor worship. She also knew that his way out favorite among the more than one hundred gods that most Chinese paid homage to over any given year was the God of Wealth. He especially liked this god, and at least faked cultivating its favor every year at this time, on the sensible theory that no one can have too much wealth.

The next day, New Year's Day, was normally for us a happy, fun-filled family day spent at home. It was a day traditionally first spent visiting relatives and close friends, then in the late afternoon, joining together at home to pay brief, casual homage to the past three generations of our ancestors.

This was usually followed by also paying light-hearted homage to a few of the more important household gods, such as the Gate God, the Door God and, especially the Kitchen God. Grandmother was serious about all this and scolded the rest of us furiously at our cheerfully making light of these traditional ceremonies.

That was what our family "normally" did on the first two days of the New Year's Festival! On this New Year's Day, however, after Daddy's bombshell announcement of the after-noon before, our household was as somber as if a death vigil was taking place.

Mother, Concubine Silver Lotus and Grandmother all spent the day in their respective rooms. Betty and I, tiptoeing quietly around the house, could hear both Mother and Silver Lotus sob-bing much of the time, especially when the maids opened their bedroom doors to leave hot tea or dishes of mostly uneaten food.

Father sulked around the house early in the morning, grous-ing that his unenthusiastic family was spoiling the day; blaming everyone except himself for the depressing atmosphere. Finally, since he couldn't even get James or Paul to fake a little cheer, he angrily put his coat on to go out.

"If you all insist on acting this way I will visit our relatives and some friends by myself," he loudly exclaimed to no one in particular, slamming the front door behind him as he stormed out of the house.

He stayed away all that day and night, not returning until late afternoon the following day.

Immediately upon his return, he summoned James, Paul, Suzie, Betty, Grandmother and me to join him for his personal, annual, traditional, show-off ritual of paying homage to the God of Wealth. Mother and Silver Lotus continued to hole up in their rooms while the household servants stayed out of sight in the kitchen unless summoned for some duty.

After lining us up, he asked us to face a colorful printed pa-per picture of the God of Wealth that he had previously propped up on a small table just inside our home entranceway. He then lighted four sticks of incense, which were sticking up out of small sand filled brass dish.

Immediately pouring a small glass of wine into a good sized bowl, he ignited it, and then quickly dropped the picture into the flames.

As it burned, he commanded the rest of us to join him in kowtowing three times before it. As we did so he loudly im-plored the God of Wealth to bring our family good fortune during the coming year. He was both producer and solo actor for this show; the rest of us just kept quiet and did what we were told.

Before allowing us to disperse, he announced that the new concubine and her children would be joining our household within two days. "Since our house is small," he said, "they will occupy our present parlor and dining rooms, and we Yangs will take our meals in the kitchen." "The Second Concubine's name is Ching, and you must all show her proper respect."

"I know how crowded we will be in this house," he continued, "But work will start next week on a new and larger home that should be finished within six months. It will be located about six miles from here near Futan University, close to the intersection of Avenues Joffre and Haig, still in the French Concession." He then headed toward the kitchen as our family group excitedly discussed this latter news.

"Grandmother, why is Daddy getting a second concubine? And why does he have concubines anyhow?" asked Betty, "none of our relatives have them." "And none of my schoolmates have ever mentioned having concubines in their homes." I said.

"I hope you haven't told them that Daddy has any," Betty snapped at me, "because Mother told me long ago that I was never to talk about a concubine living in our home." "I certainly haven't," I retorted testily, "because she told me the same thing the day before I ever started school."

These questions and comments poured out among others as we joined Grandmother in her bedroom after dinner that night.

"Now, now girls," she exclaimed, "just settle down! Why don't you both sit here at the foot of my bed, and get comfortable."

Recognizing that we knew absolutely nothing about sexual relations between men and women, she started telling this story:

"Your mother and father met many years ago in Shanghai when he was a student at St. John's University and she was a student at nearby St. Mary's girls' high school. Both well known schools were sponsored by American Protestant Episcopal mis-

35

sionaries, and both were then as now, located on the same sprawling campus."

"They were attracted to each other immediately, for two reasons, " she continued. "First, because she was very pretty, a campus beauty queen, and all the girl students considered him very handsome. Secondly, because of their mutual interest in the English language, and in America as a foreign country. He was an English major, and since her well-to-do prominent Mandarin father had studied in America in the late 1800s, she too spoke English quite well."

"Did their families arrange their marriage?" interrupted Betty.

"No, they decided together that they wished to marry, and he asked your mother's father for permission. All this was most unusual at a time when most marriages, just as mine had been many years ago, were arranged by the couple's respective parents."

"I am the last of their several children," I stated proudly.

"Yes, you are, and there were several!" smiled Grandmother. "Over the years your mother gave birth to nine children; seven girls and two boys." Betty and I gasped, for we had no idea that there had been so many.

Without delay, she continued: "The first three babies, were girls. Two of them died when only a few months old. Your father, who like most Chinese men wanted sons, decided then to adopt a son to make certain he got one, in case more girls came along. Did you know that your oldest brother Guo Liang is an adopted brother?"

We both gasped in astonishment, for we had no idea!

"But, he may be your real half brother!" she added, "Because your father was so insistent on adopting him, we suspect that Guo Liang may be his real son by some unknown woman he met in Hangkow on a business tip!"

Before we could ask any embarrassing "how could that happen" questions, she quickly continued her story.

"As you know," pointing at me, "you are the last child your mother and father had. Although he got two fine real sons along the way, I think he got fed up with babies, especially after your birth – another girl! Also, he became increasingly worried that he might catch the tuberculosis your mother had contracted. Worn out after having so many babies, she is now, as you both know, not a well person."

"Yes, she occasionally coughs up more blood now than she did even last year," observed Betty, as I nodded in agreement.

"Now to the concubines!" Grandmother continued, " a subject you must never, ever talk about outside our own household. Although your father is very modern in many of his ways, in other ways, such as having concubines, he sees no reason not to take advantage of this, to him, marvelous old fashion tradition. That's why we should never mention this embarrassing subject, not to anyone!!"

"Do you both promise never to talk about it outside our home," she asked us pointedly. "Yes, yes, we promise," we chimed in unison.

Well then, some six months before you were born (again pointing to me) he brought Concubine Silver Lotus to live with us. Her poor country parents had sold her as a young girl to a wealthy restaurant owner in the city of Wuhan to be trained as a singsong girl. She studied to sing and play the Erhu, a two-stringed musical instrument, before men at banquets.

Unfortunately, as she grew older her eyes went so bad that she was forced to wear the thick ugly glasses you now see her with. That plus the fact that she turned out to be very plain looking, and with bulging eyes like a goldfish. All that didn't make her a very popular Sing-Song girl!"

Betty and I chuckled, even as we continued to sit at rapt attention, for we didn't want to miss a single exciting detail.

"How did Daddy get her?" I asked.

"He apparently bought her for 200 Yuan, as part payment, or even as a bribe for some business deal," replied Grandmother. "I don't know the full story of that, but it was legal then to acquire concubines. A year or so after she came, the Nanking government passed a law that the taking of new concubines was illegal, but not everyone paid much attention to what the government said in those days."

"How old was she when she joined our household?" I asked.

"She was nineteen when she came, only one year older than your oldest sister, Nellie, and illiterate. She turned out to be intelligent though, so your father taught her how to read and write. As you know, he likes her very much, so much so that he eats with her in her room most evenings, and spends many more nights with her than with your mother."

"I like Auntie Silver Lotus," I said, "not as much as I do Mother, of course, but I've always known her, and even when I was a small girl she would play with me, buy me candy, and let me jump up and down on her bed. And she's very good to my doggie, Mong-Fu."

"At first none of us Yangs welcomed her, "noted Grandmother, "but she's basically such a simple person, and leads such a lonely life that we have come to more or less accept her over the past few years, even though we all wish we didn't have a concubine in the house. Even your mother visits with her occasionally, although they generally try and avoid one another."

"We've never heard that complete story before," exclaimed Betty, "and it's very interesting. But why is Daddy bringing this second concubine to come and live with us?"

"I don't want her to come!" I cried.

Grandmother looked troubled as she answered with a big sigh, "I don't know, and our ancestors don't know either!"

Two days later, they moved in – Second Concubine Ching and her four boys; one Paul's age, one Betty's age, one my age and a younger one. While Ching had a pretty Marlene-Deitrich-like face and nice long black hair, she was quite skinny and not at all what a European or American would consider a sexy type woman. Like Concubine Number One she had a very square jaw. Later on Betty, Paul and I liked to sneak up behind both of them in order to judge from behind which one's square jaws stuck out most from their necks.

We Yang children all hated the four boys from the start, never played with them, and avoided them in every way possible. We also disliked and tried to avoid their mother. We were joined in our loathing and avoidance of these unwelcome intruders in our household midst by Mother and Grandmother.

The two concubines, of course, hated each other from the start. Dealing from weakness, since neither had any legal status and could be banished from our home by Father at will, they constantly bad mouthed each other to any and all of us, including the servants. When forced to communicate, it was by verbal messages via maids. They made every effort to avoid meeting anywhere face to face.

Father coped as best he could, staying as far away (at work or supervising start up construction of our future new home) as possible during daylight hours, and by spending alternate nights with them during the remaining nights in the old house. He also frequently and sharply ordered them, both privately and in front of all the rest of us, to stop their constant bickering (to little avail).

Poor Mother spent those nights alone – probably gratefully except for her great loss of face. Although Father generally avoided her and paid her little attention, she never complained openly about anything during this period. Everyone in our household regarded her with sympathy and deferred to her as the one in charge when he was not around.

Grandmother now decided that she had better do something fast to try and get in touch with our family ancestors concerning the soon-to-be-built new house that Daddy had failed to contact them about. She decided that rather than make a direct personal attempt, contact should be made through a medium.

There was no shortage of mediums, for thousands of middle aged or older women performed such services throughout Shanghai. Some were professionals, but the vast majority, like the one Grandmother favored, were amateurs who charged no fixed fee, but offered their services in return for "lucky money", a small percentage of which was always returned to the client.

On the appointed day, arranged by one of the family maids who had acted as messenger, Grandmother and I set out early one morning by rickshaw, for the two mile ride to the medium's home. Since she couldn't walk very far, she often took me along when she went out to run errands for or carry things for her. As we rode along, side by side, Grandmother fairly trembled with excitement in anticipation of this important event, and I glowed with pride at being allowed to witness this first-ever for me attempt to contact our ancestors.

"Come in, come in," said the medium, as she smilingly led us to a sofa in the small main room of her home. She was about Grandmother's age, only slightly taller than me, and walked with a stooped back and slight limp. Dressed all in black, a short, choke-collar gown with wide wrist length sleeves, and trousers; her gray-black hair was combed straight back and tied into a bun at the nape of her neck. Several jade and silver ornaments, including a long silver combination toothpick/ear wax remover instrument, were displayed on the bun.

I nervously wondered if our conversations with the dead would take place in a darkened room.

The medium soon put that fear to rest, as she confidently went to work with the mid-morning sunlight pouring in from the window across the room. As Grandmother and I sat on the sofa facing into this quite bright sunlight, the medium placed a small table in front of us, and dragged up a white cloth covered armchair into which she settled facing us with her back to the window. Because of the brightness of the light we were facing into, it was difficult to see her face clearly. Her snaggled teeth flashed as she talked however, and after a quick, secret count I concluded that she had only eight of them in her head, one of which was bright gold.

My thoughts were suddenly switched from counting teeth to mouse still and bug-eyed attention as the medium set about putting on what was to be a quite professional, jolly good hour and a half long show.

This started by her slowly and dramatically building up an improvised altar on the table in front of us. This consisted of a rice-filled tin biscuit box covered with a piece of red paper into which she poked three long upright sticks of incense, which she immediately lighted.

"What is the name and relationship of the specific ancestor you wish to contact, and what do you want to talk to him or her about," she asked Grandmother; fixing her with an unblinking stare. Grandmother's voice quavered in reply that she wished to obtain the approval and blessing of her long dead late husband for the Yang family to move into a new family mansion being built on Peach Blossom Lane.

The medium then asked her to describe the exact location and surroundings of his grave, and to tell her where the ancestral tablets were located, which she did.

"If I cannot contact him," continued the medium, "what other ancestors do you pay homage to most often in your ancestral worship?"

"Well," replied Grandmother, "I really wish to contact my late husband because he was a well-known scholar and a very knowledgeable man, and I have great respect for his advice." She then however went on to name and describe several of her other favorite ancestors.

She first mentioned Uncle Seh Soong, a never-married playboy who had died at a fairly early age from some seldom discussed in the family but apparently horrible lingering social disease. While he had scandalized his family by raping a household maid, who had hung herself as a result of the shame, Grandmother had always liked him as a young girl because he told funny stories and bought her a lot of presents.

She then described others, among whom were "Uncle Ex-Admiral," a once highly feared smalltime Yangtze River pirate whose right eye and left thumb were missing as a result of his many combat engagements; and her great aunt "Opo," so nicknamed because she frequently smoked opium. "Opo," a wealthy town belle in her city, apparently loved to dress in beautiful clothes, and had enjoyed racing about in a horse-drawn carriage knocking over any unfortunate coolies or other pedestrians who happened to get in the way.

Her tongue loosened in face of the medium's constantly interrupting questions, Grandmother spilled out details, opinions, and wishes concerning both her ancestors and members of the current generation Yang family so volubly that the medium soon had a goldmine of information to work with.

"Be silent now," suddenly commanded the medium! After a long moment – she slowly lighted three more sticks of incense. As the pungent smoke wafted into our eyes and nostrils, she abruptly stood up, clasped her hands above her head and intoned a short prayer. Then she sat down again, with her elbows on the table, and joined her open hands with the fingertips touching and thumbs separate slightly forward of and below the level of her chin.

"My hands thus form a tunnel of the Eight Directions, in one of which every spirit in the universe is to be found," she whisperingly told us. "Now you must remain absolutely still and silent as I attempt to make contact."

Grandmother and I sat frozen in place, as the medium – eyes closed, face uplifted, as though she were on a one-way radio telephone – blew into her cupped hands (to establish contact), and then started talking "to some spirits" in a dialect we didn't understand.

Since the cagey old medium didn't want to make the affair look too easy, she at first "had trouble" getting in touch with one of our ancestral spirits. A lot of questions and answers went back and forth through the "Tunnel of the Eight Directions," with several different spirits getting into the act, before specific contact was established, to Grandmother's satisfaction, with one of the family ancestors.

That contact proved to be rather startling!

"Your husband is not available right now," she told Grandmother, "but the spirit of your 'Uncle Ex-Admiral' wishes to speak to you!"

Grandmother's jaw dropped in astonishment at this unexpected contact, for her respect for him was touched with some trepidation. He had died peacefully in his sleep at an advanced age while she was very young, but a portrait of him which she had even now in her room at home, had hung in her family home, and as a young girl growing up, she had always imagined that his one eye in that portrait was always following her no matter what part of the room she was in.

And, being quite superstitious, she often felt the presence of his one-eyed ghost in other rooms of her home, especially at night, and often in dark corridors or closets during daylight hours. She wasn't really afraid of his ghost, she had often told us, but thought his fiery eye had a dirty-minded, lecherous look in it that made her feel somewhat nervous.

Her jaw continued to hang in astonishment, as the thrust of his message became clear. Rather than a stern and commanding figure, as might be expected, he seemed to come through as just a rather guerulous and doddering old man who was quite concerned that the Kitchen God was unhappy with the way things had been going in our family kitchen of late. And, not only was he concerned about the feelings of the Kitchen God; he also worried at some length about what specific plans she had in mind to keep the Door God happy in the new home.

The unexpectedness of this ancestral contact, and the type and flurry of questions from On High put Grandmother on the defensive. She kept the medium busy babbling explanations, excuses and fretful promises toward the Heavens through her cupped hands.

In due course, the medium reported that "Uncle Ex-Admiral's" spirit had checked with a few of the other ancestors, and, acting as their spokesman, was giving family ancestral approval to build and move into the new house. This approval however, was based on the condition that Grandmother live up to the promises she had just made during the "contact" to take special steps once in the new home to keep both the Kitchen God and Door God happy. Grandmother's final message was, "I promise," whereupon communications came to an abrupt conclusion.

Since this ancestral approval was exactly what she initially told the medium she had hoped to hear, Grandmother was overjoyed. The medium, of course, was pleased that Grandmother was happy; the ancestral spirits seemed pleased as well, and of course I was pleased at being considered old enough to be allowed to witness this exciting and important contact with our ancestors!

Business concluded, the medium gave back a portion of the "Lucky Money" prepayment, and Grandmother and I climbed back into our waiting rickshaw to hurry back home with the good news.

As the weeks wore on the tension in our crowded household neared the breaking point. While Daddy, the boys, Suzie and even Betty could largely avoid it by staying away most of the daylight hours, the rest of us felt trapped. Any thoughts of the Big War between the Chinese and Japanese armies to the west were almost totally overshadowed by the open warfare that raged between the two concubines right on our own homefront.

Finally, fed up with the constant complaints and backstabbing comments from everyone, Father decided to take action to force everyone into a One Big Happy Family mode.

"We will all meet together in the old parlor, now Concubine Ching's room, Saturday at 2 p.m.," he announced, "I want everyone there, including Ah Foo and the maids."

That night he slept with Silver Lotus, and told her that he wanted her to play the Erhu at the gathering, to show everyone how talented she was, and how special a person she was in his eyes. She was elated!

On Saturday, at the appointed time, all the nineteen human occupants of our household, plus Mong-Fu, crowded into our old parlor. Adults occupied all available chairs or sat on the bed while younger children sprawled on the floor, as Ah Foo and the three maids stood in the background.

"While our home is too cramped now," Daddy announced, "we will soon be in a much larger new home. In the meantime, we must live as a happy household. The purpose of our gathering today is to get better acquainted and be happy."

He then praised several of the adults, including Concubine Ching, pointing our what he considered to be their most outstanding personal qualities. Everyone beamed with pride.

Finally, he presented Silver Lotus as a "highly talented musician who will honor us with some classical Chinese music played on the Erhu." As he did so, Ching's smile turned into a sour frown.

The Erhu, with its semi-round banjo-size base and long narrow neck is a very old Chinese two-stringed instrument that is played with a violin-type bow. Silver Lotus charmed everyone with her excellent playing of hauntingly beautiful classical Chinese songs including "Birds Singing in the Mountains" and "Autumn Moon Over a Placid Lake."

Leaning her instrument against the wall, she was accepting the congratulations of several in the room when suddenly Concubine Ching's two oldest boys started rough play-wrestling near it.

The younger boy, hard shoved by his larger brother crashed headlong against the Erhu so forcefully that its long slender neck snapped in two.

"Ahhh – my precious Erhu is broken," shrieked Silver Lotus, clutching the two parts, now held together only by the two strings, against her heaving breast.

"These boys broke it on purpose," she wailed! She had seen Concubine Ching whispering to her oldest boy while eyeing the instrument immediately after she put it aside.

"She (pointing to Ching) told him to break it," she screamed! "She hates me! She's jealous of me!"

Grandmother, Mother and Suzie nodded silently in agreement, for they, like me, had seen a terrible look of jealousy cross Concubine Ching's face as everyone fell under the spell of Silver Lotus' playing. And we also had seen her whispering to her son while eyeing the leaning Erhu.

"Nonsense," spoke Father, "it was an accident! Boys will be boys, and as you can see, they are very sorry!" As always with him, boys could never do wrong, while girls (especially his daughters) seemed never to do anything good or right in his eyes.

Silver Lotus, clutching her broken Erhu, ran tearfully to her room. All throughout the evening she continued sobbing behind her closed door.

After Concubine Ching had fed her boys, she sent them to their bedroom for the night. Father always required her to do this when he wished to visit her privately in the parlor room. After Ching's maid had served the two of them a long quiet dinner, they played chess for awhile, then retired together for the night.

"Ah yaa! Somebody, come and help! Mistress Silver Lotus has tried to hang herself! Come quickly!"

These shouted, anguished words from our Yang family's young maid Mei-Ling shattered the past-midnight, sleeping silence of our household.

While cleaning up late alone in the kitchen she had heard a loud thump and the sound of an overturning piece of furniture from First Concubine's room which was located directly above. Racing upstairs, she found Silver Lotus sprawled inertly on the floor beside an overturned chair. A rope was tied around her neck, the other loose end of which lay across the bed. There was a small cut on her forehead, from which blood slowly seeped.

As everyone in our alarmed household staggered out of their beds, Father, shirtless, barefoot, struggling to button the fly of his pants raced ahead to arrive first on the scene.

"Stand back everyone," he shouted, as he knelt over her.

"She's starting to regain consciousness – give her air!"

Suddenly, she sat up – sobbing and apologizing profusely for trying to take her own life by hanging. We onlookers, crowded around her, kneeling or standing, could only gape in astonishment.

As we listened to her story; that in anguish over her broken Erhu and feeling that no one cared for her, she had tried to hang herself; several among us began to feel that it was a suspiciously botched attempt. This suspicion was fueled by the fact that the knot on the rope end that had been thrown across a room ceiling beam had certainly not been tied very securely! When she jumped from a chair underneath, the rope above had simply came loose and plopped across the bed. She had, we later suspected, clumsily tripped over the fallen chair and struck her head on the bedpost while falling – briefly knocking herself out!

If it was indeed a "faked suicide" done merely to gain Father's sympathy, it worked fairly well so far as she was concerned. He spent the rest of that night with her, and the next day bought her a more expensive new Erhu. He then apparently convinced her that she was very much his Number One Concubine.

Then he read the riot act to each of his two concubines separately, letting them know in no uncertain terms that their continued stay in his household depended on them maintaining at least a "surface calm" armistice. He then resumed spending alternate nights with them.

While this resulted in a less disruptive household situation overall, we Yangs became even more disgusted with the presence of both concubines.

And disgusted with Father as well! Why, we thought, if he insisted on keeping concubines, didn't he at least get some classy, good looking ones?

These were such ORDINARY concubines!

Chapter 4

TOMB-SWEEPING DAY FOR GRANDFATHER YUEN

My heart stopped beating for a split second, and I wanted only to melt away into a sticky blob and leave this earth forever! It was late January 1938; the end of my first fourth grade term at McTyeire, Number One School. I had just been handed my term report card, and there IT was, just as I feared – a huge "Red Lantern" – marking my flat failure in Arithmetic!

That's what Daddy called those big red marks on any of our report cards that signified "flunking" of one or more of the several required courses. He always went over end of term report cards with each of us Yang children individually and made clear to everyone: "I expect to see good black marks, not Red Lanterns, I hate seeing Red Lanterns!"

What he had failed to take into account when he engineered my double promotion from second grade directly into fourth grade the past September, was that I would miss learning third grade material. While that skipping didn't affect my first fourth grade term in Chinese reading or writing, or in English, all of which were good, it killed me in arithmetic. Since math is a "building block" process subject, I had missed out completely on third grade level tables and fractions. I never really knew from day one on in fourth grade arithmetic class what the teacher was talking about. To complicate matters further, much of the material was learned through mass-class recitation, so I simply parroted back answers along with the group to teacher questions without truly understanding what she meant. Neither my teacher or parents showed any concern over how I was doing at school, and I was too embarrassed and fearful to ask for help. I had just kept falling further behind day by day – hoping that it would somehow work itself out.

I had always been afraid to engage in one-on-one conversations with Daddy at any time about anything, because he usually treated me with indifference and ignored me as if I didn't exist. It wasn't that he particularly disliked me, it was because I was just another, costly to maintain, basically worthless young daughter. We simply tried to stay out of each other's way whenever possible.

My big Red Lantern would now give him something specific to dislike me about, and I was absolute terrified at the thought of having to show it to him!

Fortunately, like a gift from heaven, the God of Good Luck or something came to my rescue! Daddy unexpectedly, at this most opportune time for me, got into hot, hot water with Grandmother, Ah Foo and our two Yang family maids over the shocking probability that he had not adequately protected occupants of our new mansion against evil spirits.

He swiftly got so involved with this matter that he simply doled out to each of us children our second term tuition money to take to school, without first going through the usual review of our report cards.

Father's latest problem stemmed from the discovery by Grandmother and the others that he had disregarded the professional advice of a Fung Sui astrologer engaged, at Grandmother's insistence, to advise about proper pre-construction siting of the new mansion. Since ancient times, the classic Chinese art/science of Fung Sui had been widely employed to protect both the living and the dead from malevolent designs of evil spirits that lurk everywhere in the universe.

Working with a complicated, ages-old design astrological compass, Fung Sui experts act as consultants for correct burial of the dead and for the proper siting of and construction of new homes, buildings or temples, or modification of older ones where they feel a problem might exist. They advise, supposedly "scientifically," how to conform to or adapt to currents in the universe that carry evil spirits, so as to offer protection against them.

"There is an unusual concentration of brown and gray colored rock in the soil right here where you wish to place the main entrance to your new home," the Fung Sui consultant had told Father. "It will definitely attract evil spirits. To thwart them, you will have to move this entrance twenty feet over here to the right."

Since Father wasn't about to change the whole front house design, he simply thanked the man, paid the required consulting fee, and that was that.

He then went right ahead and built his mansion as originally designed, evil spirits be damned!

At first, after moving in, there was so much confusion over the war, settling in to new living quarters and the start of school that no one even thought about the possibility of local evil spirits. Even throughout the winter, with doors and windows closed, no one reflected any concern. Everyone knew that Father had consulted with a Fung Sui expert before building our mansion.

One surprisingly warm late January afternoon however, the main front entrance door, as well as the other ground floor level doors, were thrown open to allow fresh air to circulate. The maids were busy carrying bedding out to the back veranda to air, Ah Foo was slicing turnips in the kitchen, Grandmother was resting in her room and I was at school, about to be handed my report card with its big fat "Red Lantern."

All of a sudden, the maid Mei Ling, walking through the main corridor with a bundle of bedding, let out a piercing scream!

"There is a tunnel of open doors from the front street to the backyard," she yelled, dropping her bundle, and dashing frantically into the kitchen.

"E-e-e-Ah! The evil spirits will get us all!" She screamed again in a high-pitched, panic-sticken voice!

Grandmother, Ah Foo and the other downstairs maid soon confirmed the frightening situation, and in spite of Mother's attempts to calm them, remained in a highly agitated, terrified state all the rest of the afternoon and evening until Father came home for dinner.

While Mother had quickly closed off the "tunnel of open doors," thus keeping out any possible evil spirits, the damage had been done! The "believers" now knew that Father had not followed protective measures recommended by the Fung Sui expert, as they had supposed.

The end result was that Daddy, too embarrassed to again call on the original consultant for advice, quickly engaged another highly recommended Fung Sui astrologer and demanded that he make an "immediate emergency house call."

Out he came, spun his magnetic compass, measured local anticipated cyclical weather changes against the compass' inner circle Eight Trigrams markings and muttered a few incantations.

"You can solve the problem and gain protection," he announced, "by planting one tree here on the sidewalk directly in front of your main entranceway, and a second tree in the back yard on a straight line with the front one exactly twenty feet from the middle of your back veranda doorway."

"This will force the evil spirits to deflect their desired straight line path," he continued, "and will protect household members from their unholy designs."

After assembling everyone to listen, Father had the consultant repeat all this. He then announced that the two trees would be planted the following day.

The trees were planted as promised, the "believers" were satisfied that they were now protected, and Daddy felt that he had gotten off the hook fairly easily, in spite of the extra cost.

I was also off the "Red Lantern" hook, for the time being at least!

"Why should I worry any more about arithmetic now?" I asked myself. "Besides, we will soon be celebrating Tomb-Sweeping Day and Mother has promised to then tell us the complete story of Grandfather Yuen's student days in America.

Since ancient times, in China's traditional agricultural society, festivals of many kinds have served to mark the passing of time and the changing of seasons. Elements common to all these festivals is the universal desire for happiness and wellbeing, the wish to ward off possible misfortune, and the opportunity to experience the harmony between the living and the many deities and spirits of heaven and earth. Like traditional holidays in the western world, these festivals have offered the hardworking Chinese people the opportunity for rest and relaxation in a family and community oriented setting.

First among the three traditional annual Chinese festivals honoring the dead is that of Ching Ming, popularly known as "Tomb-Sweeping Day." Much like Easter in the western world, it is a celebration of life that takes place each spring in early April when the first flowers appear and trees come into bud.

It is a festival where family members gather to tidy up ancestral burial sites, to make ritual offerings of flowers and food to and to commune with those ancestral spirits who are widely believed to hover around the resting place of the dead. Like all Chinese festivals, Tomb-Sweeping Day represents a time to have fun, to enjoy the day and the family and to tell stories about the family ancestors.

April 5 was the day, and what a nice early spring day it was – sunny yet cool, a new freshness in the air, pretty blooming narcissus and daffodils, cherry blossoms and buds of the ever-present willow trees popping open all over. Several of us Yangs were on our way out of Shanghai to enjoy the annual Tomb-Sweeping Day Festival and pay our respects to family ancestors.

"That hot water depot over there probably represents our last chance to fill thermos bottles and the tea kettle before we leave the city outskirts," said James, who was driving our family Chevy.

Mother and Grandmother, sitting in the front seat, quickly agreed to stop there as we other passengers – Suzie, Paul, Betty and me shifted the baskets of food and flowers piled on our laps, eager to get out the crowded back seat for a stretch.

Inside the depot, two big drums of boiling water bubbled and steamed atop a large stove fed with kindling and wood shavings. Several people moved about filling their vacuum bottles, kettles and pots. As they did so, smiling and nodding at us, they smoked, chatted, and like us, basked in the warm sunshine. A few steps away, two women were washing their family pots and pans at a public sink. It was a typical, cheerful local neighborhood gathering spot; a nice place to briefly rest before the 45 minute remaining drive to Wing On Cemetery, and our family ancestral burial sites.

As we drove on past dry freshly plowed open countryside rice fields, gazing at plodding water buffalo and men and women laborers digging a drainage canal with shovels, Grandmother passed out fresh cut willow sprigs to each of us.

"We all have to wear these sprigs today as long as we are at the burial site," she told us. "Since willow is a symbol of light and an enemy of darkness, they will keep the evil spirits away. Anyone who fails to do so is likely to reincarnate as a 'yellow dog' in the next life." she warned!

Betty, Paul and I shuddered behind her back and mock-barked loudly while chuckling silently and smirking at one another over that horrible bad luck possibility.

"The Yang family burial site was originally very carefully selected by an astrologer in accordance with the ancient rules of Fung Sui," she told us. "This was a most important act, because one of the three souls of a deceased always inhabits the grave. If we don't bury an ancestor properly according to those rules, its spirit will always be unhappy with descendents."

"What if an ancestor's ghost decides it doesn't like me and jumps out of the air to harm me today?" wisecracked Paul.

"Ghosts come out only at night," she snapped back, they always disappear at the sound of a rooster's first morning crow."

"But what if there aren't any roosters around at the cemetery and a ghost does try to hurt me?" Paul pressed on, in a put-on worried tone of voice.

"I'll protect you by biting the tip of my right hand middle finger and threaten to rub blood on them," she haughtily replied. "Ghosts hate the sight of human blood, and that will frighten them away."

"Why blood from the tip of your right hand middle finger? Why not from your little finger?" I chimed in.

"Because the right hand middle finger is the Master Finger and blood from the heart flows directly to that finger only, not to any of the other fingers," retorted Grandmother firmly.

Suddenly, we were there – at our Yang family burial site, and light conversation ceased as we followed Grandmother's instructions about how to set up a temporary altar around which was placed ritual offerings of food and flowers for the ghosts and spirits.

Mother pitched in to help along with the rest of us, since custom decreed that married women adopt the ancestors of her husband's family.

We pulled up what weeds there were, removed a few loose rocks, and swept clean the ground around the various ancestral headstones. We then made a kettle of tea and enjoyed some of the "offering food" as we sat on and around the gravesites, relaxing as we discussed the lives of the ancestors buried there.

After some time, leaving Suzie to watch over Grandmother at the Yang family site, the rest of us drove to another part of the huge, sprawling cemetery, stopping at the Yuen (mother's family) ancestral burial site. As far as we could see in every direction, the cemetery was swarming with families honoring their family dead, just as we had been doing. All the brightly festooned small altars and bouquets of flowers made it most colorful scene.

At the Yuen site, we did not perform any of the rituals that Grandmother had led at the Yang family site. Since both our parents were educated, modern Chinese, they did not believe in ancestral ghosts, spirits or other such superstitions of the masses. While we Yang children shared their feelings, we, like them, frequently participated in all sorts of traditional ceremonies, both for the fun of it and to humor Grandmother.

We all did sit silently together for a while amidst the Yuen family headstones, not far from the most imposing one – that of Mother's father Yuen Chan Kwon. This silent meditation was our way of letting the resident ancestral spirits (just in case any were floating around) know that we honored and respected them.

Paul was the first among us to break the short period of family silence. Turning toward Mother he said:

"You promised to tell us today the full story of Grandfather Yuen, how he became one of the very first Chinese to study in America, and how he later became a very high official in the Chinese government."

"Yes, I wanted to do so today here at the spot where he is buried, because he is our Yuen family's most outstanding ancestor; one of which you can feel very proud," she answered.

"Let's move in closer to the front of his memorial headstone. You are all old enough now to comprehend the full story, so let me tell it from the beginning. Feel free to interrupt if you have any questions."

Settling down, we prepared to listen intently, our silence broken only, by the sound of Betty and me rapidly cracking watermelon seeds with our front teeth, one after the other, swallowing the inner seeds and spitting their husks into handmade newspaper cups. The afternoon sun was warm, its rays broken only by occasional large puffy white clouds passing overhead to the west.

"Stunning victories over China by the British in the Opium Wars of 1840-42 and 1856-60," Mother began, "profoundly shocked China's inward-looking, scholarly trained rulers. While awed by the power of the invaders' warships and artillery and their superior military discipline and tactics, most of these rulers stubbornly continued to resist the notion of Chinese adopting in any way the machine-based civilization of the Occident.

Only a handful among them recognized the fact that China should at least learn to build and employ technologically modern weapons of war in order to defend herself against foreign invaders.

Two unusually able and forward thinking of these leaders were the very powerful Viceroy Tseng Kuo-Fan and his lieutenant Li Hung-Chang. They persuaded the Imperial Government to hire foreign experts to come to China to teach Chinese the Occidental secrets of military prowess. As a result, by the late 1860s China had built dockyards and arsenals that were turning out modern warships, artillery and other weapons of war. Concurrently, technical schools that had also been established were turning out competent operating level machinists, shipbuilders and military technicians of all sorts.

What China lacked however, was loyal native born leaders and managers in all these areas, with the in-depth, advanced level theoretical scientific and engineering knowledge and training available only in certain European countries or the United States.

The problem was how to obtain this kind of training! Since none of China's top rulers had even traveled abroad, to say nothing of studying abroad, they didn't know how or where to even begin to solve the problem."

"Was Grandfather Yuen the one who finally solved their problem?" Betty asked. "He couldn't have," snapped James, "because he wasn't even born then!"

"That's right," acknowledged Mother, "but as you will see, he did play a valuable role in the eventual important first attempt at a solution. Keep listening, for the story gets more and more interesting."

"While pondering this problem," she continued, "Tseng Kuo-Fan heard about a wealthy Chinese tea merchant in Shanghai who had been promoting locally a personal plan for the Chinese government to send carefully selected youths abroad to Europe and America for extended study.

This individual, Yung Wing by name, was most unique in that he was the first and only Chinese at the time to have received an extended, comprehensive Occidental education. Born of very poor parents in a village near Macao (Macau) some ninety miles from the port city of Canton (Guangzhou) in South China, he had studied in Canton as a young boy under American missionaries. Taken by them in 1847 to the United States for continued studies, he eventually graduated from Yale University in 1852. Returning to China, he had prospered in the tea trade while also promoting his "study abroad" ideas.

In 1863, Tseng invited Yung Wing to meet with him in the city of Anking (Anqing). Impressed with his ideas, knowledge of Occidental ways and perfect command of the English language Tseng tested him by first assigning him the task of purchasing machinery in the United States for a proposed large new Kiangnan Arsenal near Shanghai. Upon successful completion of this assignment Yung Ying was promoted to an official rank and thus gained standing among high level Chinese authorities. He was then able to discuss his foreign study ideas more fully with them.

Finally, eight years later, in 1871, a plan sponsored by Viceroy Tseng Kuo-Fan and Li Hung-Chang to send 120 young Chinese youth, ages 10 to 16, for fifteen years study in the United States, was presented to and approved by the Imperial Court.

These students were to be sent overseas in-groups of 30 each over a four-year period. While the two sponsoring Viceroys were to be held responsible for the success or failure of the undertaking, Yung Wing and a representative of the Imperial Court, Chin Lan Pin, were appointed co-commissioners to head and manage in America what was named the Chinese Educational Mission to the United States.

The major goal of the undertaking was to educate the boys through college or university level in various technical professions associated with the military arts and sciences. Since the Imperial government was to pay the entire cost of this training, the trainees, upon return home, were expected to spend the rest of their working lives in government service. A staff of Chinese teachers was assigned to accompany the Mission to America and continue instruction of the boys in Chinese language, Confucian classics and ethics and responsibilities of loyalty to the Emperor in Peking.

A special administrative headquarters and Preliminary Training School, large enough to house and train thirty boys at a time, opened in Shanghai during the summer of 1871. Steps were then taken nationwide to recruit and select suitable candidates through the offices of local magistrates. At first there were very few applicants – none at all from China's northern provinces where parents viewed with deep suspicion any government plan to send their best sons abroad, to a country of barbarians at that, for such a long period of time.

In the end, nearly eight out of ten of the applicants selected came from the area around Canton, the longtime most important Chinese international seaport trading center, where inhabitants were more accustomed to foreigners. Your Grandfather Yuen however, lived much further up the coast, in the city of Shaoshing (Shaoxing), famous for its light wines, (similar to western sherry), in Chekiang (Zhejiang) province, some sixty miles west of the port city of Ningpo."

"How did Grandfather Yuen learn about this program?" "How old was he when he applied?" "Weren't his parents afraid to let him go so far away from home, and for such a long time?"

59

These questions and others tumbled from our respective lips as we all waited eagerly for Mother to continue with her story.

"He was barely eleven years old in early 1873 when his father first learned about the program from a leading Ningpo wine exporter who frequently visited Canton," Mother continued. "This merchant's son had been among the first group selected; a group which had sailed to the United States in the late summer of the preceding year.

Your great grandfather, a poor but locally highly respected winemaker, who had worried about his ability to pay for his son's future education, quickly realized the unique educational opportunity offered by this program. He took Yuen Chan Kwon to the local magistrate's office where he applied for him to take the required rigorous competitive examinations, which were based on physical, mental and moral excellence. Your grandfather passed, and was selected to become one of the Thirty-third Group students. Being an adventurous, high-spirited lad, he was more than ready to see other parts of the world."

"He wasn't much older than I am now," I interrupted.

"No, he wasn't," she smilingly replied, "but he apparently was a very intelligent boy. His parents were, of course, very proud of him and overjoyed at his being selected. They had to sign a paper giving the government permission to send him abroad to be educated for a period of 15 years. This paper further stated that the government was not to be held responsible for death or any accident that might befall him during those years. He told me that his mother wept all evening after signing that paper, because she feared that she might never see him again."

"Did he depart immediately for America?" asked Paul.

"No," she replied, "he and his 29 classmates first had to spend an intensive educational year at the Preliminary Training School in Shanghai. Then, in the early summer of 1874, at age 12, after being fitted out with suitable scholarly clothing outfits, he set sail with the other Third Group students from Shanghai, bound for San Francisco on America's west coast.

When I was a child I used to thrill with excitement as he described some of his adventures on that long trip. To begin with, the sea voyage took 30 long days. For these young boys who had never been on the ocean before, this in itself was very frightening.

Then, for two days, their large steamship, which had one huge paddle wheel on each side, encountered a storm so intense that the ship's bow would rise high in the air and smack down with bone jarring force. And the shifting high winds and huge waves would push it so far over on one side or the other that the opposite side's paddle wheel would rise completely out of the water.

Your grandfather described how he became so homesick, terrified and seasick at times on this voyage that he would sometimes slip into his small cabin to weep unseen. After all, he was only twelve years old!

Once they reached San Francisco however, and boarded a train for the weeklong trip via Chicago to Hartford, Connecticut, all the way across America, life became much more interesting. As their train rolled through the American west for example, they saw colorful American Indians at every stop, and countless herds of buffalo on the great prairies."

"We know about Indians and buffalo from the American movies we've seen so often right here in Shanghai," I exclaimed!

"Did he and his classmates stay in Hartford for their education?" asked Paul.

"No, " replied Mother; "they only stayed there two days before taking a half day train trip north to the city of Springfield, Massachusetts. It was from that city that students from all four groups were assigned, usually in twos, to sponsoring American families, most of whom were members of the Protestant Congregational Church. To help the boys adapt to American customs and food and to learn English as quickly as possible, it had originally been decided to scatter them over a wide geographical area. Some were placed in homes in small towns like Granby, Connecticut or Amherst, Enfield or Greenfield, Massachusetts, while others went back to Hartford or remained in Springfield.

Grandfather Yuen and his close friend, eleven year old Chow Wan Pung, were assigned to the E.R. Kagwin home in Holyoke, Massachusetts, a city with a population of around 30,000 located ten miles north of Springfield. Six others of his Third Group friends were also assigned to Holyoke families. Although the Chinese government paid board and room costs, the boys were in nearly all cases accepted warmly as full members of their host families."

"Do you remember what kind of clothing I said they had been outfitted with just before sailing from Shanghai?" Mother laughingly asked.

"I know, I know – they were given scholarly clothing," I loudly and proudly proclaimed!

"That's right," she said, "and when the slender Chinese boys showed up wearing long quilted silk gown-like garments, black skull caps with a round black button on the top, and thick soled cloth shoes, the Americans couldn't tell whether they were boys or girls, or how old they were! And all the students had long, braided, shiny black queues that reached almost to the floor.

Well, even though none of them understood even a word of English, it took the Chinese boys only a couple of days to realize that the Americans of their age were making fun of them for being dressed like GIRLS! They quickly discarded their Chinese gown in favor of American clothes, and learned English so quickly that within two years all were attending comparable age level grades in school with their American friends. They took up American sports eagerly, baseball especially, and excelled in academic studies.

In all the cities or towns, to which they were assigned, they associated with the American boys and girls on the basis of perfect equality, and were very popular. Many were given nicknames, such as "Mohawk," "Murphy" or "Turkey." Your Grandfather Yuen was dubbed "Tiger." This really pleased him, since in China, as you all know, the tiger, not the lion as in the Occident, is the king of land beasts.

Strictly enforced Chinese law in those days required all Chinese men and boys to wear their hair braided into queues as a sign of obeisance to the Manchu Emperor. Since it was a beheading offense to cut them off, the 'China Boys,' as Americans often called the students would drop them down inside the collar and back of their shirts, drop them into side coat pockets or coil them around their heads. This latter "coiling" didn't always work to their advantage however, since in football games especially the temptation for American opponents to yank the coils loose and torment the Chinese players by jerking and tugging the long queues was almost irresistible."

As we all laughed at the idea of this queue-pulling, Paul asked Mother to tell about the type of American schools the students attended, and how their continued Chinese education was handled.

"As your Grandfather Yuen described it," she went on, "as soon as the students learned enough English most entered local American public schools, others private academies. He, his friend Chow Wan Pung and some of the other Chinese boys apparently attended a locally well known private Holyoke institution, known as The Home School, run by a Mrs. Dickerson. This school specialized in preparing students to enter New England colleges, as well as for business positions.

During breaks in the American school year, and during the long summer vacation they went to Hartford where in January, 1875 a large three story building was erected as headquarters for the China Educational Mission. It had administrative offices for the commission staff, classrooms, and rooms and kitchens to house and feed seventy five students at a time. It was here that they diligently pursued their ongoing required Chinese studies according to prescribed schedule.

He also told me about some of his several holiday outings and short sightseeing trips taken with American friends," she continued. "And he described an Educational Mission tour to the huge 1876 Centennial Exposition in Philadelphia where his 113-student delegation was presented to Ulysses S. Grant, President of the United States. Most of all however, he loved to tell of a thoroughly enjoyable Saturday visit in the Hartford home of the famous American author Mark Twain. He and three other Holyoke Chinese students were guests of that large, friendly family for a whole afternoon.

"It sounds like the students were really enjoying life in America, as well as studying hard," remarked Betty. "Did Grandfather Yuen go on to college or university after completing high school?"

"Unfortunately, not all stories have happy ending," answered Mother, "and the sad ending to the American part of this story is that the Educational Mission on June 8, 1881 was abruptly canceled by order of the Imperial Court.

The result was that not one of the 120 students sent to the United States in four groups of 30 each, in 1872, 1873, 1874 and 1875 got to finish their higher education studies.

Some sixty of them were attending colleges, universities or technical schools when the recall orders came, but most of these were really just getting started in their upper level technical programs which would have meant so much to China had they been allowed to graduate. They were attending schools like Yale University, Columbia and Amherst Colleges, The Boston School of Technology and Rensselaer Polytechnic Institute in Troy, New York.

All the others, including Grandfather Yuen, were still in high school. The First Group students spent nine years in America; Grandfather Yuen and his Third Group spent seven years there."

"Why did the Imperial Government cancel the Educational Mission to the United States so abruptly?" queried Paul.

64

"During the late 1870s," Mother answered, "a strong ultra conservative majority had come to power in the Imperial Court. One of the most reactionary of them, Woo Tse Tung, was sent to Hartford as Commissioner of the Mission, replacing Chin Lan Pan, who had just been appointed as the first Chinese Minister to the United States. Yung Wing was then appointed as Chin's Associate Minister. This position, which he hadn't sought, required him to spend much of his time in Washington, D.C. although he still nominally continued to supervise Woo at the Mission. This was undoubtedly a move to get him out of the way; to give Woo the real power.

Woo Tse Tung, who had never traveled abroad, and knew only Chinese ways strongly disapproved of the overall Educational Mission concept, and found fault with literally everything he saw. His constant flow of secret reports stated: students were becoming too Americanized, they played harder than they worked, most went to church, some had become Christians, others were forgetting where they came from and even their native Chinese language!

At the same time, racial and economic resentments in the American west against Chinese laborers who had been imported to help build the intercontinental railroad, and the unexpected refusal by the American government to admit a group of the Mission Chinese students to the national military and naval academies at West Point and Annapolis further alienated the conservatives in Peking. As relations between China and the United States soured, abrupt recall of the Mission and its students in the late summer and fall of 1881 was an unfortunate result."

Oh, that's a terrible ending to such an interesting story," cried Betty!

"That's not the end of the story," said Mother, "there's worse to come, before things get better for returning Grandfather Yuen and his fellow students!"

Upon return to Shanghai, instead of being greeted joyously by officials and family members," she continued, "they were immediately herded together in an old leaky school house with little bedding or food, and not allowed to see family or friends for weeks. Virtual prisoners in their own country, without financial means, constantly shamed and humiliated by petty officials, they were completely surprised and dazed at the bad treatment meted out to them.

In time, as influential friends and relatives came to their rescue, the returnees were assigned in groups to various branches of the government: the diplomatic service, the railroad service, the army and navy, the great Kailan coal mining administration and to the telegraph administration.

These returned Educational Mission students, as a group, in spite of constant career-long opposition from the majority other old-style Confucian trained government officials, contributed much to China over the years. Many attained high positions in the service of their country: one became the first prime minister of the Chinese Republic, two held the high office of Minister of Foreign Affairs, two represented China as Ministers in England, Germany, the United States and two other countries and two became admirals in the Imperial Navy. Others became prominent physicians, educators, engineers, industrialists and businessmen.

Your grandfather, Yuen Chan Kwon was assigned to and spent his working career in the telegraph service. Before passing away in 1916 at the relatively early age of 54 he had risen to the high position of Chief of the Telegraph Section of the Board of Communications. His Holyoke roommate Chow Wan Pung, who outlived him, eventually became Director General of the Imperial Telegraph Administration.

"And that's the end of my story," said Mother, as she began picking up personal items from the gravesite, in preparation for leaving.

"You see," she went on, "as I told you earlier, the Yuen side of your family has reason to be very proud of Grandfather Yuen

Chan Kwon." We all nodded our heads in agreement as we re-entered the car and James drove us back to the Yang ancestral gravesites to pick up Grandmother and Suzie.

As we departed the cemetery, along with scores of other family tomb-sweepers, most of them on foot or riding in rickshaws or on bicycles, the sound of many airplanes filled the sky above us.

A V-shaped formation of eleven Japanese bombers, their red ball under-wing identification marks glowing dully and ominously in the late afternoon sunshine, were passing overhead toward Hankow over some 680 miles to the west where, as we had heard, a major battle was in progress.

We had thought many thoughts this "Tomb Sweeping Festival Day; about our Yang and Yuen family ancestors, the students of the Educational Mission to the United States, and about Grandmother's "evil spirits that lurked about."

Now our thoughts turned in sadness, as we drove quietly back into Shanghai, to the poor Chinese soldiers and helpless Hankow civilians who would soon be on the receiving end of those planes' bombs.

CHAPTER 5

DADDY, KING OF, OR SLAVE TO
HIS MULTI-FAMILY DOMAIN?

For a few days in late April, 1938, following that family Tomb-Sweeping Day Festival outing where we had paid special homage to Grandfather Yuen Chan-Kwon, a feeling of great joy filled the hearts and minds of all patriotic Chinese, including us Yangs.

This resulted from the exciting news that for the first time since they started invading China back in 1931, the Japanese had suffered a big defeat at the central front battle of Taierchwang. Having made the mistake of not continuing their westward drive immediately after capturing Nanking the previous December, they had allowed the Chinese time to establish a new capital at Hankow, some 680 miles upriver from the sea on the Yangtze. By the time the Japanese resumed their attack the following March, the Chinese military had regained enough fighting spirit to win this large scale mid-April head-on battle. Everyone in our household, and all our relatives and friends, cheered at the news of this morale boosting victory.

Unfortunately, our elation was short lived – since the setback was only temporary for the Japanese. Moving in force on two widely separated fronts, their southern army first captured the great South China port city of Canton on October 12. Their central army then overran Hankow on October 25 and plunged beyond to gain control of the lower and middle sections of the river. Not until they neared Ichang (Yichang), gateway to the famous Yangtze mountain gorges, 300 miles beyond Hankow, did they halt their central front up-river drive and settle in to consolidate their gains.

These two victories gave the Japanese control of the coastal gateways to all three of the great arterial rivers that flow from the mountainous interior of China to the Pacific Ocean. Through earlier victories in the Peking-Tientsin (Tianjin) areas in the north, they had gained control of the mighty Yellow River's outlet. In central China they now controlled both banks of the Yangtze 1,000 miles westward from Shanghai as far as Ichang, and from Canton now dominated the mouth of the important West River.

The Chinese national government and its once again demoralized armies, moving just ahead of the aggressor, headed west along the Yangtze from Hankow deep into the interior. There, hundreds of miles upriver, it once again set up a new capital – this time in Chungking (Chongqing), an ancient walled riverport city of 200,000 population.

Strategically this was a wise decision, since the city was the focal point of western China's road and communications network. Also, the entire region's major interior rivers joined at this point before plunging eastward through the gorges past Ichang to the sea. It was here that the Chiang Kai-shek led central government also settled in during late autumn, 1938 to regroup and fight on, determined to resist the barbaric invaders to the end.

Little did we Yangs appreciate that summer, what a massive upheaval was taking place in our country, or the extent of the great human migration toward the interior and the new wartime capital of Chungking.

All of us were deeply concerned over what we knew about this activity however, since two of our immediate family members, neither of whom we had heard from in months, were out there somewhere in the middle of it. Even before Guo Liang's departure in the waning days of December, our oldest sister Li Cheun (Nelly) and her central government civil servant husband Hu Sei Ziang (S.Z.) had fled their Nanking home with his fellow National Railway Administration's key staffers well ahead of the advancing Japanese army.

I had last seen Nellie, who was 18 years older than I, and S.Z., a graduate of Chao Tung University, back in 1932 at their Shanghai wedding, immediately after which they had moved to Nanking. Since I was only two years old then, I obviously didn't remember her!

Even Daddy did not realize at first that immediately upon outbreak of full-scale hostilities near Peking the previous year the government had secretly begun evacuating scores of key arsenals, factories, utility plants and machine shops to safety in the interior. All possible priority movable items considered vital to continuing the war had been loaded on boats or rafts, covered with leaves and branches for camouflage, and sailed, poled or pulled from the banks by coolies up the Yangtze. Lacking decent through roads, what couldn't be moved upriver had to be transported over tortuous mountain paths by man or beast; a slow moving task requiring backbreaking labor.

Most of China's universities, technical colleges, and other schools of higher learning also moved inland; professors and students joining to carry with them essential laboratory equipment and books. These, like the disassembled factories and industrial plants moved not only to Chungking, but to other interior cities such as Kunming, Changsha, Sian (Xian) and Chengtu (Chengdu).

Along with this spectacular relocation of factories and universities was a massive human migration. Not only did govern-

71

ment civil servants, factory and plant workers, professors and students, and entire hospital staffs surge from coastal areas to the interior, but many hundreds of thousands, of ordinary people as well. They moved by junk, sampan, railway, cart, rickshaw, and by foot, in long endless, winding lines. No one really knows how many millions of people participated in this great exodus to different interior parts of China, or how many scores of thousands died en route from disease, exposure or exhaustion.

The Japanese made little effort to halt or check this massive migration of material and people. They felt that it would quickly swamp whatever remained of Chinese central authority and hasten their eventual victory. Too late did they realize that it represented a national, unified, patriotic resolve to continue the war.

These remarkable large shiftings which were shaping my country had little impact on me at the time. At age eight, although I was aware of these momentous events through listening to discussions of them by my parents, older siblings, relatives and friends, I was more concerned with the ordinary scenes and happenings of life that filled my youthful everyday world.

My fourth grade school year at McTyeire ended in late June – a disaster for me! As I feared, and Daddy did not yet know, I had failed Arithmetic! All my other grades were excellent, but in the private schools of Shanghai at the time, the rules were clear that if you flunked even one mandatory subject you would automatically have to repeat the entire grade year. Daddy was far too busy with his work and with managing his "three-families" home affairs at term's end to catch on to my predicament. He would, in time; and I had nightmares nearly every night about what would happen – WHEN! But for now, I wanted only to enjoy the July and August summer school vacation months.

By late spring, and throughout the summer, Shanghai became increasingly a city of refugees. Homeless people of all ages and ever growing numbers of beggars lined nearby Avenue

Joffre, although the French led police managed to keep clear the more affluent neighborhood residential streets like our Peach Blossom Lane. Each day's early morning light usually uncovered more than one dead body nearby on that major avenue, some murdered others the result of disease or starvation. At night it was not uncommon to hear sporadic gunfire both in the distance and fairly close by. Japanese army patrols were constantly about at night, but largely kept out of sight during daylight hours.

As Ah Foo and the maids made vocally clear, market and other prices were soaring day by day, and the market areas were getting dirtier with each passing week. The normally humid days of summer were unusually sweltering that year, and people's tempers were short as a result of the political uncertainties and the heat. Everyone was required to get new inoculations to prevent disease epidemics.

But life was not all that dreary! The neighborhood backyard flower gardens and the parks were a blaze of floral colors. The hollyhocks that summer were the tallest and most brilliant that anyone could remember, and the oleander more fragrant, dahlias seemed larger in size and cornflowers more colorful than those of years past. Our Pi-Pa tree out back bore luscious edible apricot-like fruit for the first time.

Both to cut food costs and to ensure a wider, fresher variety of vegetables, Grandmother organized and supervised the planting and cultivation of two home gardens, a small one on our mansion's roof garden, and a larger one in our back yard. Paul did the heavy digging preparation and Betty and I the ongoing maintenance and harvesting. Our snowpeas, bok choy, spinach, beans, radishes and onions grew to enormous size and mouthwatering taste.

The sycamore trees that lined the curbsides of Peach Blossom Lane and most other streets in the French Concession created at least the illusion of July and August coolness. Their leafy branches vibrated with the rasping sounds of countless cicadas. Flocks of pesky sparrows perched, preened, flapped and darted everywhere.

Inside the mansion, our three basic family entities functioned strictly in accordance with Daddy's policies, procedures and constantly changing whims. He was Lord and Master of our little kingdom and his directives or slightest wishes were our command.

His control and dominance over each of us was so total, the effect on our lives so long lasting, that the story of what kind of a man he was, how he lived his adult life, and how he exercised his control and dominance is worth recording for future generations. His life bridged and mirrored the tail end of an age-old traditional way of life, and the beginnings, for educated Chinese at least, of modern, more worldly ways.

Since the Communists, who later came to power in 1949, initiated such a massive, sustained effort to eradicate so many of the traditional Chinese beliefs and customs, Daddy's ways will interest many of his today's later generation countrymen as well as foreigners. In retrospect, those ways overall reflect far more comedy than pathos!

In the summer of 1938, in the prime of life at age 49, at the peak of career success as a top Chinese executive with prestigious American run Standard Vacuum Oil Company of China; with a new, imposing home in the desirable French Concession, and three healthy sons (also four daughters), most outsiders would assume that he really had it made in cosmopolitan Shanghai! We shall see!

He was a tall fine looking, even handsome man who projected a warm, intelligent, charming and persuasive front toward superiors or others he wished to impress. Underlings were treated indifferently or abruptly.

To outsiders, he looked and acted like a Big Shot individual of considerable authority and status. He always wore European style clothes and a hat, and was very particular about his shirts, which had to be starched and pressed just right.

Although he had never traveled outside China, he was totally fluent in both verbal and written English. This English, heavy on the show-off use of not so common literate words, was a combination of the British English he had studied at university, and American English picked up through his Standard Oil work. His reputation as a grammarian was so generally recognized that his American superiors at Standard Oil often asked him to review their written reports before forwarding them to their U.S. head office.

We Yang family members including his mother; our grandmother, used other adjectives to describe him: conniving, unaffectionate, penny-pinching, argumentative, self righteous, boastful, domineering, materialistic, and flirtatious acting toward any attractive female over age 15! He was basically a coward in that he hated direct confrontation on any issue, and for all his protestations to the contrary was quite superstitious.

Avarice was the key to his personality, money his god, although he didn't know how to enjoy having it. He had schemed and worked so hard through the years for his money that he basically resented all of us because our expenses caused it to keep slipping away from him. Since none of us worked – none of us were, in his opinion, contributing anything! Thus his manner and actions toward all of us reflected his obvious attitude that we were little more than a financial drain and burden on him.

Before any further picturing of daily life for all of us under HIS ROOF however, to be fair, let's look at this yet undescribed side of his earlier life.

His father, a respected but not so well to do Ningpo scholar who taught students in his home died when he was nineteen, leaving an impoverished family of his mother, three younger sisters and a sickly younger brother who himself died soon after their father's funeral. Through his own hard work and intelligence, without help from anyone, he had supported his mother, put two of his sisters through medical school, and worked his way through St. John's University in Shanghai, first for a degree in English, and then for a diploma in Civil Engineering.

These accomplishments impressed Mother's well-to-do Mandarin father Yuen Chan-Kwon, when, during their courtship, she presented Daddy to her family. Yuen approved their marriage and for several years thereafter helped him get jobs building railroads in various parts of China.

In 1927, just after the birth of my sister Betty, he landed a position with Standard Oil on his own, and had advanced rapidly with that company to his present executive position. Superstitiously believing that her birth had been the good luck omen responsible for this career good fortune, she was the only one of us to whom he showed any signs of fondness.

While he had received some job securing help early along the way from Grandfather Yuen, we Yangs all respected Father's career success as being that of a self-made man. But, that summer, we also felt that all our above noted descriptive adjectives fit him perfectly!

Father's first and foremost tool of control over members of his household was based on the power of the purse. Since he disbursed to each entity on the first day of each month enough expense and personal allowance money to cover needs for the balance of the month, we were all totally dependent on him for our basic existence.

His largest disbursement went to Mother, who further distributed it in turn first to Ah Foo and our two first and second floor maids for wages and household expenses. This household allocation also covered expenses for Grandmother and Concubine Silver Lotus. She then gave pocket money allowances to Suzie, Paul, Betty and me.

Disbursement was then made by him to Concubine Ching to cover her household expenses, personal allowances, and other needs for her four boys and their own cook/maid. He then handed out separate personal, private pocket money payments to Grandmother, Silver Lotus, and oldest at-home son James. He either handled payment of other larger expenses such as school tuition or automobile expenses himself, or delegated the responsibility.

His basic modus operandi for living his three separate lives under one roof was to keep us separated as much as possible within our different level living quarters. His usually private access to each of the mansion's three floors was via the big, enclosed center stairwell, although he could, if he wished, also gain access to each level from a courtyard outside spiral staircase.

He slept, as whim and passion dictated with either Concubines One or Two. He never slept with Mother after we moved to Peach Blossom Lane; in fact, he for the most part simply ignored her.

Grandmother and Concubine Silver Lotus each had one of the three ground floor bedrooms. The latter had the main bathroom for private use – Grandmother had a chamber pot and portable washbasin in her room! Ah Foo and our two Yang family maids also slept on this floor in an alcove next to the kitchen.

All other members of the Yang blood family lived on the middle floor, one room of which was taken up with James' home chemistry laboratory and his new hobby – a self-built secret short wave radio set hidden behind a covering cloth in one corner of the room.

The mansion's top floor main bedroom and its private bath was occupied by Number Two Concubine Ching. Her four boys and their family combination cook/maid occupied other space on that floor.

All of our Yang family, including Grandmother frequently, ate in our middle floor parlor which with its big round table, also served as a dining room. Father never ate with us, except on very special occasions such as New Year's Eve.

Silver Lotus, joined most evenings by Father, ate in the ground floor parlor. When Father was away or dining upstairs with Concubine Ching, Grandmother sometimes kept her company. None of us Yangs ever ate with her or she with us. Food for occupants of both ground and middle level floors was prepared in the ground floor kitchen.

Concubine Ching and her boys ate in their third floor parlor, with food being prepared in their own kitchen.

A typical Yang family day's eating schedule, on weekends or other days when most of us were at home, went something like this:

Breakfast was always informal – eat from the parlor table on the run – cafeteria style, with food on the table ready and waiting. Nearly all the food items were salty things (since no one ever ate anything sweet in the morning), such as fried peanuts, or tofu (soy bean curd) with soy sauce. Sometimes we had eggs, either the chemically blackened, so called thousand-year-old-egg type, or fried eggs. And always present was piping hot congee, a watery rice gruel.

Lunch was normally another informal eat and run affair featuring a hot soup of some type plus whatever was left over from dinner the night before. Hot tea was always available throughout the day for anyone that wanted it, but never served with meals. During the colder months, afternoon tea time refreshments (also available weekdays as after school snacks) often consisted of a bowl of hot Wonton soup or big soft-dough dumplings filled with bits of meat or vegetables. During summer months, these afternoon refreshments consisted most often of sweet, ice cold red or green bean soup.

Evening dinner was always a sit-down affair where all members of the Yang family (except Daddy) who were around joined together. We had a revolving "Lazy-Susan" sitting in the middle of the table, onto which large bowls of the several four or five hot dishes and the ever-present soup tureen were placed. We would all dig in at will with our chopsticks, spinning the "Lazy-Susan" to get the farthest away dishes close, and putting the selected pieces atop our individual bowls of rice for eating. It was considered bad manners to pick and poke, so the idea was to spot the best pieces and try and get them before someone else did! Part of the art of that was to start or check the "Lazy-Susan" spin without offending anyone. This meal was always followed up with assorted fruits, but never sweets.

Daddy's clearly defined organization of his three household entities represented no small managerial accomplishment. Overall household harmony, from his point of view, and personal peace of mind, depended on the smooth functioning of each of the three integrated "family" sub-units. His management of this essentially heterogeneous organization depended on smooth-working staff-line relationships. Like the Mongol Emperors of old he exercised absolute control, as has been noted, in all policy and financial matters, and was the court-of-last-resort for all disputes.

Within this framework, we lived, more or less contentedly, our respective family and individual lives. Even though the old social system of China was breaking down even then, and most households consisted only of husband, wife and children, many households functioned like ours, with additional sub-units. In our case, for example, Number Two Concubine Ching and her children formed such a sub-unit. In other cases, relatives and their families, such as a married son with his wife and children might live as a sub-unit within the son's father's household.

Under this tradition, among members of the blood family, the family was expected to educate the children, settle its disputes and take care of its sick and aged. Since loyalty was primarily to the family rather than the nation, this had in the past usually resulted in the lack of any strong, deeply felt Chinese national patriotism. The new, major 1937 Japanese attacks, victories and string of atrocities, especially the brutally savage "Rape of Nanking," forced a striking change in Chinese attitudes. Now suddenly, for the first time in centuries, millions of Chinese felt the stirrings of national patriotism.

This loyalty to family concept, meant that everyone had obligations: father to family, elder brothers to younger brothers, and respect between husband and wife. Children were expected to honor and obey their parents. And everyone, especially the children, was expected to honor and pay homage to the aged. This Confucian concept, of course, was pretty loosely adhered to much of the time and in many ways within our family.

Under this traditional system, Concubines were accorded the rank and privileges of wives, the only real difference being that they were not legally married.

Father, in effect then was the head of three different "families" within our larger household. He was the master of our Yang blood family (including Grandmother) and its servants; of Number Two Concubine and her children and their combination cook/maid; and he was also master of the sub-unit formed by himself and Number One Concubine.

Within the overall household, sub-units lived independent lives to the greatest extent possible and attempted to stay out of each other's way. In smaller homes, such as the one we had moved from so recently, this was not easy. Father's three-storied architectural plan of our new mansion represented a very practical, although expensive, way to handle the problem of being head of three separate households under one roof.

Within our mansion, Number Two Concubine Ching and her family, in their third floor apartment, lived so independently that we rarely saw them. Mother and Concubine Ching seldom met face to face, and when they did conversation was strained and limited. Whenever possible, communication was via respective maids. Apart from Father, no one in our household liked Number Two Concubine and had absolutely nothing to do with her children. Father was responsible for supervising her boys within their sub-unit, just as he was for his own children within our blood family group, and of course paid all expenses connected with them and their mother.

Number One Concubine's situation was a bit different. Father had brought her into our household so many years back, and at such an early age, that she was frequently considered and treated at times almost as part of the Yang blood family. While they never shared meals or Yang family gatherings time together, Mother accepted her to the extent that the two of them occasionally spent afternoons playing chess together.

Grandmother and Silver Lotus enjoyed a fairly cordial relationship, drawn together in part because they as lone individuals lived more or less outside the mainstream of our Yang family activities. We younger Yang children liked Number One Concubine, and treated her much like an older sister.

Not enjoying any legal status, either concubine could, of course, be sent packing at any time by Father. Their only "protection" was that offered by tradition and the degree of social pressure felt by him to conform to it in taking care of them in a responsible way. That, plus two other weapons used over the centuries to great advantage by Chinese wives and concubines alike – one being a "loud and eloquent" tongue, the other the threat of suicide!

While in theory, our household living system was workable, in practice it was somewhat flawed, especially from the point of view of Grandmother and myself. From her point of view she was paid no honor by anyone, shown scant respect, was seldom obeyed, and more often than not was simply ignored – especially by all the assorted grandchildren and young people in the house; most specifically, in her eyes, by me!

From my point of view, and from everyone else's too, especially Daddy's, I as youngest child, and a girl at that, rated only slightly higher than a worm in the traditional, family and mansion pecking-order. In spite of our basic differences and often mutual-loathing, Grandmother and I often joined forces and presented a united front on issues as a means not only of common defense, but also of sheer self-preservation in the family and household group. She and I had what psychologists would call a "love-hate" relationship based on the fact that we often needed and depended on one another.

She was lonely and loved to attend Chinese operas or go shopping, but due to her bound feet, really needed assistance when she went out. Since I was usually available and eager, but too young to go by myself, we were frequently outing companions, whether we liked each other or not.

As the last of the seven Yang children, I really represented the end-all of child having to my father. Although he and mother had met and gotten married on their own – an unusual occurrence for their time; and not through an arranged marriage, as was the custom; having children, to my father at least, was chiefly an end toward having males that could carry on the family line.

To his traditional way of thinking, the birth of a female was sort of an insult to his ego and virility; and besides, girls were pretty expensive to maintain and marry off, worthless things anyhow. I suspect that after his delight over Paul's birth he tried for one more son; got Betty, tried again, got me – and quit the whole business in disgust! At any event, he went out of his way to ignore me, and I spent most of my early years like a half-frightened rabbit trying to stay out of his way.

I was impressed with Father's power, authority and commanding physical presence, but was quite literally afraid of him. In later years I came to understand the frustrations, fears, and complications he faced in managing his business, family, and personal affairs during all those troubled years I lived under His roof. But since he never showed any love, affection or even gentle human kindness toward me, my feelings toward him, as toward Grandmother, remain quite mixed.

I basically grew up on my own, underfoot and largely ignored by everyone in our household most of the time, much like my dog Mong-Fu. That's one reason he and I were such great pals – youngest girl and only beast in the house, more or less in the same boat!

Several paragraphs back the point was made that to outsiders Father, with his big job, big house, three fine sons and apparently plenty of money had it made in cosmopolitan Shanghai. That was certainly the impression he worked hard to create.

Observant insiders of our household however, gleefully appreciated both the sham of his theatrics and the comedy that often resulted from his constant battle to "keep the lid on" his three families under one roof. We saw him more as a busy-bee, frequently harassed man chasing up and down either his interior or exterior stairwells, finding at each level not desired peace and tranquillity, but constant complaints and never ending problems.

To give a few examples, here are just some of the many frustrations and problems he encountered during those hot sticky months of July and August that year:

As Ah Foo scrubbed the first floor back entrance concrete veranda early one morning, I (by design) engaged her in conversation. This allowed Paul and Betty, peeking down from the second floor, to poke off her wig with a long bamboo pole. It fell into her pail of water. For some reason this really enraged her! As she yelled and screamed, I ran for cover, and Paul and Betty melted into the woodwork until lunchtime.

As soon as Father got home from work, Ah Foo volubly expressed her outrage to him and demanded that he punish us. Hating confrontation of any kind, he simply retreated to the room of Concubine Silver Lotus for the rest of the evening, and did nothing.

Then, twice during the period he had to take Mother, Grandmother and Silver Lotus out together with Betty and me in the car. Always, in such cases, "face" was gained by the adult female who got to sit in the front seat. Since it was always a "first come, first serve situation," we children would always try and get to the car first so as to hold the front seat for Mother.

No matter which of his females won, when leaving the car, Daddy would simply quietly sit tight in his seat, letting all the other occupants noisily jostle over precedence in getting out of the vehicle.

Second Concubine Ching and her boys were never involved in this type situation, since none of them ever rode in the car at the same time as any of the rest of us. When it came to the car, it was always either them or us!

At age 17, Suzie who was becoming increasingly pretty and vivacious, began attracting boyfriends, and, unknown to Father, started going out frequently on dates. Like all lively Shanghai teenage girls of her school and social group, she began to dress stylishly, wear high heels and experiment with makeup, all abetted by Mother and Grandmother.

One evening, as she was going out and Daddy was coming home, they unexpectedly crossed paths in the mansion's front entranceway. Completely unaware of his daughter's "growing up" and dating, he was both stunned and shocked beyond belief at her attire and "painted face" appearance.

Flying into a rage, he shoutingly chased her back into the second floor parlor and whacked her so hard across her backside with a ruler that it broke. He then sent her sobbing hysterically into her room for the evening, forbidding her to ever go out on dates again without his personal prior permission.

The result wasn't what he expected! Mother, Grandmother and Betty, first collectively, then individually, then Concubine Silver Lotus privately, all excitedly read him the riot act so loudly that he retreated to and sulked in Concubine Ching's apartment for the next three evenings.

He finally relented a bit when Suzie, with his permission brought home her favorite boyfriend – a fine looking 22 year old named Logan Lo who had just graduated that June from Shanghai University with a combined B.A. degree in English and Education. Father immediately approved of him; impressed by the fact that he was then the swimming champion of Shanghai, and came from a well-to-do family.

Early one evening I happened to look into James' second floor laboratory room and spotted him squeezed close up behind and with his arms tightly around our rather cute, long haired 17 year old maid Mei-Ling. Little realizing that they were simply feeling a little mutual youthful glandular attraction, I blabbed about what I had seen to Mother. Not wanting any of "that kind of problem" in our home, she promptly told Father.

Once again he flew into an indignant rage, and berated them both loudly. He ordered James to register as a weekday boarder when his university classes resumed in September, and visit home only on weekends. He had no idea how inwardly pleased James was with this "punishment." Daddy was the one who felt "punished" when he finally discovered the high extra cost of this dormitory boarding he had foolishly committed himself to.

One of Daddy's favorite managerial cost-cutting techniques was to buy things in bulk at one time. This included food, such as 20 watermelons at a time which would be lowered into our backyard well to keep cool, one stop shoe buying sprees at Wing On Department Store, with the whole family in tow, and each August, clothing enough for everyone in our household to last through the coming school year.

This annual clothing splurge required his careful prior consultation with Grandmother since she kept in her room the family copy of the Farmer's Calendar. This calendar, to be found at the time in the home of nearly all Chinese families, dated back to the time of Emperor Yao in 2254 B.C. It contained annual astrological predictions for the coming year about nearly everything concerning daily life activities.

Among other things it pointed out was 1938's lucky and unlucky days for tailoring. While Daddy protested that consultation of this calendar for such things as buying clothes for the family was nonsense, he always reviewed it carefully with Grandmother. They found, this year, to his great satisfaction, that while bad luck would occur if any required cloth was cut on August 4, cutting it August 5 would likely bring a windfall of unexpected new money.

The calendar also noted that trouble could be expected if fittings of tailor made clothing took place on August 11, but if done on either of the following two days, one stood likely to be rewarded either with something valuable or precious.

Figuring that he had nothing to lose, and hopefully new money or unknown valuable items to gain, he arranged for two tailors and their assistants to come to our home from their Yates Road shop August 1. Their job: to measure all in one day, everyone in our household for assorted new clothing. He ordered specifically that first cuttings for each garment be done August 5, and that everything be brought back for individual first fittings on August 12.

While no unexpected new money or precious gifts from the gods came to him as a result of this planning and organizing, no bad luck resulted either. We all got our nice new clothes by late August, and he, as usual, saved a lot of money by buying in quantity at one time in this way.

On September 2, with autumn school terms due to start in a few days, Daddy called us Yang children in one by one to review our last school year's final report cards, which he had not yet seen. Suzie, Paul and Betty all of whom had earned excellent grades and were continuing at their same schools were "processed" quickly. Each was given money to pay their own next term's tuition fees. Since James was to be a weekday boarder at Shanghai University, Daddy arranged to go there with him to negotiate costs.

I was the last to enter HIS PRESENCE! I tiptoed in as invisibly as possible, eyes downcast, knees knocking, with butterflies flapping furiously in my stomach. He was seated in front of a parlor window with his back to the incoming bright late afternoon sunlight. I could hardly make out his face – his crisp, freshly pressed shirt almost glowed an unusually bright white.

"Well, well," he said unsmilingly, "do we have any Red Lanterns to look at this time?" I tremblingly held out my report card with its big red one next to Arithmetic! An ugly look of rage crossed his face.

He immediately hit the ceiling and berated me shrilly and expressively at length for my dumbness, lack of diligence, laziness and the fact that he was cursed with a daughter who was just draining his money and giving him nothing in return. While he had never laid a hand on me, he really enjoyed, in a quite sadistic way, as now, cutting me to ribbons verbally and reducing me to a whimpering, tearful blob of flesh. I was given no chance to offer any explanation, only to hunker down in front of him like a supplicant, and take whatever he dished out. It was so humiliating!

He went with me the next day to see the McTyeire Principal – to try and talk his way out of having to pay a whole year's tuition for me to repeat fourth grade. Since he had put so much pressure on her the previous year, with the tables now turned, she haughtily refused to budge an inch. So, I was again entered in fourth grade, as I properly should have now been anyhow if he hadn't forced me to skip third grade in the first place. It was all his fault, and it served him right to have to pay the cost!

Later that night, after returning from seeing the McTyeire Principal with Daddy, I entered Grandmother's room, complaining about my terrible headache. Springing into first aid action, she had Ah Foo hard boil an egg for her. Shelling it, she pushed a silver coin into its center and instructed me to press and hold the egg against my left temple. She assured me that this centuries old home remedy would quickly banish my headache.

An hour later, with my head still throbbing and tired of keeping the egg pressed to my temple, I complained to Mother that Grandmother's remedy wasn't working.

"Here's something that might help," she said, handing me a package of Wakamoto Yeast Tablets. "The Japanese make these to cure headaches, dizziness and fatigue in old people," she continued. "They are all I have, so take two tablets. They've got to be better than that silly egg!"

The tablets worked and I soon fell asleep, with Mong-Fu curled up close beside me – exhausted, but glad that my school problem confrontation with Daddy was at least over for now.

Chapter 6

THE FOREIGN DEVILS MADE US DO IT!

As the final days of 1938 drew to a close, Grandmother became increasingly visibly agitated. It was only to me that she finally, confided the reason for her discomfort. "Do you remember when you and I visited the Medium several months ago, to ask permission of our ancestors for your father to build our new mansion, she nervously asked; "and do you remember what Uncle Ex-Admiral, my ancestor who appeared and obtained that approval from our other ancestors, made me promise to do on behalf of our family?"

"Yes, I remember; he was really worried that the Kitchen God seemed unhappy about the way things were going in our kitchen," I replied, "And you promised him that you would take steps to appease both it and the Door God!"

"I know," she muttered, "and I was going to do it at the proper time during last year's New Year festivities, but was so shocked over the news about second Concubine Ching's arrival that I forgot. Now the new (1939) New Year is almost here, and I am terribly worried that the Kitchen God will report most unfavorably to the Jade Emperor about our family during its seven day annual visit with him in the heavens just before New Year's day!"

"Ahhh – it's all my fault," she wailed piteously, as she fell sobbing and trembling into my arms. I felt immediate concern, for I had never seen her so truly distressed and convulsive.

Since Grandmother was the only Buddhist in our family, and had taken upon herself the solemn (to her) responsibility of honoring, on behalf of all of us, the many traditional gods and deities, she now truly felt that she had seriously let us all down.

Her concern was heightened by the fact that the Kitchen God, whose garishly colorful printed picture hung prominently above our kitchen sink was considered the most important of the several household gods. Believers considered that its presence acted as a check on the behavior of the family, and a special ritual was usually followed by them to recognize its presence and purpose during each New Year period.

Why don't you pay special homage and make unusually nice offerings to the Kitchen God right now?" I suggested. "You still have some two weeks before it is due to take off and make its report.

"That's a very good idea," she exclaimed. "I will see Ah Foo in the morning to prepare special food offerings, which we can present the following day."

Suzie, Betty and Paul were only too happy to join me in helping her pay special homage to the Kitchen God on this occasion, because we knew that Ah Foo would prepare some extra special food "goodies" to appease this god, who was also special to her.

The morning of the appointed day, we helped Grandmother set up the required special effects before the two-foot tall "altar" that was always in place in her bedroom. Painted a bright red, it looked like a miniature wooden temple, within which sat a one-foot tall bronze statue of Buddha on a small, raised platform.

Two medium-size candles were placed on each side of it, and four half-pencil size sticks of incense were placed upright in a large sand filled bowl in front; ready to be lighted at the proper moment.

As Grandmother sat on her bed directing operations, Paul took down the portraits and the pictures of her ancestors from a nearby big wooden bureau top and from her nightstand table. We girls busied ourselves setting up a larger table with rice bowls for each of her ancestor's spirits whom she wished to have sit in on the event.

Knowing that she was the only true believer in the family, she deliberately invited only the spirits of her own direct family ancestors to attend this very special ceremony – no in-law spirits allowed!

"Put the portrait of Uncle Ex-Admiral over here on the right," she commanded Paul. Since her last "contact" with him has been when I was with her, taking no chances – he was to be the "most important," spirit attending the event. She then had Paul line the other ancestral portraits or pictures to the left of it – all facing toward both the alter and the table. They were there as "witnesses" to her ceremony!

We girls were instructed to place only one chopstick to the left of each of the rice bowls on the table. This was because, as she told us, ghosts eat only left-handed with one chopstick! All this shifting and placing was done in high spirits on our part, with much gleeful chatter, as we cheerfully followed her directions.

Then, as a final act, prior to arrival of the hot and cold festival food dishes from the first floor kitchen, Grandmother had Suzie fold several small pieces of gold and silver paper into the shape of gold nuggets, similar to those that were used as money in the olden days. These were placed into the large incense bowl. Also placed there, were miniature paper replicas of a boat, carriage, pair of shoes, and a suitcase – which had been purchased earlier. All these paper objects were to be burned later in a symbolic act of sending them off for use by the Kitchen God on its journey to the Heavens.

The maid Mei-Ling then appeared with a huge tray containing the bowls of food. Once they were placed on the table, she was ordered from the room and the door was shut tight. Paul was posted in front of it, within the room, to make certain that no one else entered while the ceremony was taking place.

After Grandmother lighted the candles and incense sticks, she faced the altar, her eyes blinking convulsively towards heaven, rapidly fingering her jade prayer beads. As she did so, she began intoning prayers in a quavering, loud, high-pitched voice: "Na-Mo, O-Mi-To-Va; Na-Mo, O-Mi-To-Va;........." She then set fire to the paper money, and other paper replicas. She then beseechingly asked the Kitchen God to report favorably on our family both to the Jade Emperor and to the Door God. While she was doing all this; as previously instructed, we onlookers appeared one at a time, Paul first, to stand beside her for a quick deep bow before the altar.

We each did this in turn as noisily yet slowly as possible, without talking, to cover up for the others who, standing behind the table were snitching and gobbling down bits of food as quickly and quietly as possible, and stealthily moving the chopsticks about to different locations. As the last of us made our bow, and rushed back to stand upright and well back of the food table, with the others, Grandmother finished her prayers and turned back to face us.

"Who took the food and moved the chopsticks!" she quickly asked as she suspiciously eyed the disarranged feast table. "The ancestors, Grandmother," we all laughingly declared in near-unison!

Grumblingly accepting our explanation, she sent Betty to fetch Mei-Ling to clear the table, as the rest of us replaced the ancestral portraits and pictures to their original locations, cleaned out the incense bowl, and snuffed out the altar candles. The ceremony was over, and hopefully both the Kitchen God and the Door God were appeased.

We helpers left Grandmother to rest and reflect in her own thoughts, as we raced down to the kitchen to polish off the remainder of the "ghost's leftovers."

That lunar year, the Kitchen God was due to depart on a certain night around the last week of January, seven days before Chinese New Year Day. During that period, since our household was supposedly free from its supervision, Grandmother and Ah Foo smeared some sticky sweet red bean paste on the mouth of its kitchen poster portrait, and then burned it. A new picture of the god was hung above the kitchen sink early on New Year's Eve, the night it was due to return, and a bowl of food placed beneath it in case the Kitchen God returned hungry.

Grandmother then relaxed to enjoy the rest of the New Year's festivities. Confident that she had done the right thing by the Kitchen God, she rested secure in the belief that it would now preside benignly over our family kitchen throughout the New Year.

The evening of the first Friday in February, the last day of our respective school terms, we Yang children once again had to present our first term report cards to Daddy – one by one! Once again I was last, but this time I marched into HIS PRESENCE with more confidence than ever before – due to a good "all-black marks" report card, and the fact that I had suddenly become, on January 23, a more mature (in my eyes), one year older.

"Well, now, are you going to shock me again with more Red Lanterns, like last term?" he sternly and unsmilingly growled at me. I silently handed him my report card. He grunted, looked at it briefly, and handed me an already prepared envelope of money to take with me to school the following Monday as my next term's tuition payment.

My success in passing arithmetic this time was due to the fact that he had directed Paul to help me learn my missed third grade numbers and tables. My brother had worked with me evenings throughout the just concluded term, and I now ranked safely in the middle of my class.

"I want Betty and you to meet me immediately after Saturday morning assembly at McTyeire's main school gate" he ordered. "I will first pick up Betty and you, then we will pick up

13 year old Jennifer Farley, an American girl, who is the niece of one of our American Standard Oil executives."

"She's staying with his family this year and attending Shanghai American School while her parents are traveling in Europe. As part of her school studies she has to spend some time in a home of a Chinese family. I would like for Betty and you to take care of her tomorrow throughout the rest of the afternoon and evening." I murmured my acceptance of his directive, and was dismissed.

After picking us up at McTyeire the next day, Daddy drove us over to the American School on Avenue Petain where we collected Jennifer, a tall bubbling, blue-eyed blonde, about a year older than Betty. Something of a chatterbox, it was clear that she would be full of questions!

She got a very prompt introduction to one of the strange ways of our particular Chinese family when we drove on to a nearby French bakery on Route Louis Dufour just around the corner from Avenue Petain. Located near our old home, it had long been a favorite shop for Betty and me due to the wonderful aroma of freshly baked bread that permeated its interior. Here, Daddy initiated one of his usual managerial cost cutting techniques by buying the largest possible quantity in order to get maximum extra bread loaves as a bonus. I've often suspected him as being the original inventor of the "baker's dozen" marketing concept!

Jennifer and I giggled all the way home as we sat in the Chevy's back seat almost buried under a mountain of wonderful smelling long French bread loaves, bagels and assorted hard rolls; enough to feed our entire 18-member household for the next several days!

Once at the mansion, after introducing Jennifer to all other first and second level Yang family occupants and servants; Silver Lotus was presented to her as "our auntie." Heaven forbid if she should tell her uncle about a concubine (or two) in the Yang house! All except Silver Lotus and Daddy then sat down at the parlor round table for lunch.

"You all speak such good English," Jennifer commented, "how did you (pointing at me) and Betty especially learn it? And how is it that most of you seem to have western style Christian names?"

Betty replied by explaining that while she and I, the younger ones, understood English fairly well, due to our limited vocabulary we often had to resort to sign or pidgin language.

"Since few foreigners bother to learn the difficult Chinese language," Mother interjected, "many Chinese have developed pidgin or "business English" as a means of communicating not only with all foreigners, but often with each other. While all literate Chinese understand the same written language, only relatively few speak the official Mandarin spoken language. The rest speak all sorts of different dialects, most of which sound as unfamiliar as foreign languages."

"In pidgin English, one word often does duty for three or four," noted Suzie. "So the word 'my' can also mean 'I, me, mine, our and so on. Pidgin involves simply stringing words, mostly nouns and verbs, without any prepositions or articles, into a form of sentence, usually illustrated with physical gestures.

"If, for example, I wanted to say to our maid: 'Mei-Ling, go upstairs, get a handkerchief, put some perfume on it, and bring it to me,' I most likely would say to her in pidgin English: 'Mei-Ling, fetchee one-piece nose rag, puttee stink water, bring my side.' "

"Yes, but you all speak mostly good, grammatically correct English, not pidgin." Interrupted Jennifer. "Where do you learn it?"

"We learn it at home, at school, through music and movies and from each other," continued Suzie. "At McTyeire for example, we have a one hour English class everyday from fourth grade on. And during our Saturday morning assemblies we sing lots of American Protestant church songs, such as "Jesus loves

Me' and 'Rock of Ages, 'and on the lighter side, fun popular songs such as 'Home Sweet Home.'"

"Here at home, Mother reads many British and American classic books such as 'Wuthering Heights' and 'Tom Sawyer' to us in English, and explains both the story and difficult words," remarked Paul. "We often sit around her evenings after dinner for these readings, and she usually has us speak only English at dinner time two or three days a week. This really has helped us all improve our conversational English. And we also sing English and American folk and popular songs together here at home, around the piano downstairs."

"And you are helping us improve today through your visit with us, Jennifer," I exclaimed. This pleased her very much.

"But where do your English Christian names come from," Jennifer questioned, "and can you help me understand how your Chinese family names are organized! It's all so fascinating to me!"

"Perhaps I can best answer your question about Chinese names," volunteered Mother, "for it is one frequently asked by foreigners. It is a question that requires a somewhat lengthy and complicated explanation."

"Surnames are highly important to Chinese people, just as they are to westerners – Yang, in our case," she began. "But there are only a limited number of surnames in all China. Known as the "Hundred Family Names," they break down into only 408 single and 30 double clan names, of which Yang is one. Thus there are many thousands of Yangs all over China, relatively few of which are related to other Yangs by blood.

"Each related clan or family passes on to each generation of boys (girls not included) another lineal name," she continued. "Then, each boy will be given a book name. My husband's name, for example is Yang (surname) Tseng (lineal name) Yee (book name).

Since he works with Americans he, like many Chinese, has adopted the western practice of using initials instead of his book and lineal names. This is partly due to the fact that foreigners often find the Chinese names hard to pronounce and remember. Thus at Standard Oil, your uncle and the other Americans know him as T.Y. Yang. Among Chinese of course, he is known as Yang Tseng Yee; the surnames, to Chinese, always coming first, followed by two additional characters, the lineal and book names which is the equivalent of your Christian name.

His sons, like James and Paul here at our table were all given the lineal name Liang, and each a different book (or sometimes called school) name; for example, for them it is Yang Chia Liang (James) and Yang Ping Liang (Paul)."

"Oh, it's all so complicated," exclaimed Jennifer, what about the girls' names?"

"Girls are not always given lineal names but they are given book names – usually two of them. These book names have no real meaning as such. Many are names of flowers; others have a classical or poetic implication," replied Mother.

My Chinese name is 'Bei Sie' which can be translated as 'Honorable Goddess." I proudly announced.

"That's why she adopted Bessie as her western name, just as 'Sou Sie' (Pure Goddess) did in naming herself Suzie," James said. "But we don't call her either Bei Sie or Bessie. These are official names for school and legal documents. She is called 'Shiao Bei,' her milk name, by family members, relatives and close friends."

"Does this milk name also mean Honorable Goddess?" Jennifer asked.

"No, 'Shiao means little and 'Bei' means baby. Since she was born after Betty who was already given the milk name of 'Bei Bei,' we had to call her 'Shiao Bei'. I guess if we had another baby sister we'd have to name her 'Shiao Shiao Bei!" chuckled James.

"When a new born baby is about a month old," he continued, "a feast in its honor will usually be celebrated (most definitely if the baby is a boy). Family members, relatives and close friends are invited. A milk name is given to the baby at this event. It will be known by this milk name in this family circle

97

for the rest of its life. Then a book name will be given when he or she ready for school."

"Good gracious, my head is spinning," cried Jennifer, in mock horror.

"But that's not all – there are other names as well," exultantly chortled Suzie, "nick names are also common in our family, as among other Chinese. These are usually related to some physical peculiarity. Betty, for example, (pointing jokingly to her sister) was dubbed "Duck Lips" because of the way she pouted as a small child."

Betty made a quacking sound and pursed her lips into a pout, in mock retort to Suzie's comment.

"But you haven't yet explained why you each have, and sometimes call each other by still other Christian or western names," cried Jennifer, with a small slightly confused pout of her own lips.

"Oh, these western names, adopted by nearly all of us Yang children, except our oldest brother Guo-Liang, are pure inventions," chimed in Paul, who had taken little part in our name explanation conversation up this point. "Right now," he whispered to Jennifer, "James here thinks he looks like the American movie star James Stewart, that's why he calls himself James. Talk about imagination!"

"We, like most of our schoolmates, " he continued, "select and change our western names frequently, based on fads, which are usually influenced by American or other foreign movies. We do so because we are fascinated with things foreign."

"It's disgraceful how you are all influenced by the Foreign Devils; our ancestors must be turning in their graves!" muttered Grandmother. Although she did not understand our conversation, she caught a word here and there, which with our gestures and expressions caused her to suspect that we were extolling the westerners' ways.

"Yes, the Foreign Devils made us do it!" I shouted gleefully. "We change our western names often; for instance, I used to call myself Loretta Yang after the movie actress Loretta Young. But when I discovered that there is a western name "Bessie" which sounds almost exactly like Bei Sie, I changed Loretta to Bessie immediately. What a perfect match!"

"And we call our father 'Daddy,' among ourselves. That's a common American name that sounds much like our Shanghai dialect word for Father, 'Dya-Dya,' by which we always address him face to face," noted Paul.

"My, oh my," shuddered Jennifer, "I asked 'why,' and got far more than I bargained for with all these most comprehensive explanations. What on earth will I ever do with all this new knowledge, now that you have so kindly imparted it to me?"

"Well, whenever you find yourself through life feeling the urge to counter some conversational bore, at a cocktail or dinner party, for example," jokingly commented Mother, "you can usually render them speechless with your indepth knowledge of how the Chinese name system works!"

"Unless it happens to be a Chinese bore," chuckled Paul.

With that we all relaxed around the parlor table to enjoy hot tea and the tray of warm chewy sesame balls that Mei Ling had just brought from the kitchen. These were delicious golf ball size snacks, featuring a sweet red bean paste center inside a rice flour outer skin, that had been rolled in sesame seeds and deep fried.

We then took Jennifer over to meet Father Nicholas and his family, see his interesting bird aviary and listen to the sidesplitting pidgin English of their cook Ah Liu. This was the first time she had ever met White Russians in a home setting. English was, as always, our language of communication with them.

Ever anxious to impress the young niece of a top American Standard Oil executive, Daddy granted us the most unusual honor of His Presence at our Yang family dinner table that evening. Charming, witty, flirtatious – the perfect host, he impressed all of his seldom dined with family members, as well as our guest!

After dinner, we all adjourned to the first floor apartment and gathered around our imposing large antique piano, which had been Daddy's original wedding gift to our Mother. There he put on his Big Act of playing several American Stephen Foster songs such as "Old Folks at Home" and "My Old Kentucky Home," on black keys no less! Mother had taught him to memorize and play that way by ear only during the early years of their marriage. Mother then played beautifully as we group-sang English, American and Chinese folk and popular songs.

It was the nicest single Yang family social evening together that I had ever experienced!

Several events took place over the next three months prior to Suzie's mid-June high school graduation from McTyeire that served to keep our family on edge.

First came the announcement from Logan, Suzie's boy friend with whom she was now head over heels in love, that he was departing for Chungking almost immediately to accept a proffered commission in the Nationalist (central government) army. The hasty departure was due to the fact that he would be traveling more safely with two of his recent university graduate friends who were also being commissioned.

While Suzie was crushed over this decision, the couple pledged their love and she promised to join him in Chungking as soon as possible. Father gave his permission for this, based on their promise that they would marry there, and provided that he would decide on the safest timing for her departure. Logan agreed, and within days secretly departed Shanghai.

Almost concurrently with Logan's departure came an official Japanese announcement that a man named Wang Ching-Wei had been appointed Acting President of a new Chinese Government (a Japanese controlled puppet government) being formed in Nanking. This government, made up of Chinese collaborators and traitors, was to rule over our Yang household's day to day lives until arrival of the Americans in 1945. Wang was a renegade former official of the Chinese national government.

Closer to home, so close in fact that it was within our home, Father fell ill for three days from some virus that was floating about, and holed up with Concubine Silver Lotus. This prompted Grandmother to fly into action with her traditional medications.

To get rid of his fever she quickly came up with an ages old Jewish/Chinese mothers' "chicken soup' prescription! She and Ah Foo went to great lengths to make sure this was "hen-soup," since they firmly believed that such a sick bed soup, if made from a rooster, would poison the patient!

Then, to rid him of the virus, she had a local Chinese Natural Medicine Shop proprietor prepare a special balm made from dried, finely ground, small black and gold Coin Snakes and Sea Horses.

Surviving all this attention, he had to face a much more mentally stressful situation a few days after returning to work. Then he had to referee an especially noisy backyard battle of words that broke out between violently jealous Second Concubine Ching and smugly "superior-acting" First Concubine Silver Lotus over his staying with the latter during his illness.

Finally, in June, came Suzie's graduation from McTyeire, where to the proud tears of Mother and Grandmother, and the trying to catch her eye smirks and funny faces of Betty and me, she did her diploma pickup march across the stage to, what else, but the strains of that grand old British musical classic "Pomp and Circumstance!"

Shortly after Suzie's graduation a furtive stranger, dressed in the ragged clothes of a peasant, knocked at our mansion's servant's entrance. When Ah Foo answered, he quickly shoved an envelope into her hands, whirled about, and strode rapidly away without looking back. It turned out to be a hand-carried letter from Guo Liang in Chungking – our first from him since his departure in late December the previous year.

For the reading of this most welcome letter, Daddy assembled all the Yang family, including Betty and me, in our second floor parlor. Swearing us all to secrecy, he read the following aloud to us:

Dear Honorable Father,

For the first time since arriving here late last December, I have hopes that a friend will be able to carry this letter back to you and our family. After leaving home, I safely passed through Nanking ahead of the Japanese army and found work as crewman on a sampan headed west up the Yangtze. It was heavily loaded with machine tools from an important factory near Shanghai. It took weeks of terribly hard work to drag and pole it through the gorges against the fast moving current. The river was very crowded with other sampans, junks and boats, many of which were dashed against the rocks and sank with great loss of life and cargo.

By the time we finally passed Ichang and reached the river town of Tzekwei, after negotiating Ox Liver and Horse Lung Gorge and the Hsin Tan rapids, I was completely exhausted from overwork and lack of adequate food. I left my sampan and stayed there for a week just to rest. Along with thousands of other refugees crowding the boats and riverbank pathways, I slept on the ground and subsisted mostly on a handful of rice each day. Eventually, I managed to make my way by foot to Chungking.

I quickly found employment here as a supervisory engineer in a factory that is highly essential to the war effort. The city's population has exploded fivefold, to nearly one million people, in the last six months. They have come from everywhere in China, mostly of course from the seacoast regions. Everyone is so patriotic – even Communists from the north have come here to help fight the Japanese.

The thick damp fog that always enshrouds this city six months of the year protected us all winter from bombing attacks. Unfortunately, it started lifting three weeks ago and on May 3 we had our first big air raid, which caused little damage. A much bigger one followed two nights later – wave after wave of bombers! Since we have little antiaircraft protection their bombs caused heavy civilian casualties. Our factory, like other key ones, is located deep inside a bomb proof cliffside cave, so most of the widespread destruction was in the city's residential areas. We now get nighttime air raids often.

I live with eight other young unmarried engineers in a small, very crowded bamboo, mud-brick and thatched roof hut near the factory. We usually work around the clock in 12-hour shifts seven days a week. While we had little snow, the con-

102

stant damp cold of the past winter caused much sickness. We have no heat at work or elsewhere except for small charcoal braziers in our dining hall and rest areas that we crowd around to warm our hands. Girls constantly bring hot tea to our work area however, so that helps; that and the four layers of padded clothing most of us wear and sleep in.

Our daily food consists mostly of soups plus rice and vegetables, with added shreds of pork, chicken or water buffalo twice a week. On our rare days off, my friends and I usually go fishing in the Yangtze – for relaxation, and if we are lucky, a few small fish to eat.

Nellie and S. Z. are safe and well here in Chungking. They live and work quite some distance away, so I've only been able to see them once so far.

My respects to Mother and everyone else in the family. We here are working hard for victory!

Respectfully, your Eldest Son
Guo Liang
May 20, 1938
Chungking

One most interesting occupation for Betty and me that summer, apart from again tending to our Grandmother-supervised family garden, was observing and assisting Paul in his pigeon whistle project.

For generations, older Chinese men especially have loved to breed, contemplate and display pets such as goldfish, and caged crickets, cicadas and small songbirds. Others have engaged in the hobby of fitting tiny whistles to pigeons – sometimes to an entire flock. These hobbies are preserved out of a basic aesthetic and friendly appreciation of these living creatures, which are objects to be admired.

Many bird lovers often go for walks carrying their now uncaged pets on a stick, to which one foot is attached by a long but strong thread. This allows the bird enough freedom of motion to fly up to and perch on lower leafy branches of nearby shade trees. Often such bird owners, and passersby, will spend hours sitting, chatting and watching these tethered birds enjoy their limited freedom.

Since pigeons were almost as common as sparrows in Shanghai, Paul had been able to capture two young ones. We had seen him with them the evening before when he mysteriously refused to answer our questions as to what he was doing with them.

Early the next morning we found him in the back yard of our mansion attaching a tiny, strange looking set of tubes to the tail of one of the pigeons by means of a fine copper wire.

"What on earth are you doing?" Betty asked. "Please don't hurt that poor young pigeon," I pleaded nervously.

"I'm not hurting him," Paul replied, "I am simply fitting a very lightweight whistle to the tail of each pigeon. Then I'll tie a long thread to one foot on each one, and while holding one end, let them fly. As they fly, the wind passing through these tiny tubes will cause a vibrating whistling sound."

He went on to explain that the fitting of pigeon whistles had long been a popular hobby in Shanghai, as in other parts of China, that he had bought his whistles, and learned how to attach them, at a special bird pet shop.

"There are two different types of whistles one can buy," he continued, "one made of bamboo tubes placed side by side, and this kind I bought, which consists of tubes attached to a very small gourd. You will notice that this gourd whistle has a mouthpiece with some small tubes clustered around it."

"Does each tube make a whistling sound?" Betty questioned "And how many tubes can there be?" I chimed in.

"Yes, each tube makes a whistling sound," continued Paul, "and the number of tubes is dependent on the size of the mouthpiece. I saw one at the bird store with 13 tubes. Others had anywhere from two to ten tubes, each type having a different name. The whistles I bought, each having one mouthpiece and ten tubes are named "The Eleven-Eyed One.""

"Will these whistles protect the pigeons against any birds of prey that try to attack them?" I asked.

"Not really," he answered, "their real purpose is to please the human listener who enjoys the windblown tunes they produce."

Both the two pigeons and their whistles performed beautifully for us for the remainder of the summer. Just prior to start of the autumn school term Paul removed the whistles and gave the birds their freedom. It had been a most interesting summer project for all of us – humans and our feathered friends alike.

Autumn, 1939 started off with the exciting news of Germany's unprovoked September 1 blitzkrieg attack on Poland. Two days later Britain and France responded by declaring war on Germany.

While all this was certainly big news to everyone in Shanghai, to most Chinese, including us Yangs, it was also more or less "so what else is new" news. After all, the Japanese military had started pecking away at our country as early as 1931, and had been trying to kick us to death for the past two years. We were sick of hearing about war!

Besides, for Betty, Paul and myself the big activity of September 3 was not talking about the new war in Europe, but registering at Bei Tsun Chinese School, just a few blocks away from our Peach Blossom Lane mansion.

Due to the continued influx of impoverished refugees into Shanghai, the increase in grasping beggars and disease-ridden homeless people, the rapid rise in daylight street crime and new political uncertainties, Daddy felt that we should change to this close-by school.

Since it was within walking distance of our home, we could avoid the daily to and from rickshaw rides to our respective previous schools. Bei Tsun was considered a good school, having been started some years earlier by professors from nearby Chiao Tung University.

While we "Three Musketeers," as we sometimes called ourselves, were pleased at being able to attend the same school together, we agreed that we would miss our schoolday rickshaw ride interludes. Even though we often simply took for granted the always colorful sights of Shanghai's crowded streets, we knew that we lived in one of the most exciting, interesting cities in the world. One constantly had a sense of anticipation that the diverse, fast-moving street scene could quickly produce any kind of an unexpected situation.

Always there were the ancient sounds – squealing pigs, cackling chickens, bawling babies, gossiping women, yelling men – and the eternal singsong chants of coolies carrying, pushing or pulling their heavy loads.

And the newer sounds – the blare of the unbelievably bad sounding brass bands hired to lead funeral or wedding processions, grinding crowded trams and buses, the wails of native flutes or violins, honking automobiles and trucks, and the staccato sounds of bamboo section drums.

And the other sounds – the rhythmic beating on a block of wood by the cotton yardage salesman, and the different, specific chants of the brassware salesman, the night soil collector, the scissors and knife sharpener, and the sidewalk barber.

People watching could easily become a full-time avocation! Rich, poor, sick, wretched, fat, thin, old, young people – beggars galore, tall Sikhs from India followed by their womenfolk in colorful flowing saris, and black robed monks. Old Chinese ladies tottering along on their bound feet. Japanese women in colorful kimonos and obies. And the brilliant scarlet outer garments of young Chinese infants.

And the smells – raw sewage, rotting garbage, fresh garbage – coupled with the delightful odors of cooking food of all types – including fresh-fried foot-long hollow breakfast rolls called "oil sticks." Mobil stores (pushcarts) as well as the regular streetside open-fronted ones, by the hundreds, sold everything from socks, straw hats and lemonade to five-cent one-course dinners.

Yes, we would miss our twice a school day regular rickshaw rides, but we had only to stroll around our Peach Blossom Lane local neighborhood to experience a microcosm of all these street scenes, sounds, and smells. The color, tang and zest of Shanghai lay not in its temples and flower-filled parks, but in its crowded streets!

Chapter 7

THE BRITISH ARE LEAVING – HIP, HIP, HOORAY!

"The British are leaving, the British are leaving! Hip, Hip, Hooray!" Paul exuberantly proclaimed early on the morning of Wednesday, August 21, 1940, as he pounded on the door to the bedroom where Betty and I were sleeping.

"Are all the British leaving today?" Betty called out in sleepy reply. "Nope, only their garrison soldiers, but it will be a very colorful parade with thousands of people lining the streets to see them off," he replied. "What time will the parade take place?" I asked.

"The actual march won't start till noon, but we have to catch our tram by 9 a.m. to get to The Sincere Co., on Nanking Road in the International Settlement, in time to get a front window viewing spot," he announced loudly from the other side of our closed door. "Father has gotten permission from Mr. Wong, the manager, for us to watch from their second floor which overlooks the parade route. Up and at it sisters, this is too good an event to miss!"

The three of us soon met at the parlor table to wolf down a quick breakfast snack of cold fried dough sticks wrapped in pancake-size shape and thickness "Da-Ping" – a pizza-like dough that prior to baking had been sprinkled with sesame seeds and scallions.

As we washed our food down with cups of hot water served by Mei-Ling, Paul excitedly described a most interesting event involving these troops that he and James, along with 20,000 other people, had witnessed at the Shanghai Race Course two nights earlier.

There, as part of the early ceremonies connected with this day's parade, the combined Drums and Pipes of the bands of the departing East Surrey Regiment and the Seaforth Highlanders put on a "Retreat," one of the finest and most colorful of all British militarydrill spectacles, as a farewell salute.

"The crowd expressed its appreciation by donating enough money, into collection boxes passed around by the British societies, for one quart of beer each for the hundreds of soldiers," he told us. "These soldiers will actually depart Thursday on the ship 'S.S. Taksang,' along with other British garrison troops from Tientsin; boarding today at the end of the parade."

Shortly before noon we were happily positioned right in front of a wide second story window of The Sincere Co., where Daddy had just joined us. He informed us that James and two of his university student friends would also be watching the parade; from the rooftop of the Capitol Theater Building overlooking Garden Bridge at the north end of The Bund. That was near the moored troop transport, where the day's event would terminate.

Below us, the street was being cleared by tall, red turbaned Sikh policemen, as the jostling crowds on the sidewalks packed close together in ever increasing numbers. Scores of onlookers jammed overhanging balconies or, like us, peered out from crowded upper story windows.

As the parade formed up inside the Shanghai Race Course grounds a few blocks west of us, where hundreds of fashionably dressed British and other foreign ladies and their men-folk watched from the stands, a file of French soldiers began lining both sides of the wide avenue below us – one every ten feet. Further east on Nanking Road American Marines were doing the same, and beyond them, north along The Bund, Japanese and Italian Marines were doing the honors.

Suddenly a flag-carrying column of the Shanghai Light Horse, part of the 2,000 man, international Shanghai Volunteer Corps (S.V.C.), trotted into Nanking Road toward us from Bubbling Well Road. Martial music from a French army band following just behind swelled over them, as the crowd started cheering.

Other token foreign military units followed – from forces of countries stationed in Shanghai's International Settlement and at other points in China by (forced) agreement with the Chinese government. These included a company of American Marines, a goose-stepping Japanese army unit, French Foreign Legionnaires, and some Italian Marines. Intermixed among these were larger units of the S.V.C., an entire battalion of professional White Russian soldiers, carrying their rifles left-handed, a Portuguese company full of Eurasians, a Chinese company and The American Troop (a light Calvary unit).

Then, to the stirring sounds of their leading massed instrumental and bagpipes and drums bands, over 100 musicians in all, marched the two departing British units, each a full battalion strong. As the kilted Highlanders passed by under our vantage spot the street crowd cheered extra loudly. The troops responded by cheering back!

It was quite a stirring sight – to see all the flags, bands and snappy marching troops of so many different nationalities all at once, and we Yangs, like the thousands of other Chinese onlookers laughed, waved and cheered excitedly. It was a splendid, colorful 'happening;' and after all, everyone loves a parade!

But throughout, we all inwardly asked ourselves, "how would any of you foreigners here today like to see your major city and so much of your country occupied by foreign troops like these – no matter how friendly they try to appear?"

By late afternoon James had joined us and, surprise, surprise – for the first time in at least two years Daddy invited us to join him for coffee and cake at Manhattan Restaurant. This American style restaurant, located on Yu Ya Ching Road two blocks from Shanghai Race Course, was a favorite of his. The cake was delicious; our cups of coffee a quite different and rare treat, into which we, like most Chinese "red tea drinkers," stirred extravagant amounts of evaporated milk and sugar.

As we relaxed, James described the colorful final part of the day's parade as observed from his vantagepoint.

"As the parade turned into The Bund from Nanking Road, 'Big Ching,' the huge Customs House clock chimed a farewell," he recounted. "Further along, just past the British Consulate-General, the band of the American 4th Marine Regiment played farewell salutes of 'Marching Through Georgia' and 'Swanee River.'"

"Then, on Garden Bridge," he continued, "as an honor guard of The Russian Regiment (S.V.C.) presented arms, the British troops filed aboard their ship, after passing through two lines of Japanese Landing Party (marines) troops standing at attention.

It really was a nice sendoff, but after such a long march, I guess the 'Brits' looked forward to their farewell gift free quarts of warm beer!"

Over continued cups of coffee at first, and then an early complete dinner, we engaged in probably the longest and most serious discussion that any of us, including James had ever had with our father. Our topic concerned how China, such a great civilization and world power for over 3,000 years, had sunk to the point where today foreign armies could occupy large parts of our country and push us around so seemingly at will. Daddy reviewed and brought us up to date on some historical details that we younger ones especially had not known before.

"The century of relative peace in Europe that followed the end of the Napoleonic Wars," he explained, "set the stage for the revolutionary changes of the 19th Century, which China's inward-looking rulers were unprepared to accept or even seriously try to understand. The Industrial Revolution especially, created new wealth and stimulated a demand for raw materials that European nations suddenly sought to gain through conquests worldwide. Along with their explorers and empire-builders went energetic missionaries, both Catholic and Protestant."

"European traders, diplomats, travelers such as Marco Polo and missionaries had of course, been more or less continuously visiting China since before the birth of Christ, especially during the Ming and Ching (Manchu) dynasties. It was always apparent to such visitors that China, the most populous and one of the richest nations of the world represented a gigantic sellers' market, as well as a major source for raw materials. First, Europeans, and later Americans, began descending upon China in ever-increasing numbers throughout the late 18th and 19th Centuries – their merchants eager to trade; their missionaries eager to convert!"

"They faced one major problem however in trying to crash China's gates; the fact that the Chinese authorities simply weren't interested in foreign ideas, inventions, trade or missionaries. These rulers tried to keep China's doors shut against the 'barbarians' by requiring all trade and official business to be conducted only through a government-monopoly organization located at the south China port city of Canton."

"This state of affairs proved especially irritating to the British who had the largest share of China's foreign trade. China was so self-sufficient economically that British traders' were hard-put to sell enough to pay for sought after Chinese tea and silks. They had been making up the difference with difficult to get silver, but sale of opium from British-controlled India offered easier and far greater profit potential. The Chinese government, greatly concerned about the rapid increase in opium

111

addiction and the loss of silver income, formally attempted to stop the trade. British traders however illegally continued to push sales of opium; aided and abetted by the British government."

"The Emperor of China appealed to Queen Victoria to stop this illegal sale of opium, which is corrupting our people and sapping their health. 'Where is your conscience?' she was asked."

"When this appeal failed, and the lucrative trade continued," Father went on, "the Chinese, in desperation, seized 20,000 chests of opium from British warehouses in Canton and set them on fire. Arguments over this led to China's cutting off all trade. As the powerful British navy sailed out to 'teach the Chinese a lesson,' British merchants fled to Hong Kong for protection. This started the First Opium War (1839-42), which the British, largely through naval action, decisively won against ineffectual Chinese resistance."

"This war ended in August, 1842 with signing by China and Britain of the Treaty of Nanking. Under its terms, China was compelled to permit the unlimited importation of Indian opium, cede the island of Hong Kong, pay an indemnity of 21 million dollars, and open five so-called 'Treaty Ports' to foreign trade. These were Canton, Amoy (Xiamen), Foochow (Fuzhou), Ningpo and Shanghai.

"What happened to the massive opium trade?" Betty questioned. "While I've seen one of the old style opium couches, on which addicts apparently lay to smoke their opium pipes, in Grand Auntie Lan Fong's home, I don't know of anyone buying or smoking it today!"

"And can you tell us more about the 'Treaty Ports' agreements," asked Paul, "especially how they have affected Shanghai!"

"Since that unfortunate 1842 treaty, nearly 100 years ago, poor militarily weak and politically divided China has almost been taken over by foreign powers – divided up between them as sort of an informal colony," Father answered. "We finally freed ourselves from the opium curse, but are still occupied by all sorts of foreigners. Let me explain the two problems separately."

"First, concerning opium; as addiction grew throughout the country after the Treaty of Nanking, China's rulers kept voicing protests to the British government. Continued friction finally led to a Second Opium War (1858-60). This time an international army, under a British general, in 1860, even captured and held the then capital at Peking itself for a time. After losing again, China decided that if it was to be turned into a nation of drug addicts, that it might as well grow opium poppies within its own borders and stop the money drain out of the country. Large land areas were soon given over to poppy production."

"In 1906 the Chinese government made another supreme effort to throw off the curse of British-instigated, widespread national opium addiction. Through the aid and support of some wealthy Americans, and a growing self-consciousness on the part of the British public, China and Great Britain finally signed an agreement whereby the British would cease all exportation of Indian opium to China, if China would stop producing her own. As a happy result, by 1917 the opium problem in our country ceased to be a major problem.

But educated Chinese will never forgive the British for their quite calculated, nearly three quarters of a century long, government supported policy of trying to turn millions of Chinese into dope addicts through their mind and body destroying opium exports," angrily snorted Daddy – as he pounded his fist on the table.

"Do you recall the several other than opium importation humiliating conditions imposed on China by the 1842 Treaty of Nanking, that I just mentioned?" Daddy then asked. "Chief among them was the requirement that they open five 'Treaty Ports,' including Shanghai, to foreign trade. That most advantageous 'trade plum' for the British quickly caught the attention of, and envy of other foreign powers. Like vultures they all descended on helpless China."

"Ever more 'rights and privileges,' including the opening of additional Treaty Ports, were won by foreign powers as a result of forced treaties signed following the Second Opium War (1858-60). For example, Peking was opened to foreign diplomats' residence, foreign missionaries were allowed to evangelize and own property in the interior and foreign shipping was permitted on the Yangtze."

"How did Japan manage to obtain the same 'most favored nation' rights and the other privileges that Great Britain had won?" questioned Paul. It wasn't involved in either of the two opium wars!"

"The Japanese won their concessions here in Shanghai and elsewhere in China, and their other rights and privileges, under terms of The Treaty of Shimonoseki of April 17, 1895 which ended the First Sino-Japanese War (1894-95)," answered his father. "That treaty also forced China to recognize Japan's control over Korea and to give Japan the island of Taiwan, which China had ruled since 1683."

"The first British Settlement in what is now Shanghai," he continued, "was established in 1843 as a residential/ business/warehouse area. It was located on marshland just north of the then small waterfront walled city of Nantao, 13 miles up the Whangpoo River, a tributary of the Yangtze. Later, a strip of land between Yang Ching Creek and the Chinese city became the French Concession. While the United States never accepted a special formal concession, some Americans leased land nearby – an area that informally became known as the American Settlement."

"Today, there are actually three cities in Shanghai," Daddy went on to explain, "each with deepwater Whangpoo River frontage. First, and most important, is the International Settlement – formed when the British and American sectors joined in 1863. With its largely British-style architecture, it is not only the cosmopolitan, world famous, commercial and financial center of Shanghai, but is also the economic and financial capital of China itself."

"Covering 8.3 square miles in area, its population of around 1.5 million includes representatives of some 40 foreign nations, plus hundreds of thousands of Chinese residents. Governed by an international Municipal Council, which is controlled by the British, it has its own police force, plus the S.V.C. private army that paraded today."

"The International Settlement is basically subdivided into two sections; the Settlement proper and its Hongkew section which is largely inhabited by Japanese – currently around 200,000 of them. Hongkew, which has its own informal Japanese 'Mayor,' is barracks location for sizable Japanese troop contingents. Surprisingly, that is the district in which most of Shanghai's estimated 14,000 Jewish inhabitants reside. A high percentage of them are refugees from Germany, Austria and Poland.

"What about the French Concession, where our home is located?" asked Betty.

"The French chose to remain apart, and today's French Concession, with its population of around 550,000, is a separate self-governing 3.9 square mile area," he replied, "many foreigners as well as Chinese live there since the quiet tree-lined avenues of its European district make it the preferred residential area of all Shanghai."

"As you know, while the names of its avenues and streets are French, and there are many French style buildings, the general character of the place sometimes seems more Russian than French. Most of Shanghai's estimated 16,000 White Russians live there, and many shops and stores display Russian signs. The French Consul General, as chief executive and administrative officer of the Concession government, is assisted by a Municipal Council with only advisory powers. He controls the French-led Concession police – a force which includes many White Russians as well as Tonkinese and Annamite natives of French Indochina."

"The third, city within the city of Shanghai, is the 320 square mile so-called Chinese Municipality. It includes all the Chinese districts such as Nantao (the old walled city), Pootung (Pudong), Chapei, Paosham and all land bordering and surrounding the settlements. This political unit, run by Chinese, like the other two, has its own Municipal Council and police force."

"While Chinese are allowed to reside and pay taxes in both the International Settlement and French Concession," he added, "they are not allowed voting rights. Nor are they allowed membership in the several foreign private clubs, although some of these do allow their members to bring in Chinese as guests."

"Of the 40 or so foreign nations represented in Shanghai's foreign population," asked James, "how many are citizens of countries that have been granted 'extraterritorial rights' through treaties with China?"

"Besides the large number of Japanese civilian residents that I just mentioned, Greater Shanghai's total overall population of around 3.5 million includes some 55,000 foreigners of many nationalities," answered Father. "Approximately 85% of them are citizens of the 14 countries that enjoy such 'rights and privileges.' These countries are Great Britain, the United States, France, Japan, Belgium, Brazil, Denmark, Italy, the Netherlands, Norway, Portugal, Spain, Sweden and Switzerland."

"A few of these countries, by treaty agreements with China, have until now maintained units of their own military both here in the International Settlement and in some cases, at several other points in China," he continued. "Although the British are, by choice, now removing their troops, American, French, Italian and Japanese military and naval forces still remain. Japanese authorities announced only yesterday that American and Japanese troops will take over the former British defense sector in the International Settlement as soon as the British troops depart."

"What is the most influential foreign country here in Shanghai?" asked Paul.

116

"I would have to say Japan right now," exclaimed James.

"But I like the Americans best." I proclaimed.

"The British continue today to be the most powerful economic force here, as always, " he replied. "They have by far the largest investments in China, and are financially the most powerful. The Americans are second because they didn't really start large-scale competitions with the British until around 1900. There are roughly three British residents here to every one American. The Japanese rank third economically."

"While most patriotic Chinese wish to be free of all foreign occupation and control," Daddy continued, "the Americans are generally the most respected and best liked of all foreigners. Japanese are the most hated of course, with the British quite disliked because of their past Opium exports and the several unfair, humiliating treaties they forced China to accept. The Americans, through their missionaries, are the only foreigners to have really 'given' something back to China – such as some good universities, schools and medical colleges, as well as 'taking' through profits from trade."

"Well, at least a start was made today in getting rid of the foreigners," cheerfully spoke Paul. "Tomorrow the British soldiers will sail away! That's why I awoke you girls this morning with my shout – the British are Leaving, the British are leaving! Hip, Hip, Hooray!" We all laughed.

As we all stood up to depart the restaurant for home and bed, James, after thanking Daddy for his most informative historical and factual summations, made a final observation that caused us all to nod in solemn agreement.

"Now if we can just get rid of the Japanese soldiers as well, China will, at long last, have a chance to regain its national freedom and pride."

Earlier that year, one day after school near the end of February, well after the New Year's festivities had ended, I wandered into our Mansion's kitchen in search of Grandmother. She and Ah Foo were sitting beside the large corner country-style brick stove warming themselves against the damp winter chill of the outside thickly overcast day.

As Ah Foo, who had been under the weather for the past week with a bad cold, broke into a fitful, hacking spasm of coughs, Grandmother eagerly began offering advice on how to get rid of both cough and cold.

"You should be drinking one cup of hot Golden Griffin Bronchial Tea as soon as you awake in the morning, and another just before bedtime," she authoritatively announced. "You have bronchitis; that's why your cough sounds so terrible!"

"That's nothing but a fragrant herbal tea," snorted Ah Foo, "what I really need to be taking is Bee Boo Kon Loguat Cough Syrup. That's made to cure chronic bronchitis as well as common colds; and besides it provides good nourishment, and will help cure the tiredness I've felt all week."

"If you want to cure tiredness," retorted Grandmother, "you will be better off taking the Tibetan remedy 'Bramckaria;' you can get it in either pill or liquid form at the Natural Medicine Shop."

"You are a crazy old woman," shrilled Ah Foo, "that fake stuff is also sold at the Sex Shops as a cure for all kinds of sexual disorders, such as impotency!"

"Maybe that's your real illness!" snickered Grandmother.

"I don't need anything like THAT; but what I really do need is something that will make my hair grow back. I am sick and tired of trying to cook for so many people while trying to keep my wig from falling into the wok," came the reply.

Jumping into the conversation, I asked: "Is it true, Ah Foo, that there is a Barber's Ghost who often slips into people's rooms at midnight when they are sleeping, and shaves their head?"

"Yes, yes," excitedly interrupted Grandmother, "there is such a ghost, and after such a shaving the hair never grows again, and the head always remains totally bald and shiny – just like Ah Foo's!"

"No such ghost shaved my head – when very young I had a bad illness that caused permanent loss of my hair," sniffed the cook, as her yellow and green parrot let out a loud squawk from its corner of the kitchen perch.

"I've heard that if you can dream while sleeping that you are inside a high surrounding wall, that ghosts like the Barber's Ghost can't get inside to harm you, " I said.

"But what about the Wall-building ghost?" exclaimed Ah Foo; "that's the one who surrounds travelers and keeps moving – never allowing escape! If you dream that you are sleeping inside a surrounding wall it may be that ghost's plot against you. I'd rather get my head shaved!"

"You can always protect yourself against the Wall-building ghost simply by squatting down, looking straight ahead without blinking, and whistling three times in succession," snapped Grandmother, in a superior-sounding tone of voice.

"Out with both of you," laughed Ah Foo, brandishing a broom in mock disgust. "I've got a big dinner to prepare!"

A few days later Daddy called all us Yangs together inside the girls' bedroom. Closing the door and lowering his voice, he announced that he had approved Suzie's departure for Chung-king early the next morning.

"While it will be a long and dangerous trip, " he announced, "there are still many thousands of travelers and refugees on the move all throughout east-central China, so there will be safety in numbers. Also, she will be traveling with two female second year university students, and two young recent university graduate males who, like Logan last year, are to be commissioned in the army. They will be dressed as peasants, and will be following an inland route that avoids the larger Japanese controlled cities and towns."

Once again, as we had done previously with Guo Liang, we females all hugged her and cried a lot. Then, after we had all bid our farewells – we quietly went about our family business for the remainder of the evening as though nothing had happened. We later told the other mansion occupants that she had accepted a suddenly offered important job in Ningpo.

That spring of 1940, Betty , Paul and myself were all at-tending Bei Tsun Chinese School, with an enrollment of 1,000 students in grades one through twelve, located just a short 15-minute walk from our home. Betty, age 13, was in 8th grade, Paul age 17, was in 11th grade, and I at age 10, was in 5th grade.

At this school, which had two 40-pupil mixed (boys and girls) classes per grade level, one stayed in the same classroom all day, with different teachers (all Chinese) coming in for dif-ferent subjects or classes. We sat two to a desk; girls sitting to-gether in the front of the class; boys sitting two together at the back. Our 8 a.m. to 4 p.m., Monday through Friday class days always started with massed calisthenics in the school courtyard. Saturday mornings we had classes until noon, sometimes broken by infrequent all-student or age/class groups assemblies.

The worst assembly I attended was the funeral service one for our school principal who had died after a long illness. Our entire student body, after sitting through the service, had to pass in single file past his open coffin. Those younger superstitious students who believed in ghosts were terrified! His wasted-away, half-open jawed appearance caused many of the others, including me, to get sick at the stomach.

Since parents had to pay tuition, school in China in those days, for those students lucky enough to be able to attend, was serious business. Discipline was seldom a problem, but was sometimes applied with the smack of a ruler across an extended palm. One went to school to get an education, and there was always one or two hours of homework to be done each evening.

I had daily one-hour classes in English, Chinese, Mathe-matics, History and Science. Other classes, once or twice a week, included Geography, Handicrafts (knitting or sewing for girls, woodworking for boys), Japanese, Music and Physical Education (usually volleyball).

I excelled in English and in Music, where I was beginning to display superior natural vocal talent, and did well enough in eve-rything else except Mathematics, where Paul still continued to help me keep up. While the Japanese military authorities re-quired everyone to study Japanese, the class was a joke. We all patriotically hated it and wanted to fail! This attitude terrified our Chinese instructor, to the point that he would just give us in advance answers to examinations. Most of the time we just sang interesting Japanese folk songs, learning considerable vocabulary in the process.

School uniforms were not required. In winter girls wore below the knee length silk or cotton padded chong sam type dresses of their color choice with long self-knitted socks and woolen coats. Since classrooms were unheated, chilblains of hands and feet, especially of ungloved hands, was a constant problem. Hands and fingers which became red, swollen and lumpy from the constant damp cold, would hurt terribly when cold and itch like crazy when warmed. In warmer weather we girls wore color-of-choice cotton chong sams. Year around, on dry days, all students wore homemade, thick cloth soled slipper-like footwear; on wet days we wore rubber store-bought galoshes over them.

We three Yangs walked home for lunch. The other not so lucky ones brought their own lunches which had to be eaten in their classroom. All students had to take turns after school cleaning blackboards, classrooms, hallways, toilets, and playground areas. The biggest overall problem for all girls at Bei Tsun was the quite limited number of single stall toilet facilities. We all groused constantly at having to spend most our short recess periods lined up awaiting our turn!

Late spring and early summer brought troubling news from Europe where war was also raging. In May the Germans swept through the low countries and French channel ports as the British Expeditionary Force in Europe barely escaped destruction through its seat of the pants Dunkirk evacuation.

Italy entered the war June 11 on the side of Germany and immediately attacked France's exposed southern flank. As their touted Maginot line of fortifications along Germany's borders were rapidly being rolled up from behind by Nazi Panzer divisions, the shocked, beaten, demoralized French surrendered on June 23.

While these events aroused great consternation among much of Shanghai's foreign population, we Yangs like most Chinese viewed them with mildly interested indifference. After all, we had already been experiencing our own full-scale war for just under three years. In fact, many Chinese were smugly satisfied that the British and French especially were finally getting a taste of what it was like to be on the receiving end of sudden success-ful military attacks. We Chinese had certainly endured enough of their unprovoked attacks on us over the past 100 years or so!

We were all quite proud of the fact that while the French had totally surrendered after only about six weeks of serious fighting against the Germans, we Chinese were continuing to battle on alone against Japan. We Yangs patriotically agreed with Chiang Kai-shek's defiant late 1937 pronouncement that "China will keep fighting."

Most of all, China was too preoccupied with its own war to worry much now about that other war in far off Europe. By now the battle lines from Mongolia in the north to the Indochina and Burma borders in the south wiggled and squiggled in ragged, ever shifting lines along assorted rivers, plains and mountain valleys deep in the interior. The great movement of China's people, factories, hospitals and universities to Chungking and other interior cities was long over, and the war had settled into one of long term attrition.

The Japanese, miffed at China's unexpected unified spirit of national resistance, settled in to exploit their already enormous gains. Their strategy now was to wear down that resistance at minimal financial, material, or personnel cost to themselves. They kept the numerically larger but poorly equipped Chinese armies off balance with sudden massive, usually mechanized attacks at different locations all along the bow-like 3,400-mile north to south front. Attack, fall back, attack somewhere else, fall back – constantly ready to exploit any unexpected success with massive force! This strategy kept the Chinese who had al-most no mechanized vehicles, trucks, artillery or aerial support, constantly confused and frustrated.

And their ceaseless bombing – of Chungking, day and night, and of other cities and strategic centers! Where was help to come from? The Japanese were moving quickly to occupy French Indochina after France's collapse, thus closing off the railroad into China from there. And the British, under pressure from Japan, had just announced that they were closing the Burma Road – the only land route to Kunming, China from south Asia and India. The Americans seemed to simply be sitting on their hands watching the world go by.

While the will to fight still remained strong, especially in Chungking, morale of the Chinese as a whole had already fallen to a new low from the defiant days of 1938.

We Yangs, like most other Chinese in Shanghai, knew these things from Chungking and foreign shortwave radio news broadcasts and from the constant flow of refugees into our city. Father especially kept quite well informed through frequent field reports from Standard Oil's many employees in both occupied and unoccupied parts of the country.

To make matters even worse, the summer weather, always hot and humid at that time of the year, turned even more unbearable as a result of one typhoon after another.

Mother, Betty and I got thoroughly drenched by a thunderstorm one late July afternoon while attending an outdoor concert at always-crowded Jessfield Park, not too far from our home. The locally well known and popular Italian conductor Maestro Mario Paci was energetically conducting a program of western musical show tunes when the heavens opened and rain fell in torrential sheets.

As the Maestro and his musicians, most White Russians or Jewish refugees from Germany and Austria, scrambled to protect their instruments, we three made a mad dash for shelter across the way under a roofed Winter Garden kiosk. We heard later that many stores on Nanking Road and Kweichow and Kansu Roads had been flooded by that rain.

During August we played it safe by taking in American movies at some of Shanghai's many indoor theaters. We saw, among others, Martha Raye and Allen Jones in "The Boys From Syracuse," at the Nanking; Laurel and Hardy in "The Devil's Brother," at the Roxy; and Sidney Toler in "Charlie Chan in Panama," at the Nanking. Before each movie of course, we had to endure a half-hour Japanese propaganda film! At least we kept dry! We also enjoyed an indoor performance of the famous Olympic Circus later that month.

Just after start of the September school term, another ragged, mysterious stranger suddenly appeared at our Mansion servants' entrance. He wordlessly handed an envelope to Ah Foo, and immediately strode away. It turned out to be a long awaited letter from Nellie in Chungking, our first from her since before they fled Nanking just ahead of the Japanese army in late 1937.

Would it disclose any news of Suzie? We Yangs all sat around breathlessly in Betty's and my closed-door bedroom, as Daddy began reading it aloud to us.

> Dear Mother and Father,
> Since you probably haven't heard, Suzie and her friends reached Chungking safely two weeks ago after a long and difficult journey. She was quite thin and had suffered a lot from dysentery along the way, but is otherwise in good health.
>
> After resting several days to regain her strength, she and Logan wasted no time in getting married last week. It was a simple but nice wedding held at Army Central Command Officers Club. They rushed the wedding because Logan is being transferred to Kunming shortly. Suzie will go with him.
>
> Guo-Liang and his girlfriend Chow Ping attended the wedding. She is a college graduate from Chekiang (Zhejiang) who works in his factory. She is two years younger than him. Both are well but seemed tired from their long 12-hour workdays. They plan to get married early next year.
>
> S.Z., the children and I are all well. He works 12 hours a day six days a weeks and four hours one day a week at his government bureau. That gives us some time together as a family. Wei Joan is a bright, beautiful five-year-old now, and Wei Lih a delightful, mischievous three year old boy. We live

in a tiny four-room government apartment without electricity or running water.

Japanese bombers attack day and night, but we always get enough advance warning to get to our nearby safe cave shelter in time. The heat and humidity of Chungking is already stifling, and the clouds of mosquitoes at night drive us crazy. While our diet is quite bland, the basic government supplied rations are adequate, and we have good medical care close at hand. We are happy, and think of you all often. Take care!

Respectfully, your Eldest Daughter

Nellie

May 27, 1940

Chungking

That 1940 year came to a rather somber close for our Yang family. While we had much to be thankful for, especially the knowledge that our Chungking members and their spouses were safe, and that all of us except Mother were in good health, the war, both at home and abroad seemed to be pressing ever closer upon us.

One disquieting late in the year event was the November 21 sailing from Shanghai of the last scheduled special American evacuation ship, the "S.S. Washington," with 500 women and children abroad. This was the largest number of such evacuees to date, bringing the total to 1,000. While 150 of them were members of missionary families from Japanese occupied areas, most of the estimated 2,300 American missionaries scattered from the Great Wall to the Indochina border so far had refused American Consulate warnings to evacuate. After all, they said, "American missionary work has gone on in China now for 111 years!"

We were well aware that living costs were steadily increasing and that the price of rice had soared sharply since spring. Barbed wire entanglements had recently been stretched across most streets crossing Avenue Foch in the French Concession and Avenue Edward VII in the International Settlement, some only a few blocks from the Shanghai Racecourse.

American and Italian Marines had begun patrolling the western sectors of the city not far from our Mansion, and the boundary between the French Concession and the Nantao river-front Chinese section was now quite heavily guarded.

The nightly midnight curfew that had been imposed for some time by Japanese occupation authorities was now strictly enforced. Any houseguests overstaying that curfew had to stay overnight. Many nightclubs in the French Concession stayed open all night to accommodate patrons who overstayed the curfew time.

"What does the future hold? Would conditions get even worse?" We wondered; and worried!

Chapter 8

"MOON GODDESS" EUPHORIA TURNS
TO FEAR AFTER PEARL HARBOR

Just three weeks earlier; during the waning days of December, with Shanghai's economic conditions worsening and new fires of war raging in Europe, we Yangs had wondered aloud together about what the future might hold for our family, our city and our country. "Would conditions get any worse?" we had asked one another.

We didn't have to wait long for one answer to that question!

While we weren't able to learn enough details to form even a partially clear overall picture for some weeks, an event took place the first week of January, 1941 that profoundly affected both China's immediate war effort and its eventual post World War II political future.

It was an event that few Europeans or Americans knew of or cared about at the time, preoccupied as they were with the conflagration in Western Europe. But it would greatly affect them in the years ahead – Americans especially!

To encapsulate many long years of history into a few words, China's Communists, who by August, 1937 effectively controlled large areas of the country's northern provinces, and the National Government of the Republic of China, controlled by the Kuomintang Party under Chiang Kai-shek, had for years been basically engaged in a bitter civil war. Japan's full scale attack on China then, and its rapid military successes, caused the two Chinese factions to join together in resisting the invaders. Top Communist leaders, including General Chou En-lai, (Zhou Enlai), came to Chungking to help coordinate joint military plans. At long last, China seemed to be a unified nation once more.

As part of its commitment to the effort, the central government promised to pay, supply and agree to operations by what was called the New Fourth (Communist) Army in an area north of the Yangtze. While the bulk of that army had already crossed over to its planned zone of operations by the end of December, its headquarters detachment, including the commanding general and staff, supply personnel and some combat units, about 5,000 troops in all, still remained on the river's south bank.

Suddenly, for reasons that still lie hidden in the mist of history, during that first week of January, Kuomintang troops surrounded and launched a fierce surprise attack on this force. Most of the unprepared Communist soldiers were massacred; those captured were treated as brutally as if they had been hated Japanese troops. Many of these rear echelon Communist troops were women – serving as nurses, political officers and signalers. Most of these were savagely raped. In the end, by some accounts, only 300 of the original group survived to eventually rejoin the Communist main force.

While each side blamed the other for "causing" this incident, the unfortunate result for the Chinese nation, as a whole was an immediate, permanent breakdown of relations between the two sides; all cooperation promptly ceased. Twenty divisions of Chiang Kai-shek's best troops were quickly deployed, facing not east against the Japanese, but in a northern direction to choke off and isolate the Communists.

For nearly three years during 1938-40, it had been a unified, all-China war against the Japanese. Now it was a three-sided war: Kuomintang Chinese against the Japanese; separately, the Chinese Communists against the Japanese; and the two factions of Chinese against each other – in their own war within a war! And this is the way it was to remain until the surrender of Japan in 1945.

As news of the unfortunate event reached and circulated wildly about Shanghai, Daddy was alternately furious and depressed. He believed the events happened as described above, and blamed it mostly on Chiang Kai-shek personally. He knew how much the Generalissimo hated the Communists; since they represented the only sizable political force within the country that he could not control.

Chiang had always felt that he and the Kuomintang alone represented China, and that the Communists must eventually be destroyed before China could ever unify and become strong enough to defeat Japan. Did he personally order the attack – or were others to blame? Neither Daddy then, nor history now, knows for sure!

Our father's major depressing concern, now shared by his entire household, was that China's chances of ever defeating Japan suddenly seemed quite remote. A second concern was that the now bitterly divided thousands of Kuomintang and Communist secret agents and sympathizers in Shanghai might turn on one another in destructive local civil war.

For the first time since "Bloody Saturday" we all shared a real sense of uncertainty and fear locally, as well as for our country as a whole.

We had hardly digested news of the sudden permanent Kuomintang-Communist rift when another one of those mysterious, ragged strangers appeared at our Mansion to silently and quickly drop off another letter with Ah Foo. This one turned out to be our first one from Suzie, who had left for Chungking during spring of the previous year.

Although nothing had been, or ever would be said to us by those secretive, poorly dressed "mailmen," we now realized that they were part of the vast Kuomintang "underground "that

129

formed the national government's "resistance movement" all throughout occupied China. We never knew, of course, how many letters failed to get through to us – or how many "mailmen" were shot, beheaded or died of fatigue or illness during their long, slow, tortuous journey by foot and/or boat.

Once again, Daddy called all us Yangs together behind closed doors and read aloud the following;

Dear Mother and Father,

Shortly after my friends and I wearily dragged into Chungking just before the middle of May, Logan and I were married. Nellie said that she wrote you about it. I hope that you received her letter – we have no way of knowing if our messages get through. Neither she, Guo Liang or I have ever heard from any of you at home.

Logan, now a Captain, had already been alerted to his impending transfer to Headquarters, Southwestern Army Command, Kunming, Yunnan Province, so we had a simple, hastily arranged wedding at a nice Officers club.

Two days later we departed in a mixed army/civilian 30 vehicle truck convoy with Logan in command. While Kunming is only 420 miles or so from Chungking as a bird would fly, our trip took 18 days of hard driving over very poor dirt, gravel or clay roads that wound mostly through very high mountains. Fortunately it was the dry reason! The roads are so poor; the unmarked drop-offs so steep that truck drivers in these parts are called "Suicide Drivers."

On a typical day, we would arise at 6:30 a.m. for a quick breakfast of puffed cereal rice in hot water, flavored with brown sugar, and depart at 7:00 a.m.. Around 11 a.m., we would stop for a hot lunch of rice, vegetables, scrambled eggs and soup – cooked beside our trucks.

We would then drive until reaching a planned village night stop over location where we would sleep in terribly dirty, smelly, rooms in small inns. Each tiny room had two to four hard beds with straw mattresses. Men and women slept in separate rooms. Each of us had our own pugil (quilt) which we folded into a sort of envelope, and slid into from the top. Each room had one simple oil lamp for light and a small centrally placed charcoal brazier for heat. The toilets were unspeakable! We ate evening meals in local restaurants.

Fortunately, Kunming, with its perpetual spring-like weather, is ideal for plants and flowers. Beautiful camellia, magnolia, azalea and fairy primrose blossoms are everywhere. We hope soon to be able to visit the nearby famous Stone Forest, where strange high peaks and odd-shaped rocks stand straight up from the ground like trees.

We have a quite small but nice two-room apartment in an officer's family residential building, with clean mountain fresh running water and electricity.

I have just enrolled in two courses at nearby National Southwest University, which is a composite of three former Peking area "refugee universities." Hundreds of their professors and students got out just ahead of the Japanese invaders and trekked by cart and foot all the way here, bringing with them as much laboratory equipment and essential library books as they could carry.

Logan and I are happy, and think of you often.

Respectfully, Your Number 2 Daughter

Suzie

Kunming, Yunnan

August 15, 1940

One cold Friday evening in late February Daddy and I crossed paths, for the first time in at least two years, on the center Mansion stairwell. I was on my way down to the first floor kitchen to ask Ah Foo what she was preparing for our usual 8:00 p.m. Yang Family dinner.

He had just arrived home from work and was on his way up to the third floor apartment of Second Concubine Ching. With eyes downcast as we lightly brushed past one another, I softly muttered "Good evening, Dya-Dya." He grunted at me without looking my way, and the doors soon slammed as we each entered our respective apartment levels. I don't think we even saw one another again until early April. He led his life – I led mine, separate and unequal!

Grandmother, who was just leaving the kitchen as I was entering, caught me by my sleeve and brought me to a halt.

"How would you like to accompany me to a performance of Peking Opera tomorrow afternoon at The New World Opera Hall?" she asked. "James will drive us there after lunch in time for its 2:00 p.m. start, but we will have to return home by rickshaw."

I didn't have anything else planned, since Betty and Paul would be off visiting their older friends, but being a true daughter of my God of Wealth worshipping father, decided to test her, in hopes that she would "sweeten the pot" with a little extra bribe.

"Well," I replied cagily, I was planning to go with Mother to Auntie Peony's home where they will be playing mah-jong. Auntie usually serves delicious warm Sesame Bean Paste Puffs with afternoon tea! But ..."

Biting hard, and with a half pleading look in her aging watery eyes, she took the bait, "I'll treat you to some of your favorite Sesame Seed Candies, if you will!"

Feeling inwardly guilty since I knew that no one else would go with her, and that she couldn't go alone, I nonchalantly voiced my agreement.

The large Opera Hall of The New World, one of Shanghai's spacious entertainment complexes at the corner of Nanking Road and Tibet Road, was freezingly cold as we took our place on one of the long bleacher-like seats. Fortunately these had backs, and there were holders where we could place our paid for in advance glasses of hot tea, which were constantly kept refilled by serving girls.

"We will be seeing a very famous drama based on an ancient Sung Dynasty historical story," Grandmother whispered to me. "It's called 'Shih Tseng Kwei (a man's name) and Wong Pao Zwan (a woman's name)'."

Promptly at 2:00 p.m. the mind-numbing loud classical opera-orchestra, which Chinese people love, started up – and kept up incessantly, with only a few intermittent breaks, for the entire "nonstop" three hours of the opera. The orchestra consisted of several assorted old-style Chinese string, wind and percussion instruments, helped along by a half dozen ear-shattering cymbals and gongs.

The lead actors wore beautifully colored conventionalized versions of ancient court dress, richly embellished with gold and other embroidery. Their mask-like faces were heavily made up, their movements stylized and formal. Many of their arias ran five or six minutes in length. The minor actors, mostly dressed as brightly garbed acrobats, or soldiers in massive outsize headgear, with fiercely painted faces; hopped about energetically as they engaged in noisy horseplay or mock swordplay.

"In the old days," said Grandmother, "all parts were sung by men. They would sing the women's parts in a falsetto voice. In this opera, the women's parts are being sung by women. It's all getting too modern for me!"

"I can't understand half of what they are saying or doing," I complained. "That's because they are singing in the old Classical Chinese language," said Grandmother. "Since I know most of the lyrics from childhood, I'll keep you informed."

And she did – chattering away loudly for the rest of the show! Between the gongs, drums, cymbals and her "keeping me informed," I soon thought my head was going to split.

As the show ran on and on, the constantly laughing, talking all-Chinese audience sat, stood or moved about happily in their thickly padded clothing, as if attending an outdoor stadium sporting event. Most kept busy cracking sunflower and watermelon seeds, eating peanuts in shells or fresh hot roasted chestnuts out of cone-shaped cups made from old newspapers, purchased from circulating vendors, and drinking glasses of hot tea.

Among the many children present were several infants, most of whom kept cheerfully active sucking away at their mother's bared breasts. Scented damp hot towels were available from vendors for a small fee. Patrons energetically used them to wipe their faces, necks, hands and some men, even their hair. The used towels were collected from time to time, briefly re-dipped into boiling scented water – and resold, again and again!

When the long opera "finally" ended and we "finally" got home, after a long, bone-jolting open rickshaw ride through crowded, bitterly cold rain-swept streets, I complained of a stomachache from having eaten too many sunflower seeds.

That was a mistake, because Grandmother's bedtime traditional spoonful remedy of chicken livers, dried and ground to powder, chased by a tumbler of hot water – tasted terrible!

I compensated by sucking my way to sleep on one of the hard, peanut brittle-like Sesame Seed Candies that Grandmother, as promised, had bought for me.

The third Sunday in March, the traditional Kite Flying Festival day, turned out to be perfect for the annual event; sunny but cool with gusty winds pushing large, fluffy white clouds westward across a clear blue sky.

Betty, Paul, Mother and I excitedly headed for Jessifield Park's large open area around midmorning, to join the sizable crowd already there. Many of the people represented clubs, societies or other types of groups sponsoring entries for the organized kite fighting, highest flying, largest kites or most colorful or unusual kites competitions.

Most of the participants however, were children – of all ages, out with their parents for the sheer fun and joy of flying their own hand made individual or purchased kites. The vast majority of people were merely onlookers out to watch the excitement. Betty and I, had helped Paul make a beautiful yellow and green Butterfly Kite, and were eager to help him fly it for fun, not competitively.

Soon the sky was filled with kites of all sizes, sorts, shapes and descriptions. There were long colorful fish kites; kites resembling bats, dragons, and birds of many types. There were butterfly kites like Paul's; and kites shaped like centipedes, snakes and lobsters. There were multicolored, multi-sail kites – some with no tails, others with long tails. There were many-layered box kites, and kites towing flags and banners of many types.

By early afternoon the increasingly large crowd, now numbering in the low thousands, laughed, cheered and waved as the more than 400 kites fluttered, wiggled, dipped, soared, got entangled with one another and often crashed.

Most exciting to watch, flying high above the others, were the group sponsored ultra-large Festival Kites, some requiring several men to handle, that were vying for prizes. Other exciting competitors were the Fighting Kites, with knives attached, that were manipulated by their owners to dive and sever the strings of rivals.

Especially pleasing to the ear were the musical harps, called Yao Chin, that were attached to many of the larger kites. These were small harp shaped bamboo frames with thin slivers of bamboo stretched across them like strings. These harps, when airborne, vibrated with pleasing musical sounds as the wind rushed across and through their strings.

As we four slowly made our way back home in the late afternoon, we all agreed that this annual Kite Flying Festival was the perfect way to help us forget the war – for one day, at least!

As school terms came to an end that June 1941, we had two graduates from our Yang family. Paul graduated at age 18 from Bei Tsun Chinese School and promptly applied for admission into a first year premedical program the following September at Tung-De medical school. James, having completed his studies at Shanghai University and awarded his degree in Chemical Engineering, was once again living at home full time, and starting to look for a job.

Betty and I sat in on one early morning conversation between them over breakfast, as they discussed their respective new postgraduate situations.

"Even with my degree from highly regarded Shanghai University," said James, "it is very difficult to find a good job in or around Shanghai. The traditional major employers here in recent years have been the banking, shipping and textile industries. But after the Japanese moved 1,000 miles up the Yangtze, to Ichang, commercial access to the interior has become almost impossible, and the city is dying economically."

"Daddy would agree with you, " replied Paul. "I overheard him tell Concubine Ching on the stairwell landing just the other evening that due to the war and near stoppage of normal Yangtze commerce that Shanghai has lost its main source of past wealth."

"No matter what, our first priority must be to keep from either being drafted into the Nanking Puppet Government army, or into local war industries controlled by that government or the Japanese," said James emphatically, as Paul nodded his head in solemn agreement.

A short time later I walked down to the first floor kitchen to find Ah Foo, who had just returned from a buying trip to our nearby open air street market, filling Grandmother in on the latest market gossip.

"The price of rice was lower today than last week" she reported, "because a shipment of it from Indochina, ordered earlier by the French Concession Municipal Council to help relieve the rice shortage, arrived just yesterday."

"It's about time," retorted Grandmother, "Ah Liu, Father Nicholas' cook, saw a Chinese translator for the Japanese Gendarmerie shot to death on Kiangsi Road just the other day. Two policemen who had just caught him involved in sideline rice profiteering, made him kneel down and shot him in the back of the head, right then and there on the street."

"The live chicken vendor told me this morning that poisonous snakes have recently been found in open spaces less than a 15-minute walk from the busiest traffic spot on The Bund," noted Ah Foo with a slight shudder.

Not to be outdone, Grandmother retorted, "I've heard that a lot of them have been found recently around old Chinese tombs in the Wayside area that were blown up during the 1937 hostilities."

"Did you know that eating snake meat makes one cunning?" she continued. "Our ancestors knew that as far back as the Yellow Turban Rebellion time during the days of the ancient Eastern Han."

"I don't know about that," replied Ah Foo, "but I do know that the best way to cook skinned snakes is to boil them in a broth."

"Ugh, what does boiled snake taste like?" I exclaimed in a disgusted tone of voice.

"A bit too oily to my taste!" chuckled our cook, as Grandmother and I fled from the kitchen, grimacing at the very thought!

On June 23, news came both from American and British shortwave radio broadcasts from San Francisco and London, and from local stations, of Germany's invasion of the Soviet Union.

We kept up on both world and local events on a daily basis in this way; secretly in the case of our shortwave set which none of the servants, Grandmother or the two concubines knew anything about. James or Paul would usually listen quietly to this set through headphones late at night and report any new important news to us on an individual basis.

Within days we learned via our neighbor Father Nicholas that the large number of White Russians living in the French Concession, and elsewhere in Shanghai, were both elated and pessimistic over this news. They were elated over the thought that it might be the beginning of the end for the hated USSR Communist regime. Their pessimism stemmed from the agony they felt, as deeply patriotic Russians, over the death and destruction that would now afflict Mother Russia.

Shanghai's White Russian population, in our Yang family opinion, could use some morale boosting of any kind! Having neither consulate nor political rights, they were little more than stateless exiles. The older majority had fled Russia in 1917-18 with little or no money or belongings. Those able to raise a little capital had mostly opened shops or restaurants, many of them along Avenue Joffre, some quite near our Mansion. A sizable number of the others, especially the women had become cabaret singers, entertainers and dance hall "hostesses."

One sunny Sunday morning in mid-August, Mother, Betty, Paul and I took the long tram ride from near our Mansion east along Avenue Joffre and Rue du Consular to the French Consulate on the Whangpoo river bank. A cooling breeze from off the river nicely cut the normally sticky, humid air.

From there we engaged rickshaws to take us north along The Bund (an Anglo-Indian word for "quay" or "embankment"), that splendid, world famous, waterfront boulevard heart of Shanghai's bustling commercial district. Imposing buildings, reminiscent of London, lined the way: banks, business firms, newspaper offices and exclusive foreign private clubs – like the well known Shanghai Club (no dogs or Chinese allowed as members! The latter "sometimes" as guests of members).

Stopping at the Maritime Customs Building whose famous tower clock "Big Ching" had so recently saluted the departing British troops, we left our rickshaws and ambled slowly along by foot, talking, laughing and enjoying the surroundings and beautiful summer day.

Suddenly, looming up directly ahead of us, only a block away, one of Shanghai's tallest buildings, stood the grim looking, 16-story red brick structure housing the Japanese Military Headquarters in Shanghai. Formerly known as Broadway Mansion Apartments, the large prewar built structure at the confluence of Soochow Creek and the Whangpoo, was commandeered by the Japanese immediately after their "Bloody Saturday" takeover of our city. Armed soldiers and two manned machine gun nests guarded its front entrance – under a huge Rising Sun battle flag.

Shuddering at the sight, we quickly turned right, crossing the road bridge to the imposing, many-windowed Capitol Theatre Building on the river's east bank. There we paused briefly to look at the still photographs advertising the currently featured American film "Moon Over Miami," starring Betty Grable and Don Ameche.

Moving closer to the bridge from the theatre's marquee, and looking south at the scores of ships, boats and bustling water taxis on the river, we noticed three small foreign gunboats anchored midstream close by. Upon request, a smiling policeman told us: "One is the American 'USS Wake,' the middle one the British 'HMS Petrel' and the third is the Italian gunboat "Emillo Carlotta."

Looking the other way, we spotted a much larger warship moored not far past the west bank Japanese Military Headquarters building. Our friendly policeman said that it was the Japanese cruiser "HIJMS Idzuma," flagship of the Japanese China Fleet, and that the building very close by it was the Japanese Consulate. We all noticed that the cruiser had a clear commanding view of the three gunboats anchored only a short distance upriver.

Continuing our stroll from the theatre north, we admired the beautiful Union Church spire, the imposing next door British Consulate General building, and its neighbor, the modern 20 story Cathay Hotel, Shanghai's finest. Entering its lobby we window-shopped the several glittering arcade shops. Beautifully stocked, they displayed expensive Peking rugs, jewelry and jade ornaments of all descriptions, silks, Chinese antiques, and porcelains and curios galore.

Taking the elevator up to the rooftop Cathay Grill, we observed fashionably dressed foreigners and Chinese lunching in style under a lofty black pyramid tent. We took a quick look at the Grill's extensive menu and the astronomical (to us) prices, and quickly moved on! We peeked into the hotel's main ballroom, where couples glided about the early afternoon packed dance floor, and were entertained by singers and dancers during intermissions.

Most fun of all for us, was observing the stylish attire of so many foreign men and women at one place, from so many different countries. And modern young Chinese in foreign clothes were everywhere – the men often wearing horn-rimmed glasses, with slicked-down, brilliantined hair and glossy black patent leather shoes. Most of their fashionable young Chinese female companions while wearing silk stockings and spike heeled shoes, still preferred to wear body-clinging, colorful Chinese gowns with stiff, high collars and side slits to the knees (some, shockingly to us, slit even higher)!

This was a sampling of the "high life – often fast life" glittering world of Shanghai known to most resident and visiting foreigners, and to many wealthy Chinese. While it was not our Yang family's world, we enjoyed observing how the "other top few" lived in our city and country.

On this sunny mid-August Sunday in 1941, the people we observed at the Cathay Hotel and along The Bund, seemed not to have a care in the world!

Once back at home that evening, Betty and I talked about how we couldn't forget the day's sights of the ugly Japanese Military Headquarters, that big mean-looking Japanese cruiser and the three small foreign gunboats anchored so close by up river from it.

Soon it was back to school time again! Betty and I entered our September start of term new grade levels at nearby Bei Tsun Chinese School – 9th grade for her, 6th grade for me. Paul entered his premed freshman year at Tung-De medical school. James still continued his so far unsuccessful job search.

Just two days later I was called into the Principal's office, where I also found the school music teacher, Miss Ping, standing beside his desk.

"If I can come quickly to the point Bei Sie," said the Principal, "we would like to celebrate the approaching annual Moon Festival this year with, for the first time ever, a school play to be named, like the famous classical story, 'CHANG-ER FLIES TO THE MOON.'

"There will be one quite nice song in it" he continued, "to be sung by the starring 'Moon Goddess' character. Since Miss Ping tells me that you have a beautiful singing voice, we would like for you to be our 'Moon Goddess'.' Will you do it?"

Almost too stunned to reply, I finally blurted out "But, ... I've never done anything like that. I wouldn't know what to do!"

"I will be producer and director of the show, as well as coaching you," said Miss Ping. "Our biggest problem is that we wish to stage it before the entire student body and invited parents just four weeks from today. But, I know you can do it! Will you accept the challenge?"

After I answered "yes," she gave me for study a copy of the famous classical Chinese fairy tale, based on which the script of our 12-student characters school play had been written by Miss Ping. The story was as follows:

CHANG-ER FLIES TO THE MOON

Prince Houyi, seeking eternal youth, obtained the elixir of immortality from Xi Wangmu of the Kunlun Mountains. Returning to his palace, he confided the good news to his beautiful, beloved wife Chang-Er. He told her that if one was to drink the entire potion, immortality could be gained; that to drink but half a potion would make one youthful for the rest of his or her natural life on earth. They agreed to drink a half potion each and thus remain youthful together on earth for the rest of their lives.

One day however, when Houyi was out hunting, Chang-Er secretly swallowed the entire potion, selfishly hoping that she would gain immortality.

The result was quite unexpected! She felt herself becoming light, so light that she flew up and up in spite of her efforts to stop – drifting and floating ever higher in the air, until she reached a beautiful palace on the moon. There she became a deity, known to everyone back on earth as the immortal "Goddess of the Moon." But she was soon very sorry that she had swallowed the whole potion, for she now had to spend eternity alone in her palace on the moon, with nothing else there except a rabbit and pine tree.

The play came off as scheduled on a mid-October Friday evening; our school auditorium packed to overflowing with fellow students and parents. My entire family was there, including, to my great surprise – Father; and of course, Grandmother. The school had rented quite beautiful classic Chinese Opera gowns for the cast – mine the most magnificient of all.

My finale solo, a melancholy and beautiful classical song, with new words written by Miss Ping, sung by the Moon Goddess at the end when she realized that she was doomed to be alone in her palace forever save for the rabbit and the tree, brought the house down.

As a result, for the next several days "little old, never before recognized for anything, me" was the most talked about, complemented and envied person at Bei Tsung School. Even my mathematics teacher seemed to regard me with new respect! I went about, for a time, in a state of blissful euphoria!

Back at home, later that night after the show, my family, including Daddy, also heaped praise on me, as we gathered around the second level parlor table, which was piled high with traditional festive, golden brown "Moon Cakes." These pastries, with fillings, shaped like small crumpets, were stamped on top with the emblem of the Moon God. The most common filling was sugared red bean paste. Other varieties included assorted nuts or Lotus seeds; still others were embedded with salted duck eggs. Traditional, festive candle-lit red paper lanterns illuminated the table setting.

This Moon Festival celebration, much like the western Thanksgiving, traditionally takes place during the period of the Harvest Moon in the 8th month of the Chinese Lunar Calendar. Crops have been gathered and it's time to relax and celebrate life and good fortune – which we were doing!

Unfortunately, a diabolical war-hungry gaggle of Japanese Generals and Admirals was even then busily completing plans that would cut short my days of euphoria!

By November, everyone in Shanghai felt an unusual tenseness in the air. Most American women and children had already been evacuated from the city, and American personnel of most American business firms reduced to a minimum.

While the British government still had not ordered any Britons to leave, it had for some time been advising the departure of women, children and nonessential male employees of British firms. Since Shanghai had enjoyed immunity during World War I and through other subsequent troubles, compliance to date had been half-hearted. Too many British and other foreigners were reluctant to leave; feeling that "nothing serious will happen here."

Concerned, the British government sent the ship "Anhui" to Shanghai – outfitted to accommodate up to 1,000 evacuees; and again strongly advised citizens to depart. She sailed from Shanghai with a full load of passengers at the end of November, just 10 days before the Japanese attack on Pearl Harbor.

Bound for Australia, she first put in at Manila, where most of the passengers were summarily put ashore for supposed "safety's sake." Unfortunately, they were all interned a short time later, following Japanese occupation of the Philippines, and spent the rest of World War II in Santo Thomas Internment Camp just outside that city. The "Anhui," with its remaining evacuees, eventually reached Australia safely.

On the Whangpoo fronting The Bund, during those final tense November days, Japanese authorities, ordered the Italian gunboat "Emillo Carlotta" to be moved some distance upstream. Then, in early December the Japanese brought in a large, powerful river gunboat and moored her alongside the Public Gardens on The Bund, close to the cruiser "Idzuma." Both Japanese ships now had a clear, unobstructed view of the small gunboats "USS Wake" and "HMS Petrel" which, serving as communications relay stations for their respective country's nearby Consulates, were still anchored only a short distance upriver.

Daddy, who was spending his days full time during this period at Standard Oil headquarters, located two blocks west of The Bund not far from the Maritime Customs Building, was well aware of all these activities. He kept James and Paul informed on a daily basis; they in turn kept the other members of our Yang household informed.

Whereas the Japanese attack on Pearl Harbor took place Sunday morning, December 7, Hawaii time, due to International Date Line and time differences, hostilities in Shanghai commenced early the morning of Monday, December 8. The action began when a Japanese patrol boat, bearing a boarding party, approached the two British and American gunboats and demanded their surrender.

None of the "Wake's" small compliment of officers was aboard, and she was quickly captured without resistance. Her total American crew, officers and men numbered at best only 30 or so plus a few Chinese crewmen. She was the only American warship on station in Shanghai or on the Yangtze at the time; all others having sailed a few weeks earlier for the Philippines. She was later given a Japanese name and incorporated into that country's navy.

The tiny "Petrel," the only British naval ship in the area, also had only a small compliment of British officers and men plus a few Chinese crewmen. Her skipper, a Captain Polkinhorn, who was aboard ship, promptly and courageously refused to surrender. As he set about destroying his secret codes, both the nearby large Japanese gunboat and the cruiser Idzuma opened fire on his ship at point blank range. "Petrel" promptly sank at her moorings. While only one British seaman was killed in this attack, several others were wounded while abandoning ship. After swimming ashore, the Captain and crew were quickly taken prisoner by Japanese troops lining the riverbank.

Within hours of the capture of the "Wake" and the sinking of the "Petrel," all key points in both the International Settlement and French Concession were taken over by Japanese troops. Consulates of Great Britain, the United States, Holland and Belgium were closed, their military personnel made prisoner, and their civilian officials placed under restraint.

Awakened early that morning by the sound of heavy gunfire from the direction of The Bund, as Daddy hastily left for the Standard Oil office, the rest of us Yangs crowded around our hidden shortwave radio set. Some of us stayed there all the rest of that awful day, and late into the evening, as the bad news kept unfolding.

The Japanese also began several other major attack operations that day on the Asian mainland. Over the next three weeks we learned of the December 10 sinking of the British battleship "HMS Prince of Wales" and the battle cruiser "HMS Repulse" off the coast of Malaya, the fall of Hong Kong on December 25 and the occupation by Japanese troops of the neutral country of Thailand during December.

By December 15, notices had been posted on American and Allied property throughout Shanghai to the effect that the land, buildings and all contents were now under control of Japanese military authorities. The public was warned of severe consequences to anyone who might try to destroy, remove or sell anything covered by the notices.

Daddy came home that evening to say that all Standard Oil holdings, including oil installations, warehouses, docks, barges and boats had been taken over by the Japanese, but the employees, both American and Chinese, had been ordered to continue reporting to work as usual.

The first Americans and British to be interned, that we heard about, were news correspondents and reporters. These went into a notorious local prison known as Bridge House on December 20. Over the next few days, rumors flew wildly of ever more arrests – of Americans, Allied and other foreigners; and of Chinese employees of foreign business firms. We could tell that Daddy was becoming increasingly concerned!

The knock on our Mansion door came around 7 p.m. the evening of December 27. James answered – to find himself facing two Japanese officers, a Chinese interpreter and four armed Japanese soldiers.

"Is this the home of T. Y. Yang, an executive with the American Standard Oil Company?" the interpreter asked.

When James replied in the affirmative, the interpreter, speaking for one of the Japanese officers, said "Tell him to join us – immediately!"

Not knowing which concubine Daddy was with that evening, James scrambled to find out. Ah Foo told him Daddy was with Concubine Ching. He ran up to fetch him, as the rest of us Yangs clustered nervously on the second level stairwell landing.

When Daddy came down and was identified, the same Japanese officer again speaking through the interpreter, brusquely ordered: "Come with us – Now!"

As Daddy was led away to an army truck parked close by, we all rushed down to the front entranceway to silently watch in disbelief and horror.

He turned and gave us a half wave as soldiers roughly pushed him into the canvas enclosed guarded back of the truck. It immediately roared off in a cloud of smelly black exhaust smoke, followed closely by a staff car bearing the officers and the interpreter.

"Where were they taking Daddy?" we asked one another.

"What will happen to him? Will we ever see him again?" We were all filled with fear!

Chapter 9

ROCKS N' RICE: THE WAR RAGES ON

For four days, after Daddy was taken away so suddenly and forcibly from our home by Japanese soldiers that evening of December 27, all we Mansion occupants were filled with fear and foreboding. We had no idea where or how he was, or if we would ever see him again!

Since it was now time for him to pass out his usual first of the month January, 1942 cash disbursements to our various household sub-units, no one had any money at all to speak of. "If he doesn't come back soon, how will any of us eat, pay the utilities, pay our soon due school tuition fees – or anything else?" we asked one another. Harsh reality was that all occupants of his household were totally dependent on his monthly financial largess. We had no fall back positions!

Suddenly, around 7:00 p.m., at almost the exact same time he had been whisked away four days earlier, the same Japanese

147

army truck again pulled up in front of our house. Two armed soldiers rather unceremoniously pulled someone from the dark, canvas covered back interior of the vehicle and roughly pushed a rather disheveled middle aged man onto the street. As before, the truck then immediately roared off in a cloud of smelly black exhaust smoke.

As his Yang children, his mother, Concubine Number One, Ah Foo and our two Yang family maids clustered wide-eyed and silently just inside our Mansion's front entranceway, the man – Father – slowly picked himself up and walked nonchalantly in amongst us.

"I've got to go to the bathroom, and I am very hungry!" he announced. Looking at Ah Foo, he continued, "I'll take my dinner with Silver Lotus as quickly as you can serve it!"

Without a further word to any of us other stunned onlookers, he wheeled and headed straight for the first floor room of Concubine Number One.

Other than to merely say that the Japanese authorities had taken him to Bridge House for "some routine questioning as an employee of an American firm," Daddy for some days said nothing about his experience. As we learned later he had been warned not to do so, and was fearful of both retaliation to himself and to other prisoners still there if he did. In time however, and via the countless rumors that were flooding Shanghai as a result of so many arrests, we did learn what had happened to him and to so many others.

The infamous Bridge House prison where the Japanese secret police took those arrested for questioning and detention, was, prior to "Bloody Saturday," 1937, an eight-story apartment house located not far from the Garden Bridge end of The Bund. These Japanese secret police, called Gendarmerie, who were said to report only to the office of the Emperor himself, had converted the building into numerous small cells and torture chambers.

Both foreigners and Chinese, men and women, were thrown together regardless of sex into small crowded cells, usually with

148

only one infrequently emptied small bucket toilet for up to thirty people. No bedding was provided; prisoners had to sleep as best they could on the damp concrete floor. Food, when offered was terrible. Due to lack of shower facilities, occupants quickly attracted lice and other vermin. Conversation between prisoners was forbidden. Medical attention and facilities was non existent. During interrogations, most prisoners had to totally strip and kneel before their tormentors. Most had to endure assorted types of torture.

Daddy was very lucky! Most prisoners were "guests" of their captors for at least two to three weeks; many were never heard from again! His short imprisonment was as much a warning to him as anything. It was meant to frighten him – and it did!

The Japanese were well aware that this key Chinese executive of American-owned Standard Oil could be of use to them. They just wanted to alert him to what could quickly happen if he didn't conform to their instructions.

There was, however, amidst all the gloom, doom and imprisonment's of Shanghai's immediate post-Pearl Harbor Day shock – one small bright spot that provided enough chuckles and delight to help people keep their sanity. That was the fact the one lone British sailor from the sunken "HMS Petrel" was still at large, and search as they might, the Japanese couldn't find him! As rumor had it then, a rumor that became a cheerful fact at war's end in 1945, the sailor was secretly and successfully hidden by his White Russian sweetheart "somewhere" in Shanghai throughout the rest of the Pacific War.

Some more good news unfolded for us Yangs the month following Daddy's release from interrogation by the Japanese. One of Mother's two younger half brothers, a Paris educated, highly regarded neurologist, Dr. S.T. Yuen, was suddenly appointed Director of Public Health for Greater Shanghai, by the Chinese puppet government in Nanking. Having always been in private practice, and strictly non-political, the appointment came as a complete surprise to him as well as to the entire Yuen and Yang families.

While acceptance meant possible stigma as a "collaborator," one had to survive, and the Nanking puppet government represented the only civil authority permitted by the Japanese. Also, there was the fear of what might happen to him and his family if he did not accept! So, he accepted! Actually, his appointment was welcome news to our family as it was to most informed citizens, first because he was highly regarded professionally, secondly because the public health situation in Shanghai had deteriorated alarmingly since Japan's recent declaration of war on the allies.

Immediately after their December attacks some weeks earlier, the Japanese had dismissed all foreign members and department heads of the former British controlled Shanghai Municipal Council, which governed the International Settlement. One immediate result was that the daily collection of nightly scores of new corpses along the streets and in the alleys came to a near standstill in the Settlement. This alone posed an immediate, grave public health problem.

Also, public health conditions in the French Concession were going downhill fast. After France's surrender, the Consul General of France who ran the French Concession, allied his Shanghai office with the Vichy French government, which was now collaborating with Germany. Realizing that the days of French control were undoubtedly numbered, and short of funds anyhow, the Consul-General and his subordinate French officials began to cut back sharply on all government services in the formerly well-managed, clean French Concession.

Not only was our Peach Blossom Lane Yang family happy that "Uncle Dr. S. T." was going to get the corpses picked up on a daily basis again, but were even happier when he hired James to join his staff as Engineer-Inspector of greater Shanghai's several different water supply systems. Since James had been unemployed since his graduation from Shanghai University the previous June, everyone was glad to get him out of the Mansion during daily working and school hours.

In late February, Daddy hired a refugee peasant and his wife to work full time at turning our Mansion's large back yard into a fully utilized, intensively cultivated crop area. Since fresh vegetables were becoming increasingly expensive and at times hard to get in local markets, his idea and theirs was to raise corn, sugarcane, potatoes, eggplant and soybeans in addition to the garden vegetables we had been cultivating under Grandmother's supervision.

A small backyard hut was built for this couple to live in, and Daddy instructed Grandmother to "keep an eye on them," as well as continuing (with the help of Betty and me) to cultivate the usual rooftop garden. She promptly took his words to mean that she was overall "farm boss."

Her first move to "take charge" involved preparations to celebrate properly the "Feast of the Excited Insects," an annual celebration which falls some two weeks before the Vernal Equinox – in early March on the western calendar. This is the time when hibernating insects suddenly come to life, and signifies imminent awakening of the soil, source of all crop fertility, for spring planting.

"The first thing we must do to celebrate this feast properly," she announced to me as her just appointed First Assistant, "is to go out and buy three or four paper tigers, which we will place before an alter the night before the feast."

"Why tigers?" I asked, in a tongue-in-cheek manner. "Wouldn't paper worms be more appropriate? After all we are going to honor soil, where worms live, and celebrate the awakening of insects – who will most likely be hungry after hibernating all winter!"

"Silly girl!" she angrily retorted, "don't you know that the tiger who is king of all Chinese land beasts, offers the best possible protection against demons who eat awakening insects, and diseases that kill them while they are still weak!"

I had to confess that this information was news to me!

Off to the market we went the next day, where we purchased three inexpensive paper tigers and several sticks of a special

151

kind of incense that she favored. This type of incense was made by powdering dried aromatic Oleander leaves and then wetting the powder until it formed an adhesive mass. Small sticks were then rolled in this and put out on frames to dry in the sun before being offered for sale.

Back at the Mansion, Grandmother had me bring the red altar from her room. Placing it under a sheltered area in the back yard, she then positioned the paper tigers and incense sticks in their sand filled containers around its front. Assuming a prayerful attitude, she lighted the incense and waited silently as they burned out.

We then left the area "as was" for 24 hours so the tigers could "acquire more power" through being left alone with the Earth God for that period of time. Small food offerings of sliced hardboiled eggs and bits of pork fat were left in covered containers beside the tigers.

When time was up, the paper tigers were burned on the spot, and the "Feast of the Excited Insects" was over and done with for the year. Grandmother was satisfied, and I now knew that each spring insects just awakening from a winter's hibernation have to be concerned, among other things, about being eaten alive by demons. No wonder they awake all "excited!"

Some days later, the following letter from Suzie reached us via the usual "underground" message system. Father once again read it in private to our Yang family group:

Dear Mother and Father,

Although I have remained settled here in Kunming since my mid-August letter to you of last year, Logan, who was recently promoted to Major, has been quite busy. When France capitulated to the Germans the month before I wrote, the Japanese moved quickly to seize several ports in French Indochina. They then cut the narrow gauge railroad from the port of Haiphong to Kunming – one of China's only two remaining links to the outside world. They also seized several Indochina airfields from which they commenced bombing the only other open link – the Burma Road in northeastern British Burma.

With the railroad cut, the only way to get war supplies to China from the outside world was by ship to Rangoon, (Yangon), Burma (Myanmar); then by rail to Lashio in northern Burma, and from there by truck over the winding, difficult 720 mile long Burma Road to Kunming. Just before Logan and I arrived in Kunming, the British, in July, had caved in to Japanese demands and closed the road. That left China completely cut off from the outside world.

At about that time however, the Americans announced a Lend-lease program to provide weapons and supplies to nations in both Europe and Asia that were being attacked by Germany and Japan. Cheered by that news, the British reopened the Burma Road last October – only three months after closing it.

With lend-lease shipments now on their way, the Burma Road has suddenly assumed even greater strategic importance – and that's where Logan comes in! Due to his fluent command of English, he now serves as chief interpreter to a Staff Logistical Group of high ranking Chinese and British officers plus some American civilian advisers. They are charged with planning and carrying out this important supply operation. Logan busily divides his time between Lashio and Chinese Army Southwestern Command Headquarters here in Kunming.

He is also working closely with an interesting man named Claire Chennault, a retired American Army Air Corps officer, now a Colonel in the Chinese Air Force, who has been aeronautical advisor to the Chinese government since 1937. Logan first met him in Chungking. Chennault has just started training some American civilian volunteers (all former U.S. military fliers) as fighter pilots to challenge the Japanese Air Force over the Burma Road.

Logan and I are both well, but miss all of you.

Respectfully, Your Number Two Daughter

Suzie

March 26, 1941,

Kunming, Yunnan

Receipt of this letter from Suzie disturbed rather than cheered our family members. It had taken nearly a year to reach us! The news that Logan spent considerable time in Lashio,

Burma was especially worrisome since we had heard via short-wave New Delhi, India broadcasts that on March 7 the British had suddenly pulled out of Rangoon and were retreating north toward that city. We knew that it was the key strategic point for control of the Burma Road. If he was still there – we were worried for his safety!

We were glad that he knew Colonel Chennault, for we also knew from shortwave broadcasts that the latter's "Flying Tigers" group of volunteer American aviators had been successfully flying cover over the Burma Road since just before the Pearl Harbor attack.

Paul voiced our collective hopes when he said, one evening to Mother, "if Logan gets trapped in Lashio, perhaps he will be important enough (or lucky enough) to be flown to safety by one of those American pilots."

The only cheering note in all this bad spring, 1942 news out of Burma was that two Chinese armies, the Fifth and the Sixth were apparently on their way south toward Lashio from China's Yunnan Province to assist the British. American broadcasts said that Generalissimo Chiang Kai-shek had placed these troops under the command of an American army officer, Lieutenant General Joseph W. Stilwell, a Chinese-speaking infantry veteran who had spent many of his U.S. army years stationed in China.

Our hopes quickly turned to despair several days later however, when local Japanese controlled Shanghai radio stations triumphantly announced that on March 21 Japanese bombers had attacked the main Flying Tigers base at Magwe, Burma and "destroyed most of their planes on the ground."

Then, a few weeks later, these same stations boastfully proclaimed the April 29 capture of Lashio, cutting of the Burma Road and total defeat of both the British and Chinese forces. "Disorganized remnants of these troops," the announcers said, "were fleeing through the jungle toward India in total disarray. Japan is victorious in Burma!"

We Yangs, like all our relatives and friends, were depressed and anxious at all the seemingly endless "nothing but bad news" war news. We had all been elated at Japan's surprise Pearl Harbor attack on the United States since we felt that an enraged, powerful America would quickly defeat the treacherous aggressor. But Japan's stunning December series of victories throughout Southeast Asia following that attack had unnerved us!

And the first five months of 1942 had produced an even greater number of impressive Japanese victories: Singapore's surrender, February 15; complete occupation of the Dutch East Indies by March 9, capture of Corrigidor and the Philippines May 6, and their victory in Burma of late May! The Japanese seemed to be invincible – and by the end of May their radio announcers braggingly talked of a quick, total victory.

The only bright spot during that depressing period, as short lived as a flaring match, was the April 18 attack on Tokyo by a few American B-25 bombers dangerously and bravely flown off an aircraft carrier some 650 miles out in the windswept Pacific.

In the weeks that followed, rumors raced through Shanghai that some of these planes had landed at secret airfields in China, one of them near Ningpo. Also, that some of the American fliers had been captured and brought to Shanghai where they were forced to dig their own graves. After either being shot or beheaded, the rumors went, their bodies fell right into these fresh self-dug graves. Since the Japanese surpressed news of this raid, we did not learn the true facts until war's end.

The bright clear days of early June were a welcome relief after the long, dark, cold, often wet past winter months with all their discouraging war news. The war, during this time, was of course, our chief family concern and topic of conversation. In many ways life went on as usual – the British owned busses and trams in the International Settlement, and the French owned ones in our French Concession, both now under Japanese control of course, were operating normally, as were most of the old allied owned businesses.

Standard Oil, for example, was operating as usual, under a new Japanese company name, with key American and Chinese employees, including Daddy, kept in place teaching recently brought in Japanese civilians how to run things. While it did no oil refining in China, Standard Oil, as well as some other large allied-owned oil companies, owned oil storage terminals and warehouses for finished petroleum products at several locations up and down China's coast. From these bases, oil products were packaged in tins, boxes and steel drums for distribution throughout China. Lack of railroads and trucking lines made it necessary to ship these products in small packages by junk, in small carts or even by camelback. Since all this was essential to their own war effort, the Japanese wanted the operation kept intact.

American films were still being featured in most of the big theaters, many foreign consumer products were still being advertised and sold from warehouse stocks on hand, and most Allied civilians were going freely about their business.

Nearly all foreign and many Chinese automobile owners, like Daddy, continued to own and drive their own private cars. Due however to the shortage of, and the high price of gasoline for civilians, more and more of these cars were being converted to run on foul-smelling charcoal gas. Fortunately, Daddy was still able to get gasoline through Standard Oil.

Overall though, life was getting harder and living conditions were slowly but surely deteriorating. Food was getting more expensive and scarce, due both to shortages in production and hoarding, and good quality coal and charcoal was getting harder to buy. Basic utilities such as water, gas and electricity, now under Japanese control, were strictly rationed. Due to poor supervision and reduced maintenance, these services were frequently erratic.

Although normal commercial activity had slowed way down, activities supporting the Japanese war effort hummed. Shanghai was the key support base for Japanese army operations along the Yangtze basin west into central China, and for Japanese aerial activities south and west. Japanese military air traffic was heavy into and out of the several airfields that ringed Shanghai. Bomber formations of from 20 to 30 planes flying low overhead were a common sight. At night, we could see searchlights lighting the distant skies and would occasionally hear antiaircraft gunfire.

Since Vichy France and Japan were not at war, our French Concession was still patrolled by the usual French-led police and French troops, and we seldom saw armed Japanese soldiers there. Japanese troops and Chinese Puppet Government police however, now patrolled streets of the International Settlement.

As our spring end of school term drew to a close that June, we heard via shortwave overseas radio broadcasts of a major American Pacific naval victory at what was called "The Battle of Midway." Four Japanese aircraft carriers were reportedly sunk in this engagement. Little did we know then that this obscure to us battle would prove to be the turning point in the Pacific War. The Japanese, via their local radio station and newspapers claimed it as a major naval victory for their side. We didn't know who or what to believe.

Apart from our hidden second floor shortwave radio, we Yangs got much of our news from local Japanese controlled Chinese language radio stations. We also listened on our regular household radios to local English language broadcasts of Nazi German controlled station XGRS. This powerful Shanghai station broadcast German propaganda and news, mostly in English and German, daily throughout all of Asia and Australiasia.

Japanese controlled Chinese language newspapers were available, as well as one published in English. The constant flow of refugees into Shanghai from the interior kept people informed of events along the Chinese-Japanese battlefronts, and Daddy continued to get fairly up to date reliable information from the interior through Standard Oil sources.

As soon as school was over, Grandmother put Betty and me to work cultivating and weeding our rooftop garden, which we had planted earlier. And she put Paul and us to work building some chicken coops for her along the backyard fence. We three were all she had left to supervise since the peasant couple who had been hired by Daddy to "farm" our backyard had protested vehemently when she tried to order them around. He promptly sided with them, but as a sop to Grandmother gave her permission to raise some chickens.

This decision quickly proved to be an unwise one, because Second Concubine Ching, always jealous, then wanted to raise chickens as well for her family's table. Father approved and gave her a section of the fence next to Grandmother's for her chicken coops. Her two oldest boys started building her coops at the same time that Paul, assisted by Betty and me, started ours.

The start date for these two competing projects was based on the ages-old widely believed and used "Farmer's Calendar" which, as part of one five page section, listed good and bad days of 1942 for certain specific activities including buying a horse, starting breast feeding – and, believe it or not – building a chicken coop!

The specific June day it recommended was the day that the two Mansion factions, who seldom ever saw or spoke to one another, started their side-by-side respective building projects. That too-close contact quickly led to a flare-up of our always-simmering local, within the household, war-within-a-war: Grandmother and us Younger Yangs versus the Concubine Ching's!

This "warfare," was a subtle, guerrilla type activity for the most part – loud snide words, whispered caustic comments, hiding of tools, and cold-shouldering of one another!

It heated up later in the summer however, when some of Grandmother's chickens got sick after becoming so constipated that their rear ends clogged up with a protruding mass of hardened matter. Grandmother's age-old home remedy was to get a pair of scissors and cut the mass off! Some of her chickens died as a result of this primitive surgery; to the great amusement of Concubine Ching, none of whose chickens had come down with the affliction.

Ching's repeated bragging comments about this fact, plus her continued not-welcomed-at-all "advice" about how to both prevent in the first place and then cure the illness after the fact, drove Grandmother wild. She responded with pithy comments of her own – to the extent that the two women argued loudly and fiercely every time their paths crossed at the chicken coops. Each bad-mouthed the other so constantly to Daddy that he quickly became sick and tired of what we Yang offspring were now calling "The Great Chicken War."

Grandmother upped the ante by repeatedly getting up and out to the chicken coops early in the morning before her competitor, stealing some eggs from Concubine Ching's chickens, and claiming they were laid by her hens. Since cackling of her hens often gave away the fact that they had laid an egg, Concubine Ching guessed what was going on, but could never prove it. By mid-July continued squabbling between the two had the entire Mansion household in such an uproar that the "real war" was almost forgotten.

Shanghai lies in what is known as a monsoon climate. The prevailing winds which except during the monsoon, blow in from the arid west and northwest regions of Central Asia are very dry. There is practically no rain during the time they blow, which is usually from early September to the following April. The big rains begin around early July, when the monsoon breaks, and last through August. This July-August concentration of heavy monsoon rains is also the year's worst period of stifling humidity and heat.

As the wet monsoon rains and oppressive, clammy heat closed in on our Peach Blossom Lane Mansion occupants that July, tempers, frayed by "The Great Chicken War," rose to the near-boiling point.

It was then that Concubine Silver Lotus, an observer only of the fracas up to that point, approached me on the sly to join as her accomplice in a plot to "Do-In the Concubine Chings" once and for all! The whole bunch of them!

"What is your plan?" I whispered, in a conspiratorial tone of voice!

"On behalf of your Mother and Grandmother and the rest of our household," she replied, "I have decided to ask a Spiritual Medium to help bring the wrath of the Five Demons down on Second Concubine Ching and her brood."

"That's serious business," I answered. "How does one go about doing it, and why do you need my help?"

"Well, I've found an excellent Medium not far from here who is in close contact with the Earth God who has power over the Five Demons. We are to initiate the ritual tomorrow afternoon and I need you to be present as witness to see that it is properly performed. Will you do it?"

"Yes, I will!" was my quick-response answer!

Engaging a couple of rickshaws that next afternoon, Silver Lotus and I made our way to the Native City home of the Medium. After reminding us that the Earth God is the superior deity for intimate family matters and problems, including the settling of disputes, she stated that she was the proper authority to invoke its assistance.

She then showed us the deity's shrine, which consisted of an earth color painted wooden altar with a mountain peak shaped red rock at its center symbolizing belief in the Earth God as the basic source of all earthly fertility.

"Why are you asking the Earth God's assistance in bringing down the wrath of the Five Demons on these unsuspecting earthlings?" she inquired.

Silver Lotus, backed up by me, explained how Concubine Ching and her boys came to our home, and how unhappy they had made all the rest of our family, especially my sick mother. We stated that we were asking the Earth God to have the Five Demons drive the unwanted concubine and her children from our home, so our family could live together in peace once again.

After lighting candles and incense on the altar, the Medium placed a firecracker-filled small clay pot with closed lid in between them. She then laid a good-sized white piece of paper, imprinted with a colorful picture of the Five Demons, face down over the pot. Unwrapping a hard-boiled egg from inside a large red square of cloth, she smashed the egg on the top of the pot as she verbally invoked our desires regarding Concubine Ching to the Earth God.

Asking Silver Lotus to then place atop the pot a second piece of paper, this time a yellow sheet, on which she had written Concubine Ching's name, the Medium asked us to step back before lighting a long fuse that led into the firecracker filled pot.

The resulting noisy explosion blew the clay pot and the two pieces of paper lying over it into countless small shreds and pieces. This caused the Medium to smile happily!

"No trace remains of the Demon's faces," she said, "and that is a most favorable sign that the Earth God will, in its own good time and way, handle the problem regarding Concubine Ching in accordance with your desires!"

The Medium smiled even more broadly as Silver Lotus presented her with a quite respectable, red gift wrapped sum of "Lucky Money" on our way out.

Silver Lotus and I chuckled with glee and waved to one another joyfully from our respective rickshaws all the way back to the Mansion – pleased that we had at least done "something" to try and get rid of despised Second Concubine Ching and her boys!

I did not believe then, nor do I today, many years later, REALLY believe in old Chinese gods and deities, nor do I think that Concubine Silver Lotus really did.

But, wonders upon wonders, Second Concubine Ching, to everyone's complete surprise, Daddy's especially, suddenly and secretly up and ran away one wee hours following October morning, with a local rice merchant – taking her four boys and her maid with her! We never heard from them again! Ever!

Sometimes, today, I wonder! Could such things as an Earth God and the Five Demons really exist? If so – Bless Them!

By early September, fast changing world and local events forced all us Mansion dwellers to put memories of our "Great Chicken War" behind us and focus our attention on new, often

161

frightening and threatening situations. Central to everything, was raging war – everywhere it seemed!

Of shocking first importance to us was the sudden arrest of Fredrick J. Twogood, General Manager of Standard Vacuum Oil Company in China – Daddy's boss! He, along with many other top allied national executives of large foreign companies, had been forced since Pearl Harbor to continue managing their organizations under Japanese supervision. Now, suddenly, the Japanese took complete control and tossed Twogood, the Acting General Manager of Shell Oil Company and several other such top level executives into Bridge House prison without any prior warning. To Daddy, and the rest of us Yangs, this represented an ominous turn of events. Would he be next on their list?

At about the same time, all other allied resident civilians were ordered to wear red armbands on their left arm with distinctive markings for different nationalities (A for Americans, B for Britons, H for Dutch, etc.). Each band showed individual numbers, which were registered, at Japanese military headquarters.

After enjoying relative freedom of movement since Pearl Harbor, these individuals were suddenly denied entrance to clubs, movies, public rooms in hotels and nearly all places of amusement. While they were permitted to eat out in small restaurants, checkups were frequent, and those caught without their armbands were usually sent to prison for a time.

While Japanese treatment of allied civilians suddenly became increasingly harsh, their occupation policies toward the by now over four million Chinese inhabitants of Shanghai remained relatively benign. As they proudly displayed photographic exhibits of their military and naval victories throughout the city, and showed propaganda films in all theaters, they sought to win both Chinese approval of and cooperation in their propaganda goal of "Asia for the Asiatics." While some Shanghai Chinese cooperated willingly with the Japanese, most hated, distrusted and feared them.

Along the winding, fragmented 3,400-mile interior battle-fronts of China however, where some four million very poorly equipped Chinese soldiers, Nationalists in west and southwest China; communists in northwest China, faced a well-equipped, highly mechanized Japanese combat force of one million, the front line fighting remained bitter, inconclusive and ruthless.

And, in spite of their additional two and a half million man occupation force, the Japanese were frustrated by continued behind-their-lines harassment by both Communist and Nationalist guerrilla fighters. Also they were baffled by the continued effective mass resistance of Chinese peasants in carrying out the national government's "scorched earth" policy of destroying crops, villages and everything else of value in front of every Japanese advance. As a result, the invaders reacted with systematic enraged brutality against both the organized guerrillas and the poor, helpless but determined and defiant peasantry.

With China now completely cut off from surface contact with the outside world, the allies worried that without supplies of vital war materials China might not be able to continue resisting the Japanese. The last thing they wanted at this point in the war was the freeing of those one million veteran Japanese combat troops, now bogged down in China, to invade Australia or India. They did what they could to fly such supplies over "The Hump" – that 500 mile aerial route from northwestern India to Kunming over high and dangerous mountains, but that was only a trickle of what was needed.

Elsewhere in the world, the military situation faced by the allies was equally dismal, In Eastern Europe the German armies had reached the outskirts of Stalingrad and had advanced into the Caucasus region of the USSR. In North Africa German General Rommel was at the gates of Cairo. In the Pacific the Japanese were in control from the Aleutians in the north to the New Hebrides in the south and in Southeast Asia they had reached the borders of India. The only bright spot, one quite distant from Shanghai, was the allied invasion of North Africa in November.

As all these differing events unfolded within the "Big Picture" that autumn of 1942, Betty and I once again enrolled in nearby Bei Tsun Chinese School; 10th grade for her, 7th grade for me. Paul entered his second year of premed studies at Tung-De medical school.

Betty, who by this time was becoming quite an accomplished pianist for her age, and hoped to eventually go on to conservatory, decided that she should also take singing lessons. Since Paul and I also wanted to take singing lessons, all three of us enrolled for once a week private lessons from Madame Tamara, an elderly but locally highly regarded White Russian singing teacher. She had attended Kiev Conservatory in her younger years and had sung minor roles in Russian provincial opera productions. Her studio, on Route Prosper Paris, was within somewhat lengthy walking distance of our home.

As the dark, damp, cold days of December rolled around, coal for our household apartments' heating stoves, only one on each floor level, became harder to find and quite costly. Often it was full of clay, and thus hard to ignite and quite smoky. Mother, who by this time was quite ill and largely confined to her bed, suffered the most from the cold house and often-excessive smoke. We Yangs now frequently ate in the kitchen because it was the warmest room in the mansion.

Rice, our staple food which we purchased in large sacks based on weight, was by now strictly rationed. Unscrupulous rice merchants increasingly began to mix in liberal amounts of small white rocks with their rice in order to add more weight and increase their profits.

To counter this, Mei-Ling by directive, and me by family "election" (as the youngest Yang, I was outvoted), as the war raged on, began to spend one or two evenings each week nimbly hand picking these little white rocks out of the large sacks of rice!

Our only consolation was that we kept cozily warm as we "picked away" by flickering firelight from the big kitchen stove.

Chapter 10

MOTHER PASSES ON TO JOIN HER ANCESTORS

"Oh, that poor girl," shrieked Betty, "what are they doing to her?"

"She's pregnant, and the Japanese soldier is ripping her stomach open with his bayonet," I cried in anguish.

"How can he be so cruel? Look at all the blood and stomach contents pouring down her inside pants legs and out of the front of her chong sam!" sobbed Betty tearfully.

We stood there, in shocked disbelief, at the barbed wire barricade checkpoint stretched across Avenue Haig, near its intersection with Avenue Joffre, where a Japanese soldier had just slashed open the stomach of a young, very pregnant Chinese peasant girl. As the large crowd of checkpoint passers through watched in horror, she slumped to the ground moaning pitifully – her eyes already reflecting the glaze of fast-approaching death.

We knew instantly what had happened! Due to the shortage of, and the skyrocketing price of rice, rice smuggling was commonplace. It was not at all unusual for women to stuff a large sack of rice under their short, cloth, winter chong-sam cotton padded outer garment, pretending to be pregnant, as they passed amongst the thick crowds through Shanghai's numerous military/police checkpoints.

Nor was it unusual for Japanese soldiers at their checkpoints to slash the front of pregnant-appearing women with their sharp bayonets, laughing with glee if rice spilled out onto the street.

Sometimes, like this time – a mistake was made! This young girl really was pregnant, and now lay dead on the street in a pool of her own blood, cruelly aborted fetus and guts! The offending soldier in this case, as in other such "mistakes," couldn't have cared less! He merely waved his arm, pointed his rifle, and ordered a rickshawman to remove the body.

Life was cheap in wartime Shanghai, and death no stranger to anyone present, so the large crowd promptly continued about its business, jostling past the watchful eyes of the Japanese soldiers and Nanking puppet government Chinese police manning this particular International Settlement checkpoint.

Betty and I, still in shock at witnessing our first real-life "murder," stumbled through the barricade ourselves, and continued on past the market stalls lining the street south in the direction of Siccawei Cathedral.

It was the first Sunday of January 1943; we were on our way to visit Auntie Peony and her family, and the Chinese Nanking puppet Government had just declared war on the United States, Great Britain and all the other allied nations!

"What a way to start the New Year!" we commented to one another, as we walked hurriedly on our way.

Those words were spoken too soon – for over the next three weeks other tumultuous, bad news events rocked our Yang family lives to the extent that all plans for our usual New Year's celebrations were quickly forgotten.

Most worrisome to all of us was Mother's worsening illness. She was now totally bedridden, coughing up blood and mucus spasmodically and suffering wrenching clonic spasms that were frightening to watch.

During her frequent bouts of delirium she would cry out to, or carry on fragmented, anguished one-way conversation with Suzie and Nellie. She kept asking how they were, and when they would be coming to see her. Not having heard from either of them, or from Guo Liang, in many months, there was little we could say to reassure her. Mother seemed to be slipping so fast that we wondered how long she would be with us.

Nor was Daddy his usual poised, assured self. Mother's serious illness was finally beginning to affect him – due to a delayed guilt complex no doubt! And he still hadn't regained his usual, often supercilious air of self-confidence since the sudden disappearance of Second Concubine Ching, her maid and her four boys without a word or even a note, the previous October.

This latter event did not affect his financial acumen however; for within two weeks he had rented the suddenly vacant third floor mansion apartment to a middle aged couple from Hunan with one university student son!

Most of all however, he was nervously showing his deep inward concern over the release, a few days earlier, from notorious Bridge House prison, of Fredrick J. Twogood, General Manager of Standard Oil in China – his boss.

"I've just been informed of Mr. Twogood's release after 108-days imprisonment in Bridge House," he had told us, "and learned that he is in terrible physical condition. Fortunately, he will be among the Americans who are soon to be repatriated back to the United States aboard the Swedish ship 'Gripsholm' in exchange for some Japanese citizens caught there by the war."

It was not until the war's end in 1945 that we learned that Mr. Twogood had finally reached America in such poor health, as a result of his internment, that he died a few months later.

Our collective Yang family concern at this news was that Daddy might suffer the same fate!

The event, which most shocked me personally, however, took place only two days after bayoneting of the pregnant Chinese peasant girl! Lu Fong, our second Yang family maid had, as she often did, taken my dog Mong-Fu along on a leash for exercise during one of her frequent local market shopping trips with Ah Foo. Since we had no refrigeration in those days, our cook usually accompanied by one of our two family maids, made such shopping trips at least every other day.

This time, amidst the thick crowd of shoppers, Lu Fong's fresh fruit and vegetable filled string bag broke and its contents spilled onto the roadway. As she scrambled to pick them up, Mong-Fu's leash slipped from her hand and he was quickly lost in the crowd. Although Ah Foo and Lu Fong searched the area frantically – my poor pooch, the very best friend I had in the whole world – was gone forever!

Loss of one's pet dog in a Shanghai crowd at anytime was bad joss, but to lose one now, in wartime Shanghai, with thousands of always hungry refugees around represented a "no hope" situation! Too many Chinese considered dog meat not only "good eating," but a "real delicacy."

While the public marketing of dog's meat had for years been prohibited by Chinese law, Daddy had told me when he originally gave permission for me to accept Mong-Fu as a gift from Auntie White Pearl that some shops did sell it. He told me then of a shop he had seen in the Chapei district of Shanghai where both dog and cat meat was being sold as "tinned rabbit."

"In the back of that shop," he said, "I saw with my own eyes the carcasses of over 1,000 dogs and cats. Most had been stolen by coolies who employed a wire ring on the end of a pole to snatch them. The thieves would then either eat or sell the carcass for food, and separately sell the stripped skins."

I thought at the time that he was just trying to frighten me into watching my new puppy very carefully – which I always did! But now I knew that he had been telling the truth, and I cried for days at the thought that my poor Mong-Fu had most likely wound up on some family's dinner table!

While pet dogs were not common in Shanghai at the time, Daddy had approved of my accepting Mong-Fu as a gift because it was a black and white puppy. Since he had recalled reading in the ancient "Book of Five Elements" that ownership of a black and white dog portends the birth of many healthy males into a family, this particular puppy represented a good omen. Even better, he had also apparently read that should one breed a black and white dog and get one or more black puppies with white ears as a result, one could quickly become both rich and powerful. So, by allowing me to accept this free gift, HE had nothing to lose, and possibly a lot to gain if by chance the ancient book's words came true!

The loss of my black and white dog now however, just before the New Year's Festivities, to him represented very bad luck. Good enough excuse for him NOT to put on his annual kowtow act before the God of Wealth this year – which he didn't!

"What a way to start the New Year!" Those words of only three weeks back seemed to keep coming back to haunt our household!

We certainly felt that way on the evening of January 25 when, around 7:00 p.m. three uniformed Nanking puppet government Chinese policemen appeared at our front door and demanded to see Daddy. As Paul, who had greeted them at the front entranceway, went to fetch him from Concubine Silver Lotus' room, the three officers, without invitation, followed him into the first level parlor. Grandmother and I looked up at them in astonishment and concern from our seats at the parlor table where Paul and us had been playing a game of Chinese checkers.

As Daddy and Concubine Silver Lotus joined us, Father announced who he was, and asked them their business.

"We have been informed that you are hoarding large tins of illegal gasoline for use in your personal automobile, and for sale to others! Is that true?"

The questioner, a tall, stooped, sallow-faced man with long, greasy, unkempt hair falling over the high collar of his uniform tunic, looked directly at Daddy only fleetingly as he talked. Otherwise his sharp, narrowed eyes darted swiftly about the room rapidly taking everything in.

169

"That is not true, officer," replied Daddy firmly, "I work for the former Standard Oil Company, now bearing a Japanese name and under Japanese control, and report directly to a Japanese executive who approves use of company gasoline in my personal automobile, which I use in company business. I do not have any gasoline here at home."

We other members of Father's household, listening apprehensively, knew that the authorities were after all the many speculators and hoarders who had purchased large stocks of gasoline in 1941 and hidden it away for later illegal sale on the black market. "Someone, jealous that we have a private car, must have falsely reported us," we thought to ourselves. This was serious business, because the penalties were severe!

Motioning to the other two rough-looking, also unkempt policemen to enter Grandmother's room, the officer in charge then said to Daddy, "I will sit here with you and your family at the table while my men look around."

As we all sat down, he pulled his pistol out of its holster and placed it on the table in front of him – within easy reach.

As the two searching policemen began tearing things apart, first in Grandmother's room, then in the room shared by Concubine Silver Lotus and Daddy, it suddenly became quite clear to all of us that they were looking for far more than large tins of gasoline. Could it be hidden money or jewelry they were really looking for?

Our individual thoughts now suddenly began to focus in fear on the highly illegal hidden shortwave radio in our middle level Yang apartment!

At this moment, Daddy suddenly said to the Police Officer, "Since you won't find any illegal gasoline, perhaps I can save you and your officers some time, and show our family's appreciation at the wonderful job you police are doing in enforcing the law."

"What are you saying?" asked the officer; his eyes narrowing even more as, for the first time, he looked directly and steadily at Father.

"In order to help the Nanking government's war effort, our family would like to present our private car to you police, for your official use. Will you personally accept it on our behalf, if I now write you a signed turnover note?"

Later, after the officers had gleefully driven off in their newly acquired automobile, Daddy told us what we had begun to suspect; that the whole business was nothing but an unofficial police "shakedown," and that if the officers had not been "paid off" they undoubtedly would have arrested him and made life impossible for all of us.

"Our private car is rapidly becoming a liability anyhow," he told us, "noticeably obvious to everyone that it still used gasoline since it did not have a large teapot-like converter built into the trunk to produce charcoal or Kao-liang (a grain sorghum) gasoline.

"Since I no longer have any Standard Oil protection," he continued, "it was best to simply give it to these 'gangsters in police uniforms' and get them off our backs. Had they found our shortwave radio, we would have been in real trouble!"

His "generous payoff" worked, for never again did these Nanking puppet government "extortionists" bother anyone at our Mansion; as they continually did all our more affluent neighbors, relatives and friends throughout the rest of the war.

The only cheering news for Shanghai's residents that month came in a late January announcement via shortwave radio of the great Russian victory at Stalingrad, USSR where a fierce battle had been raging since late August of the previous year. There, on January 30, German General Friedrich Von Paulus and his encircled 110,000 strong Sixth Army had finally surrendered unconditionally.

The month of February started off on a brighter note for us with arrival, via the Kuomintang underground once again, of a most welcome letter from Suzie. For its reading, Daddy had us assemble in Mother's room, around her sickbed. Fortunately, she was alert enough to sit propped up to hear its news, which was as follows:

Dear Mother and Father,

So much has happened in our lives since my last letter, written to you from Kunming in March of last year, that I hardly know where to begin. But first, to put your mind at ease; Logan and I are both safe and well here in New Delhi. I flew here in an American military plane from Kunming two months ago. How Logan got here, is a much more interesting story!

Early this year, he was at British/Chinese Burma Road army headquarters in Lashio, Burma when the Japanese invaded southern Burma in force. The greatly outnumbered British Forces, hurriedly withdrawing from Rangoon, retreated north toward Lashio. Generalissimo Chiang Kai-shek had just sent two so-called Chinese "armies," under command of the American General Stilwell, down the Burma Road to help them. If you heard about this it may have sounded like a lot, but the two "armies" combined totaled only 30,000 or so soldiers, half of them poorly trained.

Logan had been serving as Interpreter/Liaison Officer between the Lashio British /Chinese headquarters and Colonel Chennault's "Flying Tigers" airbase headquarters at Magwe, Burma when a massive Japanese March 21 bombing attack so damaged their base that Chennault and his American volunteer pilots were quickly forced to relocate to southern China. Logan was ordered to meet and join General Stilwell's staff in Lashio.

As you probably heard from news reports, the much larger Japanese force defeated the exhausted, just joined British/Chinese combined army, and captured Lashio April 29 thus cutting the Burma Road. Remnants of the allied force, in basically four separate groups, finally made their way through heavy jungle and over high mountains to safety in India.

Logan and some 114 Chinese, British, American, Indian and Burmese military and civilian individuals made up the smallest, General Stilwell-led group. The last 150 miles of their 400-mile retreat involved a 14-day trek on foot over jungle trails already slippery with the first monsoon rains. Logan had lost 17 pounds by the time their totally worn out-group reached Imphal, India on May 20, but was otherwise healthy.

Logan now serves as Interpreter/Liaison Officer on General Stilwell's staff here at the general's New Delhi headquarters. He is constantly busy since the general wears three hats; as Generalissimo Chiang Kai-shek's Chief of Staff, as Commanding General of the newly formed American China-Burma-India Theatre of Operations (CBI Theatre) and as Commander of The Chinese Army in India.

This latter force, made up of surviving Chinese troops from the recent Burma fighting plus reinforcements from China is training at Ramgarh, India, some 200 miles west of Calcutta, where Logan spends part of his time. General Stilwell wants to lead them back to Burma and reopen the Burma Road.

Enough about Logan! Your daughter, that's me, is a working newswoman now! I am employed at the New Delhi office of the official Chinese government news bureau called "Kuomintang News Agency," and enjoying every minute of it. Logan and I have a nice apartment inside a military compound on the outskirts of New Delhi. Oh yes, before I forget – I'm pregnant; will keep you posted!

We miss all of you very much, and hope that you are all well.

Respectfully, Your Number Two Daughter,

Suzie

New Delhi, India

September 12, 1942

While Suzie's letter cheered us momentarily, more bad news during the remaining days of the month proved that the "occupation screws" were continuing to tighten around us.

First came the official announcement that American and British movies would no longer be shown in Shanghai's many movie theaters. From then on, we soon learned, the only foreign films shown were very old German or French productions. Chinese and Japanese movies continued to be shown, plus, of course, the usual pre-main feature 15 to 30 minute Japanese propaganda films.

Hard on the "new foreign films policy" announcement came a public warning from Uncle Dr. S.T's Public Health Department of Greater Shanghai that most brands of canned green peas of recent months contained so much copper that they posed a major health hazard. The public was warned against these specific brands: Cock Brand, Fisherman Brand, Lion and Pagoda Brand, and Elephant Brand.

Finally, near the end of February came the proclamation that all unmarried males of allied nationality over the age of 14 were soon to be put into internment camps. This was bad news for all resident allied nationals, since they knew that this was but the first step toward internment for everyone.

Mother passed away, all alone, in a crowded, uncomfortable hospital ward at 3:30 a.m. one cold, windy, sleet-swept morning in early March. We had taken her there a few days earlier, as her condition worsened, in order to provide around-the-clock bedside medical and nursing care.

She seemed to have improved to the point that we had hired a horse and carriage in which to bring her back home the next day. Since we no longer had a family car, no taxis were available and trams were too crowded, that was the best we could do. During daytime Betty, Paul or myself had always been at her hospital bedside, but this was not permitted during midnight to 6:00 a.m. curfew hours. The hospital was unable to notify us immediately after she passed away due to the fact that we did not have a home telephone.

Since weddings and funerals are the two most important events in Chinese life, certain tradition-prescribed family decision making steps were now called for. These involved only closest family members; in this case Daddy, James, Paul, Betty and me. Our ingrained reverence for the deceased and the importance of ancestor worship in our society required us to provide as best we could for the comfort of Mother's soul as it journeyed to its final destination. This meant that certain specific formalities had to be observed.

Our first family meeting to consider funeral and burial details was held later that morning at the funeral parlor to which Mother's body had been taken. Fortunately, the owner was an old family friend; his wife one of Mother's longtime mah-jong playing companions. Daddy invited him to join us for this important meeting.

"We must first decide whether your Mother's funeral arrangements shall be traditional or more modern," stated Daddy, by way of getting our meeting started.

"Since she favored so many modern ways, I think that the very new idea of cremation might please her spirit," he continued. "That would not only be practical, but would also save the expense of a large wooden coffin and a lot of extra funeral formalities."

There was a collective gasp of shocked astonishment from us siblings at the very idea of his acting the "cheapskate" at this particular time and place!

James angrily spoke for all of us in reply!

"Mother was modern in some ways, but traditional in most other ways, such as being a traditional wife. She followed you all over China in your earlier working years, gave you child after child, and suffered great humiliation and loss of face when you brought not one but two concubines to live in our home!"

"Mother had a hard life! She experienced years of sickness, pain and sadness – and enjoyed very few pleasures," snapped Betty curtly. "She deserves the best, most beautiful, respectful traditional funeral we can give her! Our relatives and friends would be shocked at the very idea of foreign – style cremation!"

As Paul and I emphatically nodded our agreement, Daddy recoiled in disbelief at this outburst of anger from his children. It was the first time we had ever spoken in collective rebellion against him.

Basically a coward at heart, he quickly backed down in face of our unexpected unified opposition.

"Of course we will give her a proper funeral," he muttered, "and it will be a proper traditional one too! And she will have an honored spot in our Yang family Wing On cemetery site."

Turning to the funeral parlor owner, he asked, "what do you recommend first!"

"The first thing my staff will do," the owner responded, "is to wash her body seven times, since the uneven number seven is a lucky number. After that we will first wrap her body in a special cotton material, then clothe her in silk, rather than cotton, as a symbol of her status as wife of an important, well-to-do husband."

Daddy nodded emphatically in agreement!

"We must then engage a Fung Sui astrologer to determine from her date of birth, age, time of death and other key events in her life, the future specific day and date of her burial at your family gravesite. This will take time, but her body will be respectfully kept here at the funeral parlor until that time! I will handle all details of this if you so wish."

"Yes, yes, we will all be grateful if you can handle those details, plus the lying in funeral here at the parlor and the banquet afterwards," said Daddy, as we other Yangs nodded our agreement.

The next morning we close family members went to the funeral parlor for the necessary "laying out" of Mother's body prior to the formal funeral which was to be held the following day.

Her hair had been dressed and adorned with a jade ornament. This custom of putting a small jade carving or ornament in close proximity to the body of the deceased goes back to the earliest days in Chinese history. Part of the "laying out" ceremony is to assure family members that traditional customs like this have been adhered to.

We carefully looked underneath the veil of white silk that covered her body from head to toe to make certain that she had been properly dressed, including cotton stockings and embroidered satin slippers. We also made certain that her feet were bound tightly together with a gold, tassled silken cord. This ancient, traditional custom would prevent her body from leaping about should it ever be tormented by evil spirits.

I remember vividly to this day that while her eyes were closed, her mouth was open! Daddy refused to look at her uncovered face-turning away with a frightened look on his face when the veil was pulled down from her head for our inspection.

Back at the mansion, following the "laying out" ceremony. James hung a large blue and white paper lantern on each side of our main entrance doorway. Fairly wide strips of white (the color of mourning) paper were hung down on each side of those, with narrow red "good luck" strips affixed in their centers from top to bottom. This was our only formal public notice to the outside world that a death had just taken place in our household.

In China, in those days, a funeral was as big an event as a wedding! Relations and friends came not just to pay their respects, but also in the sense of a good Irish wake, to socialize and enjoy a good seven to ten course meatless, vegetarian banquet-at the expense of the deceased's family! Since no one in our family was in any sense religious (except Grandmother, a Buddhist), simple yet traditional can best describe Mother's funeral. It was the "traditional" quintessentially Chinese part that we "did up right" for her.

To begin with, everyone in our immediate family, including Grandmother, dressed up in traditional mourning outfits. For us siblings, this consisted of a coarse burlap type monk's cloak with cowl-like hood (which covered most of our head) over an inside white cloth garb. Our feet were clad in white shoes with a narrow strip of red on the heels and a piece of white burlap sewed on the front tops. The red strips on the heels represented a lamp to illuminate the way so our late Mother wouldn't stumble in the dark!

The event took place in the funeral parlor's large reception hall. As the 200 or so invited guests, singly or in groups, entered the hall, four white clad musicians blew short, loud, weird, sad-sounding "announcement" music blasts on clarinet or horn type Chinese wind instruments.

Each such awful sounding "announcement" blast was a signal for Betty, two hired female "wailers," and me, hidden behind draped white curtains on one side of the room; and Paul and two hired male "wailers" hidden behind their curtain on the other side of the room, to start bellowing and moaning loudly and sadly.

The guests would then walk to our far side of the hall where, in a wide space between the curtained enclosures of us "wailers," a large blown-up head photograph of Mother sat among many wreaths of flowers sent by well-wishers. Below it was an altar with two large white candles and a bronze, sand-filled bowl containing many burning sticks of incense. Our brother James, as white robe-clad eldest son, stood there to greet them. The coffin was not yet in the hall.

Each guest would then meekly and humbly pay their respects to Mother's photograph. Younger people would kowtow (forehead to the floor) three times; older ones (who physically could) would either kowtow, or bow low in deep respect. James would respond in kind to each, whereupon the guests would then seat themselves wherever they wished at one of the many 10-seat round tables out in the open reception hall. There, with teacups, dishes of watermelon seeds for snacks and constantly replenished pots of hot tea before them, they socialized with one another in a subdued manner.

Daddy and Grandmother garbed in white robes circulated cordially among the seated guests like good hosts, obviously pleased to see so many relatives and friends at this occasion. Many guests had either sent flowers or brought gifts of money in envelopes or other tokens of esteem.

After most guests had arrived, an eight-course banquet was served-all vegetarian, no meat-as was the traditional custom.

Then, after dishes from the last course had been cleared from the tables, the highly polished closed wooden coffin containing Mother's body was brought out and displayed before the altar for all to admire. There was no service, eulogy, or anything like that.

Considerably larger in size than western style caskets, it was closed since she had died from tuberculosis. Normally it would have been open for all to take a last look, after which the lid would have been put on and James, as eldest son present, would have driven in the first symbolic nail to seal it.

In this case, with the coffin already closed, he still drove in a symbolic first nail. Then, as everyone watched respectfully, funeral parlor personnel finished nailing tight the lid as James, Paul, Betty and me, still in our monk robes rubbed its top, in keeping with tradition, "to keep the nails from hurting her." After that, guest socializing resumed until everyone got caught up on all the gossip – whereupon they departed.

Exactly 47 days later, at the time determined by the Fung Sui astrologer, we family members and a few close relatives and friends, escorted Mother's body out to Wing-On Cemetery for a simple but dignified burial.

There, according to Grandmother, Mother's soul split three ways – one remaining with her body in the grave, a second off to circulate for eternity in the spirit world, the third to join other ancestors in the traditional family ancestral tablets.

I just hoped that she would enjoy a happier life wherever her spirit was than she had in our household during her lifetime! She was a dutiful traditional, submissive wife to my domineering father, following him all over China in their earlier married years, to jobs her influential Mandarin father got for him.

During these years she served as his uncomplaining, rather frail "baby factory" – eventually losing her health and contracting tuberculosis as a result. His bringing of not one but two concubines into our home to satisfy his lust and ego broke her spirit psychologically, and caused her heart-breaking permanent "loss of face" before relatives, friends, and the outside world. He didn't deserve her!

For several days after Mother's funeral life around the Mansion moved at an unusually slow, even somber pace. We had all devoted so much time and attention to her during the final weeks of her life that the household atmosphere without her presence seemed unnatural and depressing.

By early April however, life began to move at a more normal pace, and two noticeable changes took place. Paul moved from the room he had been sharing with James into Mother's former bedroom, and all our family household members started taking evening dinner together in the ground level parlor. That included Daddy, Concubine Silver Lotus, Grandmother, James, Paul, Betty and me.

Daddy, having dinner evening after evening with his children! We siblings could hardly believe it!

Life on the private singing lesson front also picked up! Madame Tamara, our overly stout White Russian teacher, with her jolly, boisterous personality, red-dyed stringy hair and heavy makeup quickly lifted Paul, Betty, and me out of our temporary depression.

As she lustily played accompaniment on her old, slightly the worse-for-wear piano and corrected my pitch, timing and rhythm, she soon had me singing – in English, like a canary:

From "Rosamunde" by Schubert – "The full moon rises, o'er the height – but where, my love – art thou?"

And from "Solveig's Song" by Grieg – "The winter may pass – and the spring dis-ap-pear!"

Since Shanghai was such a cosmopolitan, western-oriented city, many families, like ours, were influenced by and interested in western music. We had little interest in Chinese music, associating it most often with Chinese Opera, which, in our eyes, was music for the uneducated masses.

From our shortwave radio listening to late March war news from the outside world, we learned that Logan's CBI Theatre acquaintance, Claire Chennault, had just been recalled to duty with the American Army Air Corps as a Major General and placed in command of the newly formed American Fourteenth

Air Force. The mission of this force, the announcers said, was to help China continue battling the Japanese invaders.

Locally, after having sent most allied national males over the age of 14 into internment camps in March, the Japanese began interning families and single women. One group, consisting of families and small children, was placed in buildings of the Columbia Country Club on Great Western Road, just a short distance west of our Yang family mansion. The largest local area camp was at Lung Wha, near the well-known Lung Wha Pagoda, and airfield of the same name. This was only a few miles south of our mansion. By the end of June nearly 8,000 men, women and children had gone into these camps.

One result of this was that families of Japanese military and civilian occupation forces began moving from their normal Hongkew residential area into former homes of the foreign internees. Thus we began to see more and more Japanese residents in our French Concession. By now the number of Japanese residents in Shanghai had swelled to nearly 300,000.

Lots of Europeans and other foreigners were still moving around freely. All of these, including citizens of nations allied with Japan, such as Germans and Italians, and those of neutral countries such as Portugal, Brazil and Vichy France, had to wear badges indicating their nationality.

By the end of the June school term, Paul, having successfully completed two hard years of premed studies, decided that he would rather enter the business world than become a doctor. Fortunately, "Uncle Dr. S.T.'s " Public Health Department needed a new supervisor for its large municipal "Wan-Guo Cemetery" and Paul was selected. Offering good managerial experience, the cemetery was located only five miles west of our mansion in the Rainbow Bridge area. This job would save him from the likely possibility of being drafted into the Chinese puppet government's rag-tag army!

On September 8, two days after Paul started work, James, happily returned home from work with some exciting dinnertime news for all of us.

"You won't believe what I saw this morning, while doing inspections at the French Water Works on the Whangpoo riverfront at Que Maloo," he exclaimed.

"As you know, since before Pearl Harbor the Italian naval gunboats 'Lepanto' and 'Emillo Carlotta' and civilian passenger liner 'Conte Verdi' have been moored close by. Well, the Italian government apparently collapsed yesterday and Italian Naval Headquarters in Rome ordered these three Shanghai based Captains to scuttle their ships immediately!"

"The three ships slowly steamed midstream in the Whangpoo and did just that around midmorning. I was close enough to see everything! Both gunboats quickly sank to the tips of their masts. The 'Conte Verdi' capsized slowly, turning over on her side until only part of her hull and one propeller were exposed."

"The most exciting part was that the liner slowly went down right in front of a warehouse across the river that houses a group of American internees. As their ship sank, the Italian sailors responsible for her scuttling hung onto a guardrail cheering the American prisoners to high heaven. "

"I heard the Italians yelling – 'now we're on the same side!' as the Americans cheered and waved back," he laughed. "It was a wonderful and astonishing sight to behold!" Our entire family dinner group laughed with him and clapped for joy at his story.

Later we learned that the surprised, infuriated Japanese had rushed a destroyer to the scene and arrested all the Italians. Later on, they were able to raise the two gunboats and incorporate them into the Japanese navy. They also eventually raised the "Conte Verdi," whereupon American bombers of the Fourteenth Air Force promptly sank her again permanently.

After Italy's formal mid-April surrender to allied forces in Europe, local Shanghai Italian military personnel went into POW camps and civilians into internment camps.

By late 1943 both political and economic conditions in Shanghai had deteriorated to new lows. While Shanghai's International Settlement had already been taken over by the Nanking puppet government, the French Concession was now willingly and formally handed over to them by the French administration. The French-led police force was disbanded, and French and Indochinese native soldiers, while not interned were confined to their barracks areas.

Public sector activities of the former British and French run concessions, such as bus and tram lines, utilities and telephone systems were integrated, and a single Chinese mayor now ruled over a unified Greater Shanghai.

This didn't seem to improve efficiency of public services however – tram service was erratic, and bus service so unreliable that days could go by without seeing one on the streets. Electricity was now so strictly rationed that we used only one low wattage light bulb per room, turning those on only when the room was in use. Otherwise we relied only on candlelight.

The year finally ended on two quite personal "low notes" in our Yang household. First was the news, via our shortwave radio, that on December 5 the Japanese had heavily bombed Calcutta, India causing over 500 civilian casualties. While they had made nuisance raids over that city before, this was more serious. We wondered if New Delhi would be next, and if Suzie and Logan were safe.

The second "low note" was the rather abrupt and unsettling discovery that no one in our household was immune to the quite harsh dysentery that was now taking a heavy toll among Shanghai residents.

Chapter 11

NUMBER ONE CONCUBINE RULES THE ROOST – WHEN DADDY'S NOT AROUND!

By late February, due to constant exposure to the cold in our unheated school classroom, my poor fingers were so red and swollen from chilblains that the flesh on some burst – like carrots! Although we students wore padded gowns all day long, we had to take our mittens off in class to write, and I was not alone in my misery.

When one has chilblains of the fingers, they swell up – sometimes twice their normal size. They itch terribly when warm and are constantly painful when cold. And when the flesh bursts, like mine, the pain gets unbearable. There wasn't much that doctors, could do to treat the problem. Like all the other afflicted students – I just had to suffer and wait for warmer weather!

For now, in early 1944, it seemed like the unusually lengthy period of damp, bitter cold would last forever. To make matters worse, normally seldom seen snow had covered the ground since start of my 9th grade spring term at Bei Tsun school some two weeks earlier. I had just passed my fourteenth birthday without celebration. No one in my family, except Betty had even re-membered!

In fact, since Mother's death nearly a year ago, no one had paid much attention to me. I was growing like a weed, had few close friends at school since I lived so close by and spent most of my evenings on school homework or practicing the piano and singing by myself.

Due to unreliable tram schedules, Daddy and James, who traveled to their respective offices in the Bund area together, had to leave home quite early each morning. Their individual return home was at uncertain late evening hours. Our family dinner was usually eaten now around 8:30 p.m., after which, in our cold blackout darkened home, everyone usually soon retired for the night.

Betty's 11th grade school studies were different from mine, so our evening homework was done separately, and our piano time was, of course, separate.

Concubine Silver Lotus, "Auntie" to all us Yang offspring, was now "Mistress" of our household. With James and Paul both working, Betty and I were the only siblings financially dependent on our father. While he gave us advance money individually to cover our upcoming school and private singing lesson expenses, we had to go to "Auntie" for all other needs and wants.

As controller of, and dispenser of household expense funds given her in advance of each month by Daddy, she was our Patron. We would never dare ask Father for extra things or money. Fortunately, she gave us what "pocket money" she could spare for our tram and rickshaw rides and occasional "treats".

Betty and I still continued to go separately to our once-a-week private singing lessons with Madame Tamara. Paul had dropped out when he started work at Wan-Guo Cemetery.

As might be expected, due to these rather dreary circum-stances, our traditional lengthy New Year's Festivities were un-usually subdued. We had a fairly festive family dinner, visited a few relatives and friends and that was it.

The New Year's first real ray of cheer for our family came in the form of one of those "mysteriously delivered" underground letters from Guo Liang, from whom we had not heard in years. Again, Daddy read it to all us in the evening seclusion of Paul's bedroom:

Dear Honorable Father,

It has been nearly six years now since I left all of you at home to come here to Chungking. During all this time I got news of you and the family only when Suzie came in 1940, and then several months later when Nellie received a letter from Mother. I think often of the happier days in Shanghai prior to the August, 1937 Japanese invasion, and can only hope that you and the rest of the family are safe and well.

In case you haven't heard, and I assume that you haven't, you have a pretty little one-year old granddaughter named Yi-Jing. She laughs a lot and looks a lot like her mother Chow Ping. You may not even know that Chow Ping and I were married in early 1941. We met at the war industry factory where we both worked – the same one where we still continue to work. She was born and raised in Chekiang and graduated from university there, coming to Chungking, like me, to help in the war effort.

We both work the same ten-hour shift six days a week. Because of Yi-Jing we are allowed to take one day a week off together as a family. During work time our daughter stays in a factory run nursery. We live in a small three room factory-owned hut with bamboo pole framing and interlaced bamboo walls coated with thick gray mud. Our roof is of gray tile. We eat our main daily meal in a large factory worker's dining hall. All basic foodstuffs, material for clothing, and charcoal for workers are strictly rationed, but are adequate for our needs. We are in good health.

We work so hard that we have little time or energy for outside pleasures. Fortunately, because people have come here from all over China, there are many small restaurants serving interesting regional styles of cooking. Eating out, alone or with friends, movies, occasional government-

sponsored plays or exhibits and sometimes river fishing outings in the summer make up our recreational activities.

There are only two seasons in Chungking – six months of
cloudy cold, drizzly, always foggy winter, and six summer
months of hot, humid, usually sunny days which brings out
bugs of all descriptions and clouds of hungry mosquitoes.
While the blanket of winter fog protects us from Japanese
bombing, the streets and walls of buildings are covered with a
constant damp, slippery gray slime during the wet season.

Throughout the long hot summer, which has just ended,
Japanese bombers come often, day and night, but we have a
good half-hour advance warning system and many cave air
raid shelters close by. Nightly blackout regulations are strictly
enforced by patrolling armed soldiers. Their orders are simple
– if you see any light in a home, building or on the street –
shoot at it immediately! As you might guess, the public coop-
erates wholeheartedly in preventing any light from showing!

In case you haven't heard, Nellie, S.Z. and their three
children moved to Kwelin (Guilin) last April, following S.Z.'s
promotion to Regional Operations Director, National Railway
Administration. It was a very nice promotion for him and I
hear that Kwelin is a much nicer place to live than here.

In conclusion, here are three overall impressions from
Chungking! First, the smells, year around, from open gutters,
ancient narrow streets and old, very crowded buildings are terrible! Second, while top officials and politicians seem to be
living quite well, rampant inflation has the rest of us constantly
struggling to make ends meet. Finally, while the war seems
endless – victory will eventually be ours!

Chow Ping looks forward to meeting all of you someday.
Until we do meet again – take care!

Respectfully, Your Eldest Son,

Guo Liang

September 15, 1943,

Chungking

My raw, red, swollen chilblains fingers hurt so bad that my
eyes filled with tears as Mei-Ling and I worked away at our
twice weekly chore of picking small white rocks out of a large
sack of recently purchased rice.

It was early evening on a chilly drizzly late March day. As we worked away by firelight of the main kitchen stove, Ah Foo started preparing the family's late evening meal. We were soon joined by Grandmother, Auntie Silver Lotus, Betty and Paul. Each had come from other rooms of our already dark, chilly Mansion to seek the warmth and sociability of our family kitchen. Even in this toasty-warm, relaxed setting our thoughts soon turned to the war and the effects it was having on our refugee crowded city. Paul, who had been riding his bicycle to and from work, had just commented that it was getting too dangerous to travel by bicycle after dusk.

"Two of my cemetery workers have been knocked off their bikes while returning home after dusk just this past week," he said. "Two thieves usually work together. One bumps into the cyclist causing a spill. As this one helps the cyclist get to his or her feet, really keeping them distracted, their accomplice grabs the bike and rides it quickly off into the crowded dark street. Since streetlights are dimmed now each evening, and often go out completely, thus creating a total blackout, the thieves have little fear of getting caught." "Not only bicycles are taken," added Betty, "but often clothes, shoes and especially, at this time of the year, overcoats are stripped off the accosted – both cyclists and pedestrians."

She added that fathers of two of her school chums had suffered this nerve wracking experience while returning home from work after dark within recent days. "One was stripped right down to his underwear, and nearly froze to death trotting the rest of the way home," she laughingly noted.

"It's just not safe to go out anywhere after dark these days" added Concubine Silver Lotus. "Your father says that the puppet government municipal police are now so undisciplined and corrupt that they're as much to be feared by honest citizens as thieves and muggers." "Some dishonest police are so bold that they try and collect 'squeeze' (payments of small amounts of money as bribery) even in daylight now," chimed in Ah Foo. "I was returning home from the market by rickshaw just day before yesterday when two uniformed officers stopped my coolie-puller, and demanded to 'inspect' the bags of food and fish I had just purchased."

"They indicated that their 'inspection' might take some time unless I made a cash 'contribution' to their 'Police Welfare Fund!' So, as I told Nai-Nai (the Mandarin word for "Mistress," always used by our servants in addressing Father's concubines), nodding to Silver Lotus, "when I got home, I gave them a small amount of money, and they waved me right on. The police just can't be trusted anymore!"

"Firemen can't be trusted any longer either," interjected Grandmother. "I heard on the radio just this morning that their union told the Municipal Council yesterday: 'no special bonus payment – no water at fires!'"

"The real problem is raging inflation," remarked Paul, "working people don't earn enough to even buy rice, that's why the unions are so militant. Tram and bus workers cause constant delays for no reason as a way of protesting, and street traffic is allowed to go uncontrolled by the underpaid police to the point where congestion brings everything to a standstill for long periods of time.

As all present joined in with what they had actually observed, or heard about, the conversation turned to some of the petty theft racketeering that so many of Shanghai's wartime refugees and poor residents depended on for their pitifully small but dishonest incomes.

For petty thefts, such as "liberating" a handful of coal or charcoal here, a few wisps of cotton there, or a mere scoop of rice, could, through painstaking accumulation, add up to enough minor bulk amounts to provide a meager living for thousands of Shanghai's more unfortunate souls.

One common racket, engaged in by many poor men and women was that of cotton stealing. Mei-Ling and Ah Foo told how these people would snatch handfuls of cotton from trucks and handcarts carrying bales of cotton from wharves along the Bund area to godowns and cotton hongs throughout the city.

Often done quickly when the vehicle stopped for a red light, the thief would quickly cut a hand-size hole in a bale and pull out a handful of cotton – then run away! Stuffing the collected bits in their clothing, they would, after some accumulation, earn small amounts of cash by selling their loot at a low price to small cotton hongs.

"The cotton stealing racket is at least a much cleaner illegal occupation than the coal stealing racket," laughed Paul. "Those who sweep up coal dropped, or quickly snatched from coal trucks or hand carts are dead giveaways," he continued, "first because they carry around small straw brooms and dustpans, and second because they are always so dirty and black. I don't think they ever bathe themselves!"

"Someone told me that these coal thieves stuff their stolen coal and coal dust into laundry bags, tied around their waist and hanging down the inside of their baggy pants legs!" I chimed in. "Is that true? "

"Yes, it's true," replied Paul. "These thieves sell their accumulations to the many street side 'portable restaurant' vendors who require little fuel for their small cooking braziers. If they are 'hustlers,' these petty coal thieves can eke out a bare existence. But it's a dirty life; many of them sleep in alleyways, using their brooms and dustpans as pillows."

As Ah Foo tickled our respective senses of smell with the bubbling concoction of vegetables, mushrooms and poultry giblets she was stir-frying in a big wok, a knock came at the back entranceway by the kitchen. As Paul opened the door and peered into the rainy darkness, a dark cloak wrapped man asked if this was the T.Y. Yang residence.

When Paul replied "Yes," the man shoved a small oilskin wrapped parcel into his hands and, without another word whirled about and disappeared into the night. Later, Daddy, who had just made it home from work in time for our late family dinner, called us Yangs together in Paul's room for a reading of the parcel's contents – a long awaited letter from Suzie:

The news contained in this letter, that Logan had gone into the jungles of Northwest Burma with General Stilwell in late

December, caused our family great concern. This was due to the subsequent occasional brief New Delhi radio reports of fierce "no quarter given, or asked" jungle fighting in what apparently was a full-scale, sustained allied offensive there. Weeks and months passed with only these tantalizing bits of information as to what was really going on.

Finally, on May 18, that shortwave station triumphantly announced the surprise seizure of Myitkyina airfield the previous day. "Capture of this important Burma airfield, from which the Japanese have launched past bombings of Calcutta," said the British announcer, "breaks the back of Japanese air operations in Burma."

This news flash also announced that two Chinese regiments along with Americans of a "Merrill's Marauders" U.S. army infantry unit and some British-led Kachin Rangers had achieved this victory after a bold but secret advance sustained solely by air dropped supplies over jungle covered mountains the Japanese had considered impassable.

All this news was most exciting to us Yangs, because we had good reason to suspect that Logan was right there in the thick of the action. As we later learned, our excitement (and concern) was justified – because he was there, as part of General Stilwell's field command headquarters staff.

Now, suddenly, our family's attention was riveted on a very big, important, entirely new development in the war – something much closer to home!

Since the great Japanese victories of late 1937 and 1938, the long 3,400-mile Great Wall in the north to Indo-china in the south China-proper battlefront had not seen any really major battles. This suddenly changed on May 27 when the quarter-million strong Japanese Eleventh Army launched a major summer offensive, called "Ichigo," southward from their Hangkow base toward Changsha. Concurrently, the Japanese Twenty-third Army, one quarter that size, attacked west from Canton.

This powerful two-pronged offensive, the greatest within China Japanese military operation in six years, set off alarm bells not only in Shanghai, Chungking and New Delhi, but also at highest military and political levels in Washington, D.C.

The aim of this sudden massive effort clearly was to eliminate forward bases of the American Fourteenth Air Force, which had gained mastery of the air over southern China and far out into the South China Sea, block imminent likelihood of the Burma Road reopening and destroy the bulk of Chiang Kai-shek 's eastern front armies.

Allied leaders knew, as did us Yangs and all other informed people in Shanghai, that if it succeeded, an already grievously weakened China might be knocked out of the war. This was serious business!

Heading south from Hangkow along the railroad and Hsiang River route toward Kweiin and Liuchow (Liuzhou), heartland of the several American air bases some 500 miles distant, the Japanese at first encountered stiff resistance. But in spite of stubborn Chinese ground troops, backed up by effective Fourteenth Air Force support, they pushed steadily on through the rich province of Hunan – capturing important Changsha on June 19, and the key American air base city of Hengyang on August 8.

By now panic had set in and many thousands of refugees, heading west into the interior, were clogging trains and roads throughout eastern China. Chinese military resistance suddenly broke down almost completely; the ill equipped troops, demoralized and exhausted.

The confident Japanese were on their way to Kweilin, location of the best railway shops and equipment in all unoccupied China, and forward command headquarters of the Fourteenth Air Force. It seemed as though nothing could stop them.

We Yangs in our Peach Blossom Lane mansion had been following all these Burma and Eastern China events of the past few months with bated breath. After all, the safety, welfare and possibly lives of several of our immediate family members were at stake, as well as the future of our country.

Thinking of Logan alone in the jungle battlefields of North-western Burma was bad enough, but now we were worried sick at the thought of Nellie, S.Z. and their three young children being trapped in Kweilin. One of us Yang children, or Daddy, stayed with our hidden home shortwave radio, in shifts, from dusk until early morning hours nearly every evening during that period.

We also followed closely the local Japanese and Chinese puppet government broadcasts and newspapers. So long as they were winning victories, the Japanese kept Shanghai's population fairly well up to date on events. When losing, they either said little or nothing, or claimed victory anyhow!

During this time, as our normal respective work, backyard home gardening, school, singing lessons and household life continued as usual, we also kept ourselves informed about important war news from other parts of the world. We knew that allied troops had entered Rome June 4, and cheered at news of their successful June 6 D-day landings on the Normandy coast of France.

We also learned via shortwave radio of the June 15 landing on the central Pacific island of Saipan by American marines. Little did I know then that my future husband was one of them!

Finally, we heard about the mid-August allied landings in the south of France, and were delighted to learn of the liberation of Paris later that month.

While all this far off war news was both interesting and heartening, the "Main War" for us at this point in time was centered in Northwestern Burma and Eastern China.

"I've been inspecting the waterworks serving Shanghai's Hongkew area for the past few days, and am amazed at the large number of Jews that are forced to live there," said James, as our family relaxed around the table following a late September evening dinner.

"I thought that Hongkew was populated almost entirely by Japanese; but then, I haven't been down there for the past year or so. And I am really disgusted at how abominably these Jews are treated by the Japanese. They are all forced to wear identification insignia and live in a special Ghetto district within a run-down industrial area near the dockyards!"

"While many have permits that allow them to work during the day in other parts of Shanghai," he went on, "all Jews living in the Ghetto have to be back by 8:00 p.m. at the latest, since they are required to spend every night there. I didn't realize that so many of Shanghai's thousands of Jewish residents are being treated like that!"

"Shanghai's German Nazi allies of Japan are largely responsible for that," answered Daddy. "After Pearl Harbor they kept urging that our city's Jews be confined as possible 'security risks.' Finally, in 1943 the Japanese ordered the 15,000 or so, mostly German and Austrian Jews, who had arrived here as stateless refugees since 1937, to move into the Ghetto area you are talking about.

Other Jews, those who were nationals of allied countries, were sent to internment camps along with their fellow citizens. The fairly small number of Jews who immigrated here prior to 1937; some during the early 1900s, and others, Russian Jews mostly, after 1919, still enjoy the same privileges of our long-time resident White Russians."

"Well, Jews living in the Ghetto are probably worse off then those in the camps," snorted James, "The Japanese official in charge of the Ghetto calls himself 'The King of the Jews,' and treats the hapless residents like dirt."

"It wasn't always that way," replied Daddy. "For quite some time the Japanese both encouraged refugee Jews to come to Shanghai and welcomed them to settle in Hongkew in order to revitalize the area. Many quickly found work in newly opened Japanese-owned factories."

"I heard that after 1937 and 1938 when so many Jews fled from Poland, Germany and Austria with little money or possessions, that Shanghai was, for some time, just about the only place in the world that welcomed them," remarked Paul.

"Not only that," replied Daddy, "but it was, so far as I know, the only place in the world that did not require either a

195

visa, affidavit, police certificate or proof of guaranteed financial support in order to gain entry and permanent residence.

While Japan's leaders knew little about Jews historically, they appreciated the fact that British, American and German Jewish bankers were the only bankers in the world that offered Japan loans to help finance the Russo-Japanese War (1904-5). Since such loans were viewed internationally as being quite risky, the fact that Jewish bankers alone granted them made a deep and lasting impression on these Japanese.

For quite some time after 1937, other Shanghaiers as well as the Japanese welcomed Jewish refugees," he continued, "but since most arrived penniless by the shipload, and required expensive community provided financial assistance, the welcome grew less warm with the arrival of each new liner-full. Finally, on August 21, 1939 Japanese authorities prohibited completely any further Jewish immigration into Shanghai.

"It's my impression that the Jewish refugees, as a group, have really contributed a lot to Shanghai's cultural life," said Betty. "most of the musicians in Shanghai Municipal Orchestra, for example, are Jewish, and I've heard that most of the popular night club band musicians are as well."

"Yes, and they have also contributed a great deal to our city's commercial life," added Daddy. "Since their overall contribution as a group has been so positive, it's a real shame that the Japanese are now treating them so shabbily."

All we Yangs knew at the time about what history would later described as the "Stilwell Crisis" was from the terse October 19 announcements via both New Delhi and Chungking shortwave broadcasts about some very high level allied command changes.

These reported that the American General Wedemeyer was now commander of a newly created China Theatre of Operations (over Americans only; not any Chinese troops), and also the new Chief of Staff to Generalissimo Chiang Kai-shek. General Stilwell's name was not mentioned!

It would be several months before we learned from Logan what really happened to bring about these changes. He then told us that President Roosevelt, fearing that lethargic China was about to be knocked out of the war, made what were virtually two demands on Chiang Kai-shek: The first was that he immediately appoint General Stilwell as Commander-in-Chief of all Chinese armies; the second, that he settle the political deadlock between the Central government and the Communists, and get on with really fighting the Japanese!

Chiang, realizing that acceptance could cause him to lose both military and political control, refused – saying that he would rather break with the U.S. than accept these demands. Then, since he and Stilwell personally disliked and distrusted one another, he demanded Stilwell's complete ouster from China. Roosevelt backed down, recalled Stilwell to the U.S. and set up the new China Theatre under General Wedemeyer.

The Japanese Eleventh Army didn't give anyone much time to think about allied top command changes or personality clashes! Their offensive simply roared on and on and on!

Kweilin was overrun November 11 – the same day that the converging Japanese Twenty-third Army captured Liuchow, 70 miles to its south. This cut the last overland link between unoccupied China and the coast.

When Nanning, further south, near the Indochina border, fell to the enemy a short time later, nearly everyone in Shanghai realized that the last of the American air bases in Eastern China had been overrun! Even worse, the Japanese now had a complete interior overland communications route all the way from Korea south to Singapore!

Turning westward, the victorious Japanese then surged through Nantan Pass toward the key Chinese communications hub city of Kweiyang (Guiyang). Chinese resistance in this region had by now almost totally collapsed; panic had seized Chungking!

Shanghai's Japanese-controlled radio stations and newspapers, which had constantly trumpeted each individual fresh victory, now extolled the overall magnitude of this past summer's offensive triumph.

In less than six months, nearly half a million Chinese troops had been wiped out, and a huge eastern Chinese coastal region of eight provinces and their over one hundred million population had been wrested from Chungking's control. One third of China's landmass was now occupied by the Japanese! Was Kuomintang China about to collapse?

Not only our Yang family, but everyone else in Shanghai had good reason to remember the date and day November 11, 1944. Not only was it the day Kweilin fell to the Japanese, but also the date of the first big American daylight air raid on Shanghai! While we had experienced a few earlier small raids, nearly all at night, this was a big, all-day affair that left huge, clearly visible columns of smoke over Shanghai harbor and Whangpoo River dock and godown areas. Such raids continued with increasing frequency and intensity for the balance of the year. During that period we often heard the sound of antiaircraft fire and witnessed overhead airbursts. Twice, from our mansion roof garden, we watched distant aerial dogfights.

Two weeks later we heard via shortwave radio that over one hundred American B-29 bombers, from the recently captured Pacific islands of Saipan and Tinian, had successfully attacked the sprawling Musahi aero-engine plant on the outskirts of Tokyo. This was the first raid of what turned out to be the final strategic American air offensive against Japan.

As 1944 drew to a close, we learned from Chungking radio broadcasts that two divisions of American trained and equipped Chinese troops, ordered flown up from Burma by General Wedemeyer, plus the onset of harsh winter, had finally stopped the overextended and still summer-uniformed Japanese on the barren Kweichow plateau midway between Kweiyang and Liuchow. This later proved to be the high water mark of their highly successful 1944 summer offensive. Kuomintang China, although groggy, was still very much in the war!

198

We also heard about great Russian eastern European front victories, of the German Ardennes Offensive (Battle of the Bulge) and that Churchill, at the December Big Four Powers Cairo conference, had declared British "extraterritorial rights" claims in China null and void.

"Thank you, Winston!" was our sarcastic tongue-in-cheek Yang family reaction to that!

"Shao Je, Shao Je" (Young Miss), "Come, come!" shrilled Mei-Ling, excitedly motioning me to follow her out through our mansion front entranceway. "Father Nicholas asks you to come quickly to his house! Follow me – he has something to show you right now. Hurry, Shao Je!"

Perplexed, but curious, I followed quickly after her – out to the street and next door to and through the main entranceway of the Russian Orthodox Priest's home. "Where are we going, Mei-Ling?" I pantingly half-shouted as we rapidly walked through their family parlor heading into the kitchen.

"Lookee Shao Je – Lookee what Ah Liu found for you! " she laughingly shouted back over her shoulder.

Before I could catch more than a fleeting glimpse of the several smiling faces in the kitchen, I was almost bowled over by a terribly excited leaping, licking, yelping, crying 18 pound ball of black and white furred pooch – frantically trying to wash my face off with a wet, pink tongue!

"Mong-Fu!" I screamed – "you are alive! Oh, where have you been!" As tears of joy streamed down my face, licked off as fast as they fell by the squirming, still excitedly crying little animal, the others in the room clapped their hands and laughed happily at our reunion.

Two minutes later, with me still in tears on my hands and knees where I had been hugging him, Mong-Fu forgot all about me and trotted over to Ah Liu who was holding out a piece of cooked chicken for him. After gulping that down he frisked about saying hello again to all the others in the room who had gathered for this surprise reunion: Father Nicholas, their family cook Ah Liu, our cook Ah Foo, our two Yang maids Mei-Ling and Lu-Fong and three woman members of Father Nicholas' household.

As we all sat down on benches and floor around the kitchen, family members and servants alike from both households cele-brated by eating slabs of Chornyi Khleb (Russian blackbread) piled high with mounds of freshly made Baklazhan Farshivoran-nyi (cold stuffed eggplant).

As we washed this down with cup after cup of hot Russian tea from their big brass Samovar, Ah Liu told how he had dis-covered Mong-Fu just that morning. He had seen him being led on a leash by a young boy in the very marketplace where the dog had gotten lost in the crowd so recently.

"The boy said that he had caught the dog's leash that day, and, along with his accompanying Amah, had looked for its owner," said Ah Liu. "Not being able to discover the owner of what was obviously a valuable family pet, they had taken it home with them. They brought it to the market today in hopes of finding its owner.

I recognized Mong-Fu, and called his name," continued Ah Liu. "He broke away from the boy and raced to me, so the boy and his Amah realized that the dog knew me. I gave them some money, they wrote down my name and address and gave him to me – and here he is, back to you, Shao Je!"

The next day, Concubine Silver Lotus, Betty and I went over to Father Nicholas' home to repay Ah Liu plus giving him a nice thank you gift, and, along with members of their household, to rejoice again over my pooch's homecoming.

As we laughed and talked about what a nice ending it made to what had been a quite dreary and worrisome wartime 1944 year for all of us, Betty half-jokingly asked Ah Liu:

"What if it had not been Mong-Fu; but had been just some other dog! What would you have done with him?"

As Ah Liu winked slyly, his smiling Pidgin English reply was: "Me cookee and eatim!"

Chapter 12

THE WAR ENDS-HERE COME THE AMERICANS!

My sound 6:30 a.m. sleep the second Sunday morning of January 1945 was rudely broken by a loud, window-rattling, bed-shaking explosion, apparently originating just up the street from our Yang family mansion.

Half stunned, in a state of shock and scared out of my wits, I rushed, along with Betty, to our front bedroom window which overlooked Peach Blossom Lane.

"What is going on? Have the Americans dropped a bomb? Have Nationalist or Communist underground forces started an uprising?" we excitedly asked ourselves!

Peering north through the screened window toward the nearby intersection of Avenues Joffre and Haig, we saw, amidst a cloud of drifting gray smoke, a sizable group of Japanese soldiers and some large construction vehicles.

The soldiers suddenly broke and ran behind the vehicles, whereupon a second loud explosion completed destruction of a ground level store front building facing that intersection. Another cloud of smoke promptly obscured the scene. Then, from different directions, not too far away, came the sound of similar explosions.

Several truckloads of armed Japanese soldiers then roared east on Avenue Joffre, past our limited viewing area, heading toward Shanghai's Bund office district and Whangpoo riverfront docks. Something unusual was certainly going on! But what?

Rushing from the bedroom into our middle level apartment parlor, and looking down through the backyard facing windows, we saw Daddy, James and Paul near the garden calmly performing rhythmic, slow motion Tai Chi exercises. Executing specific stately motions in unison, they appeared entirely oblivious to all the close by noise and commotion that had so startled Betty and me.

"What are all the explosions about?" Betty shouted down at them, "and why are there suddenly so many Japanese soldiers around?"

"Part of the Japanese Kwangtung Army from Manchuria has just arrived to defend Shanghai," Daddy replied. "I think they are starting to build a concrete antitank gun emplacement at the intersection of Joffre and Haig Avenues, and some concrete pillboxes at other nearby locations. Go back to sleep, you two!"

He and our two brothers, turning their attention away from us, then moved slowly, with mutual perfect balance, into another formalized Tai Chi movement. This one, like all the others moved in a circular motion toward a specific compass direction. Daddy liked to do Tai Chi exercises – "because," as he often said, "they ease my digestive troubles."

Frustrated at their indifference, but too shaken still to even think of returning to bed, Betty and I tiptoed past the still-sleeping Ah Foo and maids to see what early-morning "goodies" the ground-level kitchen might yield. Our stealth was rewarded with discovery of half a dozen left over Mashed Date Flour Pastries.

These, plus a pot of fresh, quickly self-brewed tea soon caused us to forget, at least for the time being, all those disturbing explosions and other sounds of this new, frightening military activity in our neighborhood.

Some three weeks later, around 9:30 p.m., as we sat around the family dining table enjoying cups of hot after dinner tea, our family conversation turned to the extremely strict rationing that was making life increasingly difficult for all Shanghai inhabitants.

Ah Foo and our two maids had retired to the kitchen and their downstairs servant sleeping quarters next to it. James was in his old laboratory room listening to our hidden shortwave radio. The rest of our household was at the table.

"Nearly everything these days is strictly rationed and difficult to obtain," complained Concubine Silver Lotus. "Rice, flour, sugar, soap, matches, salt and charcoal briquettes – they are all rationed," she sighed.

"My cemetery workers who smoke complain that all the Chinese manufactured cigarettes nowadays contain very little tobacco," said Paul. "They say that all types, including the best-selling Roy brand, are mostly filled with dried, ground spinach or other types of leafy vegetables – or maybe weeds; who really knows?"

"Not only is it often difficult to find some of these rationed items," continued Silver Lotus, "but most family's servants who shop for them manage to get plenty of "squeeze" for themselves when they do make such purchases."

"How do servants get 'squeeze'?" I naively asked.

"Easy!" Chuckled Grandmother. "Since the market vendors don't issue receipts for purchases the family cooks or amahs who usually do the shopping either buy inferior quality items and quote a higher quality price to their mistress, or cheat when purchasing a given quantity or measure."

"How can they cheat since the vendor does the counting or measuring?" I asked.

"The trick is to do the counting or measuring themselves rather than letting the vendor do it," answered Silver Lotus. "For example, many of them, like our Ah Foo, carry their own scales to market – 'to keep the vendors honest,' they say. But as we all know, scales can easily be manipulated to give wrong readings!"

"Do you really think that Ah Foo gets 'squeeze' from us by doing that?" I asked – wide eyed!

"Probably – on a small scale," laughed Daddy, "but basically she's such a longtime, faithful servant, and such a good cook, that your Mother never checked up on her personally.

It's now your job as Household Mistress, Silver Lotus," nodding toward her, "to keep track of Ah Foo's purchasing spending habits!"

The concubine widened and flashed her eyes as she slightly nodded at him an agreement.

Suddenly, James rushed into the room to excitedly report:

"Chungking radio has just announced reopening of the Burma Road, and that the first truck convoy of American war supplies in over two and a half years just reached Kunming yesterday after a 24 day journey.

It seems that troops of the Chinese Army from India, which General Stilwell originally led in clearing Japs from the jungle of northeastern Burma, behind whom U.S. Army Engineers have been pushing through a new road from Ledo, Assam, in India, finally linked up with Chinese troops coming down from Yunnan Province. They met January 27 at Mong Yu on the China-Burma border, thus reopening the route.

The announcer said that the 1,000 mile long, newly joined, combined Ledo and Burma Roads have just been renamed the 'Stilwell Road' in honor of the General. He, by the way, has apparently returned to the United States."

"This is wonderful news," beamed Daddy. "At long last China's 'back door' to the outside world has been reopened!"

With the new February school term due to start in two days, Daddy called Betty and me into our family parlor together to give us our usual advance tuition payment funds.

"I've brought you two in together this time," he said, with a worried look on his face, "because I am increasingly concerned about the continued increase in the number of Japanese troops and constant building of new street fortifications both in our local area, and throughout the rest of the city.

As you both know, the allies will soon win the European war, and Japan will be fighting alone. Rumor has it that the Americans may land before winter this year on the north bank of Hangchow Bay – near where the Japanese landed to attack Shanghai back in 1937.

The Japanese appear to be building numerous gun emplacements, bunkers, pillboxes, trenches and rifle pits throughout the city, including the Bund business area, in order to defend Shanghai, if necessary, house to house. If any such battle for Shanghai turns out to be as desperate as that for Stalingrad or Manila, heaven help us all!"

Betty and I sat silently, staring wide-eyed at him.

"Even though your school is but a short walk distant, I am concerned about your safety with so many Japanese soldiers stationed right in our neighborhood area. Promise me that you will always walk quickly to and from school together; never stopping at shops en route, or to talk to friends – even on a crowded street! I want you to promise me that right now!"

"Yes, yes," we both promised in nervous unison!

"And I feel it best that you both stop your singing lessons with Madame Tamara immediately. It's simply not safe now for you to take that lengthy walk alone on different but regular schedule days to her home and back here. Rickshaw rides there are no safer. I'll tell James to inform her tomorrow."

We sadly agreed that this practical decision made good sense.

"You will graduate from high school in June, Bei Bei," he continued, looking at Betty, "and we will talk later about future plans for you.

As for you, Shao Bei," nodding toward me, "I think we had better enroll you as a boarder-student at Aurora Middle School next September. Both your cousins Doris and Dorothy did that,

205

and were happy there. If the Americans do attack Shanghai, you will be safer there with the foreign Catholic sisters than as a student alone at Bei Tsun; living here at home."

After answering our few questions, and giving us our upcoming term's tuition money, he dismissed us.

Betty and I retired to our bedroom where we sat for awhile together on her bed quietly murmuring sister talk about what the immediate future might hold for us if ground fighting were to erupt in Shanghai.

Over the past two weeks hundreds of new Japanese soldiers, arriving daily from Manchuria had moved into campus buildings of Chiao Tung University, located just across a small creek a stone's throw west of our backyard. After the Chinese faculty and students fled en masse to regroup in the interior following the August 1937 occupation of Shanghai, the Japanese had settled large numbers of Japanese and Korean civilian workers there.

These had now suddenly been replaced by Japanese combat troops, well positioned to defend against any future attempted American paratroop or airborne attack on nearby large Lungwah Airport, and to protect key roads from there leading into Shanghai central.

Due to increased tensions arising from so many surly new Japanese troops and their frantic construction of street corner fortifications all around the area, our February Chinese New Year festivities consisted only of a special low key family home dinner.

We did not feel secure enough to pass through all those coldly staring enemy soldiers just to exchange casual New Year's greetings with relatives and friends. During those tense days, one went out only when absolutely necessary for work, school or shopping.

Our only good laugh of that period came during a Saturday shopping excursion by Concubine Silver Lotus, Betty and me to visit shops along Hupien Road, between Shanghai Race Course and Lester Hospital, in search of suitable new clothing material for members of our household.

That laugh came at one visited, formerly well patronized by foreigners, tailoring and fabric shop which featured a faded, prominently hung pre-war English language (of sorts) sign that read:

"Ladies have fits upstairs!"

April turned out to be a busy, news-filled month! First came a cheering New Delhi shortwave radio bulletin: "shortly after capturing Iwo Jima, American troops on April 1 landed on Okinawa." This was truly exciting news since it seemed to indicate that the Japanese home islands themselves would be next!

Then, on the annual Tomb-Sweeping Festival Day two days later, Paul was approached as he was making a mid-morning inspection at Wan Guo Cemetery, by a poorly dressed, stooped, slightly limping, elderly-appearing male visitor carrying a handful of fresh flowers. Moving to Paul's side from out of the visiting crowd of families attending to pay annual homage to their ancestors, the man softly said, "I have a verbal message from you sister Suzie; can we talk for a few seconds alone?"

From behind a large screening tombstone, addressing Paul as if asking directions, the man, whose face up close now appeared much younger than Paul had at first thought, quietly told him:

"I've been instructed to tell you verbally, since a written message would be dangerous, that your sister Suzie and husband Logan are now in Chungking. Logan, recently promoted to the rank of full Colonel, is Interpreter/Liaison Officer on the personal staff of now Lieutenant General Wedemeyer, the top American military officer in China.

Also, that your sister Nellie and her three children were safely evacuated from Kweilin by rail as soon as that city was threatened by the Japanese. Her husband S.Z. had to remain on duty there until near the end, but was safely flown out by the Americans just in time.

All your family members now in Chungking have met together, are well, and send their greetings to all of you here."

With that, the man turned to limp hurriedly away, saying only, over his shoulder: "that's all I know, I must go quickly now!"

As Paul relayed all that good news to us over the family dinner table that evening, for a few quietly happy moments we forgot about all those nearby new Japanese soldiers and that recently completed concrete antitank gun emplacement just down the street from our mansion.

News reports from Europe over the next few weeks were most cheering: the April 12 hanging of the Fascist Dictator Benito Mussolini by Italian partisans, the suicide of Adolph Hitler in his Berlin bunker April 30, and of course V-E Day, May 7 and the unconditional surrender of Germany!

Now, if only Japan would call it quits!

But as Saipan and Iwo Jima had so recently proved, and the still ongoing battle for Okinawa continued to demonstrate, most Japanese soldiers still preferred to die for their Emperor rather than surrender. And the untouched bulk of their huge army, full of fight, was here in our country, our city and all around us in our local neighborhood!

While most Shanghai residents, including our family now believed that it was only a matter of time until Japan's defeat, we shuddered at the thought of a bitter, final house to house battle over our city.

Who could forget the orgy of brutality the Japanese army had deliberately unleashed on Nanking's hapless civilian population that not so far back December of 1937!

At this point in time – May through July 1945, our Yang family's fear of that happening was quite real – and never far out of mind!

Due to similar fears on the part of all the faculty, graduating students and parents of those students, the late June graduation day ceremonies for Betty and her classmates at Bei Tsun Chinese School were very brief and low key.

She and I had walked to the school together, as usual, earlier that morning to say our good-byes to friends. Grandmother and Concubine Silver Lotus went later by rickshaw, meeting us there in time to attend the short early afternoon diploma-presentation program held in the school's auditorium.

Afterwards, we all hurried home, Betty and I walking as quickly as possible en route, with eyes downcast, past that evil-looking new pillbox fortification at the intersection of Avenues Joffre and Haig, and the protruding snout of the cannon within.

The soldiers manning it, laughed sneeringly and made sly comments in Japanese, which we didn't understand (but could guess at), as Betty and I hurried past, our hearts thumping with fright.

During the next few weeks of summer, afraid to leave the house, Betty and I kept busy gardening, taking turns practicing at the parlor piano, singing and listening to the radio. Ah Foo and the maids kept us abreast of the many daily rumors floating about the marketplace; Daddy, James and Paul relayed their workday gathered ones over the evening dinner table. Two sets of recurring rumors were especially unsettling.

The first of these centered around unconfirmed reports of Chinese Communist troops moving down from the north along the coast toward the outskirts of Shanghai. Their purported mission was to be in place to greet and assist the expected autumn American invasion force, thus gaining greater U.S. recognition of their movement and its strength!

The second revolved around the large, well-organized and armed rival Kuomintang and Communist underground forces in Shanghai that were poised to strike at any time. For now they battled only via purposely leaked propaganda rumors!

Rumors were rumors; the one real fact of the period was that American bombing raids, often involving formations of 50 or more planes over our sprawling city and environs, had greatly intensified.

The darkness of nearly every night now was lit by antiaircraft tracers, parachute flares and distant fires caused by exploding bombs. Fortunately, most of this activity centered on outlying dock and factory areas, not over our residential section of the city.

We saw one close by, low-flying large American bomber, hit by antiaircraft fire, explode in a great orange and red fireball of flame. There were no survivors!

Suddenly, as we remained glued to our home radios, local and foreign shortwave, a series of very important events took place with breathtaking rapidity:

July 26 – The allies issued their so-called Potsdam Proclamation which demanded the unconditional surrender of Japan, but promised a just peace. It also threatened that, unless Japanese forces surrendered promptly, Japan would be destroyed.

August 6 – Not receiving an answer to the Potsdam Proclamation, the American dropped their first atomic bomb on Hiroshima – killing over 78,000 Japanese.

August 8 – Russia declared war on Japan, and launched a massive offensive into Manchuria the next day.

August 9 – The Americans dropped a second atomic bomb – this time on the Japanese city of Nagasaki – killing over 40,000, with another 25,000 injured.

August 14 – The Japanese government accepted unconditional surrender.

August 15 – Emperor Hirohito, in the first public speech a Japanese sovereign had ever made, in a strange, obliquely worded radio message during which he never mentioned the word surrender, called upon the Japanese people to accept the coming of peace.

Immediately, all 70 million Japanese accepted defeat, and ceased combat operations everywhere.

The long Pacific War had ended!

September 2 – V-J Day! Representatives of Japan and the Allied nations formally signed surrender papers aboard the U.S. battleship "Missouri" (Big Mo) in Tokyo Bay.

World War II was over!

For some 48 hours, following Emperor Hirohito's August 15 radio address, life and general activity in Shanghai slowed down to the point that we seemed momentarily, uncertainly to be living in the eye of a typhoon!

We Chinese residents literally held our breaths, awaiting the reaction of the Japanese troops in our midst. Would they accept their Emperor's message submissively – or would they turn on us in bitter, savage rage? All we could do was wait and see.

Although Daddy and James went to work as usual during that period, Daddy ordered everyone else in our household to stay quietly inside behind locked doors. And he ordered Paul to stay with us to make certain that we obeyed.

Returning home the evening of the first day, he and James both reported that the Japanese civilian supervisors at their places of employment, and apparently everywhere else in the city, were totally shocked and stunned by their Emperor's broadcast.

"They have always regarded the Emperor as devine, a supreme being descended directly from the Sun God who would never talk to his subjects in any way about earthly matters," said Daddy. "His telling them in effect that Japan has surrendered unconditionally is almost beyond their comprehension.

But it seems like they, and most of the local Japanese military, so far at least, have accepted the situation and will not turn on us as we have feared. Let's hope that it stays that way!"

After waiting another day to make certain that this was true, as daily life throughout the city began to return to normal, he took me to Aurora Middle School, where in spite of the war's sudden end, he had me enrolled as a boarder student.

In less than three weeks, for the first time in my 15-½ years I would be living away from home sharing a single large dormitory room with a great many of other female students, all of whom would be strangers to me.

My apprehension at the thought of that change in life style was heightened by the rather strained, uneasy manner of Daddy during our private interview with the elderly, very businesslike, English-speaking French-born Catholic Nun Registrar.

No "Big Shot" act on his part here! The foreign religious pictures on the wall, the near life size statue of the Virgin Mary and child Jesus in one corner of the reception room, were such unfamiliar objects! And the nun's steady, direct, unblinking gaze from underneath her crisply starched white bonnet, over which draped a black veil matching her all black habit, obviously made him feel uneasy. I found it quite refreshing to see him act so meek and polite for a change!

The Japanese soldiers and their gun bunker near our Mansion were far more familiar to us than this foreign nun in her strange (to us) religious setting. Neither he nor I had ever been inside a Catholic church or institution of any kind, or really knew anything about this brand of the Christian religion. I was immediately curious to learn more about it. He was just glad to get out of the place!

An hour later, as we walked into Peach Blossom Lane from the not too distant tram stop, we noticed a sizable crowd of neighbors and other onlookers gathered in front of the driveway gate near our mansion's main front entrance.

Parked inside, behind the iron bars gate, was the object of their attention, and subject of their animated discussion. It was an unoccupied, small, squat, four-wheeled, gray, green and black camouflage-painted military vehicle. Highly visible, full-color American and Chinese Nationalist flags, painted one on each side, decorated both front and rear bumpers.

Rushing inside to see what was going on – we were greeted by a tall, handsome, smiling young military officer dressed in a foreign style green twill fatigue uniform with a full color American flag patch on one shoulder and a full color Chinese Nationalist one on the other!

"Hello, Dya-Dya!" laughed the officer, "do you remember the young fellow who married your daughter Suzie in Chungking back in 1938? And just look at how Shao Bei has grown!"

"Logan," shouted Daddy, shaking the officer's hand vigorously, western style, "how wonderful to see you!" I grabbed both of Logan's hands as soon as I could and cried out in joy, "when did you get here? Where did you come from? Did Suzie come with you?"

The rest of our family, who had smilingly watched our greetings now crowded about as everyone started talking at once.

At the dinner table that evening Logan told how he had flown into Lung Wah Japanese military airport a few hours earlier aboard an American Army Air Corps transport plane. He, along with two dozen Chinese and American specialist army officers, a few enlisted men from both armies and three "Jeep" military vehicles had flown in as the very first advance party sent from Chungking to set up allied Shanghai military headquarters.

"Along with other officers due to arrive over the next three days, I will be concerned with setting up command headquarters for General Wedemeyer who will personally arrive in due course," he explained.

"But first, how would you all like to take a ride tomorrow in my American Jeep," he smilingly asked, "and see how Shanghai is celebrating the end of the war!"

As we all clapped our hands and cheered, he added: "and, we will be driven in style, for my Nationalist army driver/ aide is in your kitchen right now enjoying the best meal he's had in the past three years!"

After an exciting morning's drive throughout the city with Daddy and James the next day, followed by an animated family luncheon gathering at home, Betty, Paul and I piled into the back of the Jeep for our turn.

What a thrilling ride it turned out to be! Overnight it seemed, people had finally realized that the war was really over. Now they poured out into the streets in a joyful festive mood. Everywhere they cheered the strange sight of our American Jeep and uniformed Logan and his driver! And everywhere they crowded around to ask countless questions, touch the Jeep or just stare in smiling awe.

In spite of its sizable Communist underground population, Shanghai was and had always been a Kuomintang stronghold. The large middle class especially had always considered Chiang Kai-shek the living symbol of China's nationhood, and had willingly accepted his leadership throughout the long war. Now, large, youthful-looking portraits of him, hidden for years, were popping up all over the place – many surrounded by garlands of flowers and colorful paper streamers.

Scores of those small thoroughly unmusical bands hired by merchants to advertise their wares, or for funeral or wedding processions, were everywhere loudly blaring out mostly American tunes like "Dixie", "There'll be A Hot Time in the Old Town Tonight" and "Polly Wolly Doodle!"

Except for a few armed Japanese troops quietly on duty at key intersections or fortified strong points, little evidence of established authority was to be seen! The Chinese puppet government police especially, and Chinese prison guards everywhere, seemed largely to have disappeared. As a group, they had been so brutally inefficient and corrupt that fearing the wrath of the populace most had simply deserted their posts.

Yet, in spite of the absence of civil police authority, and the joyous, festive atmosphere, the laughing, shoving, mini-parade-forming crowds were quite orderly. They just seemed happily elated at this sudden feeling of freedom.

To observe all this was the real reason that Logan had taken the time to drive us all over the city. Around 4:00 p.m. we parked in front of the Bund area's well-known Park Hotel, which had been taken over from the Japanese military the day before by fellow officers who had flown in with him. By now they had established direct radio communication from there with Chunking military headquarters, and Logan took time to make his report on the situation in the city before we drove back home.

As he told us over our family dinner table that evening, the dropping of the top secret American atomic bombs on Japan and the resulting sudden Japanese surrender had caught even the highest levels of allied command by surprise.

"Overall allied planning had been based on the assumption that victory would come next year," he told us. "A large Chinese army was all set to launch a major south China offensive August 15, just the other day, with the goal of capturing Canton by mid-October. Shortly thereafter, scheduled for November 1, would come massive landings by Americans on Kyushu, the most southern of Japan's main islands.

"Rumors floating around Shanghai for months have been predicting an American landing near here this coming autumn" noted James, "and we feared that a bitter house to house battle over our city would follow!"

"Well, that probably would have happened – next year, in the spring of 1946," replied Logan. "That's when the Americans planned to land in Tokyo Bay and at other locations on the Japanese main island of Honshu."

"When will Chinese soldiers arrive in enough force to disarm all the thousands of Japanese troops here?" asked Daddy.

"The American Fourteenth and Tenth Air Forces are now in the process of assembling every available plane to quickly fly in troops of the Nationalist 94th Chinese Army from their south China Canton offensive staging points. These troops should start arriving at Lung Wah Airport within a day or two," replied Logan.

"Truly amazing, is the way the Japanese military is cooperating in every way possible, both to make the military turnover run smoothly and to maintain law and order until we can take full control ourselves.

I honestly believe," he continued, that the Chinese Communist army, located near the coast north of Shanghai would now be force-marching to beat our troops here if they were not afraid that the Japanese would attack them. The Japanese hate and fear the Communists, and would probably obey allied orders to block such an advance. And they have the force to do so!"

"Another amazing thing," added Logan, "is the way the former Chinese Nanking central puppet government and its Shanghai municipal government bureaucrats are already smoothly accepting and obeying orders from Chungking, both direct and via our underground people. Although our government has always maintained secret contacts with many of their top officials, all the rest are now rushing to try and get back into the Chungking government's good graces!"

The next few days, before start of term for me at Aurora Middle School, were a dazzling whirlwind of activity and new, exciting sights and sounds. Logan, busily observing the city scene and making radio reports of his observations to Chungking late each afternoon, frequently took Betty, Paul and me with him on these Jeep tours. As a full Colonel on General Wedemeyer's staff, he had easy access everywhere, so we went places and saw things in and around our city that we had never experienced before.

We attended, for example, the official reception at Lung Wah Airport for the first arriving troops of the Chinese 94th Army. As these tired, shabby, dust-covered, straw sandal wearing peasant soldiers stepped out of their American Army Air Corps C-54s and DC-3s they gaped in stunned disbelief at the huge, surging relatively well dressed crowds cheering their arrival. As they disembarked, to the sprightly tunes of a municipal band, welcome banners waved in the breeze and movie cameras rolled.

In the background, confined to their barracks, hundreds of still-armed Japanese air force and army personnel looked on curiously and silently.

Another day saw us greeting the arrival of the first two U.S. naval ships to tie up alongside the customs jetty on the Bund – two small minesweepers.

Some days later we witnessed arrival of the flagship and escorting destroyers of the U.S. Seventh Fleet, which was operating in the Yangtze estuary. Chiang, who didn't want U.S. ground troops to take control of Shanghai, had asked the U.S. Navy to do so temporarily on behalf of the Chinese government until adequate Chinese troops and civilian officials could be flown in.

Daddy, recharged by the sudden turn of events, was once again his old authoritative, enthusiastic self-assured self! Stunned by their Emperor's August 15 surrender broadcast, the few Japanese executives who had been sent in 1942 to assume managerial control of the then Japanese-renamed Standard Vacuum Oil Company of China simply quit functioning. Daddy quickly seized the initiative and took charge – busily reorganizing operations under the old Standard Oil name. He knew that new American executives would soon be sent over to reclaim the company's formerly extensive holdings, and wanted to have things set up as best he could prior to their arrival.

Anticipating that the rest of our family members would be arriving from Chungking as soon as they could arrange transportation, those in our mansion busily began planning for their new future. While James elected to continue his municipal water systems inspection work with Shanghai Public Health Department, Betty enrolled for advanced piano classes at Shanghai Music Conservatory.

The biggest lifestyle change was made by Paul who had immediately resigned his "dead end" job as Manager of Wan Guo Cemetery the day after Emperor Hirohito's radio address. An energetic entrepreneur at heart, in the best tradition of a "Son of Shanghai," he now wanted to "do business, make money, and get rich"! Thus he and a friend formed a low-investment company to manufacture and sell charcoal briquettes – hopefully, through Logan's connections to the American military and naval forces who would be busily repatriating Japanese troops during the coming winter.

In early September, just three weeks or so after "peace" had supposedly come, as Betty and I started classes at our respective new schools, two major new events suddenly began to shape Shanghai's future.

The first, something dread, happening at places far distant for now, was an unwelcome event that most Shanghai residents didn't even want to think about – much less talk about!

But as Logan sadly put it most solemnly, one Sunday evening after our family dinner – "full-scale civil war has already started in North China between Kuomintang and Communist forces, and although the Americans are trying to head it off, I am afraid that 'real peace' for poor China is something we can now only dream about."

The second event, just now starting to rock and roll Shanghai, was the sudden presence of large numbers of Americans – young, virile sailors and marines mostly, arriving by the shipload! The city's welcome mat was rolled out wide for these fun-loving visitors; their ships bringing holds full of mostly free to China "goodies" in and quickly transporting the unwelcome Japanese troops out – back to their homeland.

To the cheerful delight of the city's countless long suppressed purveyors of the "happy life" – bars, restaurants, dance halls, cabarets, Sing Song girls, tarts, touts, musicians, "Ladies of the Night" and to rickshaw pullers, beggars and whatever – the signal went out, "here come the Americans!"

Americans! The only people in the Far East with money, money, money to spend!

"Da Ja Fat Choy (Let's all get rich)!"

Americans! To coin the British – "oversexed, overpaid and overhere!"

"Mei Guo, Ding How (America is Number One)!"

Shanghai's citizens were delighted – forget civil war and the Communists; along with Paul:

"Let's do business, make money and get rich!"

Whoopee!!!

Chapter 13

DOUBLE TROUBLE IN NORTH CHINA
DOUBLE HAPPINESS AT HOME

"Jingle, jingle, jingle" – the sudden loud, jingling sound of the handheld morning awakening bell nearly caused me to jump out of my deep-in-slumber skin!

It was a rude shock awakening, since I was right in the middle of an exciting nightmare – mentally flailing madly away at Ah Foo's green and yellow parrot which was trying to peck out Mong Fu's eyes!

"Jingle, jingle, jingle" – the Nun shook her long wooden handled bell vigorously as some 50 of us female boarder-students at Aurora Middle School stirred sluggishly in our individual, narrow, cot-like beds.

"Jingle, jingle, jingle" – there was no getting away from that noise! So, one might as well open the old sticky eyes, run a dry tongue around the bad tasting, furry inside of the mouth and lips, have a last yawn – and peer uncertainly into the dim 6:00 a.m. late January early dawn-light that was feebly trying to penetrate our big, open, second floor dormitory room.

"Jingle, jingle, jingle" ("STOP IT" – our minds screamed)!

"Jesus, Mary, and Joseph," loudly intoned the nun in her first verbal utterance of the day.

"I give you my heart," came our muffled, individual response replies, as we all suddenly leaped from our beds in a mad dash for the washroom, and our usual cold water morning ablutions. The school time-allotment for this was short, so "everything" had to be done pretty much on the double!

A short time later, encased in our thick padded gowns (there was no heat anywhere in our large school), which were covered with our maroon trimmed black winter uniform chong sams, we quietly assembled in a long corridor just outside the dorm.

"Click-snap, click-snap" – came the sharp sounds from another nun's small, hand held metal "cricket" noise maker! Still silently, we all formed into a line facing her.

"Click-snap, click-snap" – turning smartly left in line at this signal, we obediently, still silently, followed her down a stairwell, past the convent chapel and into the dining hall.

No loud army sergeant-type barking of verbal orders in this process – just the occasional "click-snap," click-snaps" of this one little "cricket." The British army's Seaforth Highlanders would have been proud of us!

"If these nuns of the Catholic 'Society of the Sacred Heart' Order had been given the job of instilling this kind of discipline on the Chinese army back in early 1937," I thought to myself as I shuffled along, "that army might have repelled Shanghai's Japanese invaders later that summer on the landing beaches, and the whole long Pacific War might never have happened!"

No time for any more such silly thoughts – or even to remind myself that today was my 16th birthday! None of my family members had or would remember, so why would anyone take notice here at my new school, where I had now been enrolled for nearly four and a half months!

It was just another late January day in 1946 to everyone else in the world! "Why should the fact that I turn 16 today be of interest to any living creature?" I asked myself with a shrug!

Turning to one of my new found classmate friends, Inez Tan, a pretty Chinese/German Eurasian, at our eight-student dining table, I asked her to please pass along the bowl containing spicy sliced preserved turnips.

Picking some of these out with my chopsticks, I stirred them into my bowl of hot congee, a watery rice gruel, into which I had already mixed some fried tofu and shredded jellyfish. That, plus fried peanuts, and "yu tiao," a long, twisted type of fried dough stick, constituted this day's breakfast!

This same type breakfast had been and was to be for the next two and a half years of my school-year stays as a boarding student at Aurora Middle School, our daily standard breakfast meal.

Hot congee always, at breakfast; as much as we wanted, individually self-ladled out of the big pot on a nearby rice-table station – one station serving four tables such as ours. And usually, "yu tiao." That, and exactly four bowls or dishes of foods, like those of today, which were awaiting us on the table when the "click-snap" commanded us to first say grace and then sit down – in unison.

The only variation to all this was in the contents of the daily four bowls or dishes of food. One, for example might contain "Stinky Tofu" (fermented bean curd) instead of fried tofu, another hot chili radishes, or tofu in soy sauce and sesame oil with a garnish of scallions, for change.

While I sometimes turned up my nose at "Stinky Tofu," I really never tired of this basic breakfast menu and especially looked forward to those frequent days when my very favorite preserved turnips was on the menu!

While we were allowed to talk at meals, time allocated was so short that slow eaters quickly learned to concentrate first on the food! All too soon came the familiar "click-snap, click-snap" which quickly brought us "always in silence" to our feet, into line and out to our after-breakfast "free time" open area. Twenty minutes later, after assembling individually, we were seated in our home classrooms where, except for lunch and music or physical education classes, we would remain throughout the day.

At this day's "free time" period I stayed to myself, thinking of our recently reunited Yang family, finally back together in Shanghai after so many years of wartime separation, and of the joyful New Year's festivities we would soon be celebrating together. I could hardly wait!

So much had happened within our family since Emperor Hirohito's August 15 radio surrender announcement of the previous year!

Just three weeks after Logan's arrival, the Americans had flown S.Z. in from Chungking to help take over control of the railroad system from the Japanese military. He was now working night and day as a key coordinator executive, constantly bringing trainloads of Japanese soldiers in from the interior of China. These troops were still being processed around the clock for repatriation back to Japan on American ships. Outgoing trains had to be quickly loaded with the relief goods those ships had brought into the port of Shanghai. It was a busy operation!

With a Shanghai as well as Chungking headquarters now in place for General Wedemeyer, and a personal penthouse suite for him in the Tower Apartment of the Bund area's fancy Cathay Hotel as well, Logan had to stay constantly nearby. Thus he, Suzie and their two year old son Da Wei (Michael) had just moved into a comfortable large Hongkew area house that had been inhabited since early 1938 by a Japanese occupation army Colonel and his family.

Nellie, S.Z. and their three children; two girls ages 11 and 7, and a nine year old son; having arrived by Yangtze steamer from Chungking in January, had just moved into a home owned by Daddy on Sinza Road, near Gordon Road.

It was quite an experience, and a real pleasure for me to finally get to meet this sister, 18 years older than I, whom I last saw (but obviously didn't remember) at her marriage to S.Z. back in 1932! While our great age and life experience differences made it difficult to find much sisterly common ground, we did enjoy trying to get better acquainted.

Their new abode, conveniently located in the heart of the former International Settlement area, was close both to Shanghai's main railroad yards and Tung De medical school. Betty, who at Daddy's insistence had dropped out of Shanghai Conservatory to enroll in Tung De's spring term premed program, had moved in with them – as had Mong-Fu, my gift to the children!

Having evicted our Peach Blossom Lane mansion's top floor renters, Daddy turned that apartment over to Guo Liang, Chow Ping and their 3-1/2 year old daughter. They had just arrived together after a long, uncomfortable trip down the Yangtze by junk.

Now, for the first time, we learned that the top secret "factory highly essential to the war effort," where the two had worked so hard for all those long war years, and where they met, was the famous Kiangnan Arsenal.

Formerly located along the banks of the Whangpoo River in Shanghai, some 20 miles or so upriver from the city's Bund area, its vital artillery and ordinance making machine tools had been secretly moved on camouflaged junks and sampans up the Yangtze to safety in Chungking as soon as the Japanese attacked Peking in early July, 1937.

Dug deep into Chungking's bluff-side caves overlooking the Yangtze, safe from Japanese bombs, the arsenal had operated at full capacity around the clock, day in and day out throughout the war. It had been highly dangerous and exhausting work for them. He was now looking for a new type of job in Shanghai; she hoped to stay at home and concentrate on raising her daughter.

With Daddy, Concubine Silver Lotus, Grandmother, James and Paul still at home, Betty with Nellie and S.Z., and me residing at Aurora Middle School, our family now seemed settled enough to face both old and new work and living difficulties of the immediate post war period.

Unfortunately, this long unknown thing called "peace" was already giving indications of simply heaping new problems on top of the many still existing old ones!

But who wants to think of "problems" during the upcoming annual New Year Festival period? That's a traditional Chinese "enjoy the family" time, and I planned to spend my three-day 1946 New Year's school holiday doing just that!

While the traditional annual Chinese New Year festival period is, in theory, always a lengthy 15-day affair with many public festivals and fairs, most working people and students, like those in our family, had or took only a three-day holiday break to celebrate. And, like most other families, ours did its traditional New Year celebrating the first three days of the First Moon in the Lunar Calendar. That period, this year, fell in early February on the western calendar.

During this three-day period, covering New Year's Eve Day, and the two following days, storefronts of many of the closed shops, and home fronts of most Buddhist families were festooned with red (the color of Good Luck) banners and streamers. On most of these, handwritten in black characters, were greetings such as "Good Luck," "Happy New Year," and "GET RICH!" This cheerful last expression was the most celebrated overall "wish greeting" of this holiday season!

At the mansion, Ah Foo and the maids had been busy for days preparing food for our planned big New Year's Eve family dinner. To mark our first large such gathering in years, Daddy had ordered in a whole roast pig from an outside caterer. Enough advance food had to be prepared for New Year's Day meals as well, since tradition forbade the use of cutting utensils such as knives or scissors on that day. Also, servants were traditionally not asked to do much work then.

In keeping with the family oriented spirit of the festivities, all the adults, including Concubine Silver Lotus who, since Mother's death had been included in all things, "taking place within our home," as a full member of our family and Mistress of our Household, looked forward to carrying out traditional activities for the benefit of the younger children. While Nellie and S.Z.'s three children were the special focus of attention due to their ages, Suzie and Chow Ping's younger ones were kept, wide-eyed, right in the forefront of unfolding events.

The action got underway around mid-afternoon on this New Year's Eve day when children and adults alike started setting off a two hour backyard progression of exploding firecrackers. This excitement was interspersed with stories and play acts designed to chase away any evil spirits that might be lurking in the garden or elsewhere to enter the mansion from the backyard at midnight with the New Year.

Then everyone moved to the mansion's front entranceway to hang a pair of large, colorful, fierce-looking paper "Gate God Warriors," one on each side of the doorway, to guard against any wandering evil spirits on Peach Blossom Lane that might try to sneak into the household with the New Year from that direction.

Then came the lengthy, talkative, laugh-filled traditional New Year's Eve dinner, featuring our roast pig, with all members of our four generations present at the big first floor parlor table.

After all had finished eating, the three older children in turn walked around the table bowing formally and respectfully, first to their parents, and then to each of the other adults. Their parents then presented each child with special red, gold embossed envelopes of "Lucky Money."

After Nellie and S.Z., and Suzie and Logan with their young child left to spend the night at their own homes, Nellie's three children, who were sleeping over, followed Daddy and Grandmother around, assisting them in their "Big Act" of sealing all the mansion's doorways against possible entry by evil spirits.

While adults in most of our friend's families' traditionally stayed up all night New Year's Eve, we all went to bed. The tired children soon fell sound asleep – confident that no evil spirits would be able to slip into our home at midnight with the New Year!

Around 6:30 a.m. the next day, New Year's Day, which was the second day of our three-day celebration, the three children were awakened to assist Daddy, James and Paul in unlocking all the mansion's doorways which had been sealed against evil spirits the previous night.

This traditional ceremony, called "Opening the Gates of Good Fortune," was led by Daddy, who loudly and authoritatively acted out his traditional role as "Master of the Household." Prior to each unlocking, he made the youngsters busily and noisily look under all nearby chairs and tables for any evil spirits that might have slipped in. None were found, of course, but all had fun "searching."

After breakfast, with Nellie and S.Z., and Suzie, Logan and their young Michael again present, Grandmother, now in her element, conducted a brief ceremony to acknowledge and honor our family ancestors. The room was darkened as she lit candles and incense before a small ancestral shrine she had set up in the parlor. After she had intoned a brief Buddhist prayer, the entire assembled family followed her lead in silently and with reverence, bowing three times before this shrine.

She then led the now suddenly jovial, chattering entire group around the first and second mansion levels to acknowledge the important Household, Kitchen, Gate and Door gods. The children placed small food offerings before colorful painted paper effigies of each of these at little "shrines" she had previously set up for the occasion. All this activity was carried out in a cheerful, game-like atmosphere, with the adults often carrying on more like children than the youngsters themselves.

In order to encourage everyone to "simmer down" a bit before lunch, Daddy, who like most Chinese was an inveterate gambler, then proposed that everyone who truly believed in the New Year "Get Rich" greeting, join him in a game of "Lucky Red Dice." Most of the family, including Silver Lotus, promptly joined him around the parlor table, ready to play.

He quickly saw to it that the three older grandchildren got all of their yesterday's paper "Lucky Money" changed into small denomination ten-cent coins.

"As the youngest player, you get to go first," he announced, nodding to Nellie and S.Z.'s young seven year old daughter Wei Ming.

"But before she starts, everyone has to put 20 ten cent coins, out on the table as your 'into the pot' bet!"

"Now, what do I do?" asked Wei Ming, after her Mother had helped her count out her coins and place them in the center of the table with everyone else's.

"You, as lead-off player, must first put these six playing dice into this large bowl here on the table," he answered. "Notice that all numbers of dots on each of the dice are black – EXCEPT the four-dot side of each, which is RED.

Cup both your hands now Wei Ming," he went on, "scoop up all the dice, shake them around in your hands, and drop all of them into the bowl.

For each red four-dot side showing up, you win one coin from the pot out on the table.

If you should be lucky enough to have the red four dot side of all six dice showing up – you win the jackpot, and get to take all the coins out on the table!"

After winning three coins on her first throw, Wei Ming, along with all the others at the table was laughingly "hooked" on this simple, popular, widely played family game, which went on for the next two hours. As luck (or years of skilled experience) would have it, Daddy was the big winner; his grandchildren, especially Wei Ming, the big losers.

Did it bother him in the end that he had won a big part of his young grandchildren's collective New Year's "Lucky Money?" Not at all – his theory was that "business is business" and that good luck in gambling is the same as in business.

"It's never too early for your children to start learning the give and take of 'doing business!'" he loudly told Nellie and S.Z. at game's end, in spite of young "Lost Nearly Everything" Wei Ming's sobs in the background.

The rest of that day and evening was spent in small family groups, going out to visit with relatives or friends, or just visiting quietly together at home. Traditionally, an important purpose of this New Year's Day "family reunion" focus was to settle any within the family quarrels or grievances. Fortunately, we had no such problems within our family this day.

The next morning, that of the final third day of our three-day family New Year's celebration, featured Daddy's old showoff, posturing act of paying homage to the God of Wealth. He had been too depressed to do this since the Japanese occupation of Shanghai, their takeover and renaming of Standard Oil, their Pearl Harbor attack, Mother's death and Concubine Ching's running off with that unknown rice merchant! Just too long a run of bad luck even for the God of Wealth to cope with!

But this time, with his whole reassembled family as a "captive audience," and the good luck omen of the unexpected return of my black and white Mong-Fu pooch, he went all out to pay homage. We adults of course had seen his Big Act so many times in earlier years that we could hardly stifle our yawns as he again went through the familiar kowtowing and loud, fake importuning before his hallway "shrine" and effigy of the god. The grandchildren, of course, loved the half-hour long show!

Afterwards, during our informal family luncheon, James asked that we all gather around the table, since he had an important announcement to make. Once we had all assembled, he told us that he and his attractive, steady girlfriend of the past several months, Bright Jade, who was now standing beside him, would marry soon – on a specific date yet to be determined by an astrologer.

"While we decided ourselves to get married," he told us, "since her Chu family is much more tradition-minded than ours, I went formally to her father to ask his permission. That was granted, and a special approval announcement was made by him to the entire Chu family yesterday afternoon at their New Year's gathering. Our wedding will be a large quite traditional affair."

Everyone in our family was very happy and pleased at this good news, and quickly gathered around the couple to offer our individual congratulations.

Around mid-afternoon as windup to the New Year's festivities, our entire Yang family group went to a large multi-relatives gathering at the home of my Auntie Nyang Nyang (Father's younger second sister) and Uncle Mao Tou (Baby Uncle). As usual, concubine Silver Lotus was excluded from such "outside our home" gatherings of relatives or friends.

One of the two sisters Daddy had, as a young man, put through medical school, Auntie Nyang Nyang was now a prominent M.D. pediatrician with her clinic on the ground floor of their quite large mansion. Her husband, Mao Tou, my mother's younger half brother, was under Daddy, a department head in the transportation section of Standard Oil. Their mansion was only a short tram's ride away from ours, and Betty and I often visited them and their five children, two of whom were our age.

This large, over 70 assorted relatives gathering, our family's first such since early 1937, was assembled both to celebrate the ending of China's very long, (since 1931) war with Japan and Shanghai's first "peaceful" New Year in nine years.

Since many of Auntie Dr. Nyang Nyang's patients were working people, and mostly poor, they tended to bring her live chickens, or food items, either as payment for services or simply as "thank you" gifts, at New Year's time. Thus one reason for holding this "clan gathering" at her home, was due to the "probability" of having enough food (of some kind at least) available to feed so many hungry relatives.

One thing NOT readily available however, was still-strictly rationed rice; a basic staple for any Chinese meal! So, on this day, everyone had to bring their own bags of rice – which were thrown together in the communal pot, cooked and served up at that evening's banquet.

After the long, informal banquet, with its happy visiting and congratulatory toasts to long-missed relatives, and to the engagement of Bright Jade and James, the children were sent to

229

another room. Most of the adults, all the men and many of the women, including Betty and me, gathered around in a big parlor room, interested in hearing from Logan and S.Z. what was really going on in China now, some six months after the end of World War II, and what the future might hold for all of us.

"As a Nationalist liaison officer attached to the staff of the American General Wedemeyer, you must be well informed as to the current military and political situation in China," began Mao Tou, addressing Logan.

"Can you tell us honestly what the Chinese factions, the Americans and the Russians are up to in China these days?"

"Due to my officer's rank and sensitive assignment," replied Logan, "I can only discuss general facts and situations as I understand them, and not matters relating to military security."

"We all understand that," acknowledged Mao Tou, "but we want to learn the truth after so many years of rumors plus Japanese, other foreign, Kuomintang and Chinese Communist propaganda."

"Japan's sudden surrender last August caught all parties in China by surprise," Logan began. At the Cairo Conference of November 1943, Roosevelt, Stalin and Churchill had pledged return to China of Manchuria and Taiwan among other things. Later, at the February 1945 Yalta Conference, Roosevelt and Churchill secretly promised Stalin such far reaching concessions in Manchuria in order to persuade Russia to enter the war against Japan, that Russia may become dominant there.

Russia invaded Manchuria only eight days before Japan's surrender and, facing little resistance, soon assumed complete control there. Breaking earlier promises, the Russians accepted surrender of Japanese troops, arms and equipment. They have turned the latter over to the Chinese Communists, and seem to be taking thousands of the surrendered Japanese soldiers to Siberia – for reasons we don't yet understand. And, most disturbingly, they are dismantling and taking back to Russia all industrial and factory equipment that can be moved, plus destroying all the rest."

"What are the Americans doing in face of these Russian provocation's?" questioned Lu Lok, my Auntie Peony's husband.

"The Americans, so far, have done everything possible to honor both their Cairo and Yalta agreements, and their promises to Chiang Kai-shek," answered Logan. "They have rushed thousands of Nationalist troops, both by air and ship, to occupy northern cities such as Peking, Tientsin and Tsingtao. They have ordered all Japanese commanders to surrender only to the Nationalists, and have assisted Chinese national government generals in accepting such surrenders.

The Nationalists have also been helped by the fact that nearly all the estimated 1.5 million Chinese puppet government and separate old warlord controlled armies, who have been allied with the Japanese for many years, moved quickly to join the Chungking forces. These troops fear the Communists!"

"All sides right now, even with peace negotiations currently taking place between Chiang Kai-shek and the Communists in Chungking, are fighting to gain control of the all-important North China railway system," interjected S.Z.

"That's right." Logan agreed, "and two divisions of American marines, with headquarters in Tientsin are helping the Nationalists in this. Since Communist troops are also rushing to grab what they can, there have already been some minor firefights between these marines and Chinese communist troops. And Japanese troops have even helped repel communist attacks in some places!

The uncertain military and political situation adds up to big "Double Trouble" in North China right now – to the extent that I can't even guess how it will all finally turn out."

As the family gathering broke up to collect all the younger children and head off to our respective homes, the final evening's conversation had a worried tone. All agreed that while our overall family three-day New Year Festival had been wonderful, real peace seemed nowhere in sight. Full-scale civil war seemed now to lie in our future!

Weeks later, as the damp, chilly winds of winter began, slowly, to give way to the softer, warmer ones of early spring, they brought with them the first two postwar American Standard Oil executives. They found, to their delight, that Daddy had things well under control at the company's Shanghai headquarters. He in turn, immediately liked and respected Charles Sprague, the one to whom he would report. Both their working and personal relationship was to prove cordial.

Other members of our family were also adjusting well to postwar life. Guo Liang, for example, was delighted with his new employment as Technical Trade Representative at the newly formed, government funded Shanghai Bureau of International Trade.

Paul, who was now doing quite well in his new charcoal briquette business, had us all pleased with his new girlfriend Ruth Ho, a close friend and former Aurora classmate of Auntie Nyang Nyang's daughter Dorothy.

And Betty, by now only halfheartedly pursuing premed studies at Tung De medical college, was finding life far more exciting outside school, noisily riding piggyback around town astride new boyfriend T.K. Hu's rebuilt big blue 1938 Harley Davidson motorcycle!

One Saturday evening late the following month of March, when I was spending my Saturday noon until Sunday evening "free time" from school at home, all of us household members present started teasing James at dinnertime over his forthcoming marriage to Bright Jade. We could tell that he was starting to get nervous over the whole idea!

After all, one's marriage and funeral are the two most important events in the life of any Chinese, male or female!

The astrologer they had consulted two weeks earlier, after finding their mutual horoscopes to be compatible, had taken her time in predicting and recommending the most auspicious month, day and hour for their wedding. The delay, she claimed, was due to carefully double checking her prediction through use of two different methods to look into their future – the traditional palmistry method, and the more modern finger and joint method!

The "Lucky Day" date she came up with, May 5 at 7:00 p.m., had been discussed and accepted at a formal restaurant dinner gathering of several members of our Yang family and Bright Jade's Chu family only two evenings earlier.

"What did you and Bright Jade have to do in order for the astrologer to even start looking into your future?" I asked.

"We had to immediately give her 'our Eight Characters;' namely, the exact hour, day, month and animal year of our respective births," replied James. "This enabled her to determine, from specific combinations of the five elements and the twelve animals of the zodiac, whether or not we are compatible.

If it had turned out that either elements and animals or both, in our respective birth years had been incompatible, the Chu's probably would have insisted that we break our engagement."

"If her birth date had shown the element of "fire," for example, and mine "wood" he continued, "the astrologer could have foreseen marital incompatibility because the astrological charts would show that 'fire consumes wood.' And if her birth year animal had been 'Monkey' and mine 'Boar,' the charts would have shown that 'the Boar and the Monkey are soon parted'."

"Apparently, since you have set the wedding date, your respective Eight Characters must have been mutually compatible," noted Paul.

"Yes, thank goodness, laughed James, "and the astrologer is giving each of us a signed formal red and gold 'Eight Characters Certificate' stating that fact. We will display these at our wedding ceremony."

"It's all so silly!" snorted Daddy. "Since no official government records are kept of births, marriages or deaths anywhere in China, the only records are what families or individuals keep. Since these astrological charts can be purchased on nearly every street corner, if you figure out that yours and Bright Jade's birth years show incompatibility, you can just fake yours and give the astrologer a birth year that is compatible with hers! Neither

Bright Jade, the astrologer or Mr. Chu would have known the difference!"

"But the spirits of the family ancestors on both sides, who always know when people are trying to fool the gods, would know; and they could create much future marital unhappiness!" angrily snapped Grandmother.

"All is well in this case, however," James reassured her, soothingly. "Our 'Eight Character Certificates are all in order, Bright Jade and I are relieved that no problems cropped up, and, best of all – the Chu's are satisfied!"

Some time after mid-April, as the May 7 wedding date drew ever closer, James' nervous tension increased – there were so many details to be taken care of, which he, as groom was responsible for. Daddy would shoulder the costs involved, and was watching them like a hawk!

While betrothal and wedding customs varied somewhat throughout China, in cities especially, nearly all weddings at the time took place in large restaurants, which specialized in such affairs and had professional staffs to handle all details. In this case it was the well-known Double Happiness Restaurant which, ten days before the event, sent out colorful red and gold boxes of "Dragon and Phoenix" cakes as invitations.

These cakes, symbolizing a happy married life, along with a notice of date, place and time, were sent to heads of families of invited relatives and friends. The invitation covered all members of the invited family, including children of all ages. Over 400 guests were expected at this wedding. The head of each such family was expected to bring a "gift" of money in a red envelope which would be handed to Paul or me as they entered the hall. Hopefully, this cash gift would at least cover banquet costs for all attending members of that family.

Three days before the wedding Bright Jade fell under the laughing, prankish attendance of four of her unmarried best girl-friends, who stayed constantly with her, at the Chu home, until she left her parent's home for the wedding ceremony. During this time she was given a light reading "for ladies only" book, with large, colorful, graphically lurid illustrations (obviously painted by a male artist with a Huge Ego), intended to help prepare her for certain wifely responsibilities! After she and her girlfriends gasped and giggled their way through that, she had the obligation of passing it along, in due course, to the next bride-to-be of her acquaintance.

The day before the wedding, Bright Jade, and her mother came to visit Grandmother at our Yang Peach Blossom Lane mansion, and presented her "Bride's Dowry." This consisted of her jewelry and other personal items, new clothing and bedding and $1,000 cash. Since, after marriage, Bright Jade would become an integral part of our Yang family, this cash dowry gift would be turned over to James as head of their household.

Another special, traditional item accompanied her on this visit. It was a brand new, old-fashioned style red wooden chamber pot, or "Thunder Mug;" not needed in our mansion which had modern plumbing, but a traditional "necessity" still in countless Chinese homes of the day. It was filled with a mixture of dyed red eggs and pomegranates – age-old symbols of fertility!

Grandmother accepted the dowry on behalf of our family, and showed them the middle-level apartment of our mansion, where the couple would make their home. James had purchased new furniture for their two bedrooms with connecting bath. For the time being Paul would continue to occupy James' old laboratory room on that floor as his bedroom. Bright Jade would be bringing her own cook/maid to serve James and her. With all these formalities completed – it was time to proceed with the Main Event – the wedding itself!

Shortly before 6:30 p.m. on the appointed "Lucky Day," the guests started pouring into the restaurant's large wedding/banquet hall; seating themselves in family groups as they wished at one of the 40 ten-person round tables. Paul and I greeted them at the door and accepted their red envelope "gifts."

Daddy, James, Grandmother, and certain members of the Chu family circulated around greeting guests, who cheerfully cracked watermelon seeds from bowls-full of them on the table, and sipped cups of hot tea served by waiters as they greeted one another and loudly gossiped away.

Lady guests were attired in their best silken chong sams, and bedecked with their most glittering gold jewelry. Most of the men were wearing western-style business suits; the rest long dark Chinese gowns.

The large hall, cheerfully decorated in red and gold (the colors of Good Luck) featured a large altar or dais at one end, underneath a large red and gold, table-size calligraphy sign saying "Double Happiness." Two large, fat red candles were on the dais, one at each end, with a container of tall burning incense sticks in the middle. Large red, with gold written inscriptions, ancestral tablets stood upright between incense and candles: the Yang family ones' on the left, the Chu family ones' on the right. The astrologer-signed "Eight Characters Certificate" for bride and groom rested flat underneath their respective family ancestral tablets.

On a red-cloth covered small table in front of the dais was an open red and gold Marriage Registration Book, with an ink dish and brush positioned close by.

Promptly at 7:00 p.m. the "Most Auspicious Time" of the preset "Lucky Day," a huge gong was sounded, and a professional restaurant-supplied Master of Ceremonies, standing to the left of the dais, loudly proclaimed: "The wedding will begin."

James, as Groom, first took his position in front of the dais, his Best Man to his left. Both were dressed in formal long black Chinese gowns, over which was worn a waist length satin brocade jacket. Each wore a traditional black satin skull cap.

Once they were in place, the Bride, accompanied by two beautifully pink-garbed bridesmaids, appeared from a nearby private anteroom where they had been waiting in seclusion. Bright Jade was attired in an expensive, rented, beautifully embroidered, red and gold traditional wedding gown, over which she wore an also beautifully embroidered short red satin jacket. She also wore an elaborate pearl-encrusted red and gold tiara on her head, over which flowed a shoulder-length red veil which covered her face.

Around her neck, along with beautiful jewelry, was a small mirror on a chain – to ward off any approaching evil spirits – who according to tradition are always frightened away at the sight of their own image!

Moving into place next to the groom, guided by the two bridesmaids to her right, she and James solemnly stood facing the dais. A black satin brocade dressed elderly lady, her head and face covered in a red veil, then appeared to the right of, and back of the dais. A professional chanter provided by the restaurant, she launched into a loud, fairly lengthy incantation of "advice" as to how married women should properly behave. Nothing about men!

Upon signal from the Master of ceremonies, Bright Jade's two bridesmaids then stepped over to lift the veil from her face. Then, upon another signal, the Bride and Groom stepped forward and signed the Marriage Registration Book; James first.

Completing the signing, the couple turned, holding hands, and smilingly faced the roomful of guests, who clapped and cheered them for several minutes. That was it – the wedding ceremony was over – they were now husband and wife!

Now it was time for the banquet; a lengthy affair, beginning with eight cold dishes, comparable to western hors d'oeuvres, which had been preset out on each table. This was followed first by the restaurant's bird's nest soup specialty, then nine assorted hot dishes cooked in various ways. These consisted mostly of chicken, pork, duck, prawns and mushrooms; very few vegetable dishes. All this was constantly being washed down with never ending pouring of beer, the famous Shaoshing wine, Hennessy Four Star brandy, soft drinks and tea.

As this went on, the newly married couple made the rounds to greet guests at each table, to thank them for coming, and to receive the celebrants' loud, alcoholic toasts. The aim of the guests clearly was to get the couple as "tiddily" as they could, as fast as they could! During this time, Daddy and Grandmother, and Mr. and Mrs. Chu also moved happily around among the guests, also accepting liquid toasts. They would all eat later, if they were still up to it!

Following the serving of bowls of expensive shark's fin soup, and platters of mushrooms and prawns or other such dishes at each table, came a huge, whole, sweet and sour fish (carp in this case) on a huge serving plate.

To top it all off, as dessert, guests were offered cold, sweet Lotus Seed soup, fresh Lichees and sliced oranges.

Finally, after the big gong signaled an end to the banquet, Bright Jade and her parents stood before the dais facing the guests. The daughter then briefly bowed three times in formal farewell to her parents. The guests, who had all stood up at the sound of the gong, again clapped after this formal farewell was completed.

With the wedding now over, guests could stay and play mah-jongg, keep drinking and visiting or depart for home – their choice!

Many guests followed the newly married couple outside to the front of the restaurant where a red and gold gaily decorated rented car waited to take them back to our Peach Blossom Lane Mansion.

On the back seat of the car, as they entered, was another mirror, lying flat, face up – to frighten away any evil spirits who might try and slip into the mansion with them.

Paul rode back with them in the front seat; going only as far the mansion's front entranceway where he led Ah Foo, Silver Lotus and the maids in a noisy, welcoming burst of firecrackers. He then departed to spend the night with Suzie and Logan.

Alone in their newly furnished rooms, with the entire second level apartment to themselves, the newlyweds spent their honeymoon night.

Long observed ancient Chinese tradition called for new brides to hang their wedding-night under-panties above the closed bedroom door early the next morning following the couple's first honeymoon night together.

It was then the responsibility of the mother-in-law, or in this case Grandmother, to check them for expected "Virgin's bloodstains."

Did Bright Jade follow this tradition?

Did Grandmother check to find out?

If she did, what did she find?

Grandmother wouldn't say the next day, when we jokingly asked her!

But as she smiled the biggest smile I had ever seen her flash – knowingly and toothily – I couldn't help noticing, for the first time ever, that she had only half the original teeth left in her aging head!

Chapter 14

A CONCUBINE'S LAMENT AND IT'S OFF TO IRELAND!

It was still relatively quiet on the cross streets below that early Sunday morning in mid-May as I stood alone gazing down from my vantage spot atop two story Aurora Primary School.

It was 8:30 a.m. on this cool, sunny 1948 year of the Lord day, to be exact. I had just finished participating at morning Mass as one of the choir "songbirds," in Sacred Heart Convent chapel, and was mulling over the surprising words that Mother Duff had spoken to me immediately following the service.

"I've been working for you, Bessie!" she said. "I've been corresponding with the Mothers of our Sacred Heart Order in Dublin, Ireland to see if they can arrange a music scholarship for you. It looks promising – free room and board at their convent house, and tuition paid! But you will have to pay your own transportation costs to Dublin, and take care of your own personal expense needs while there."

"Are you interested?" she asked, her kindly Irish face wreathed in smiles.

"If so, after thinking about it carefully, try and let me know following school assembly next Saturday so I can arrange for a firm written acceptance from them. You will need that in order to apply for travel documents and for purchasing airline tickets.

"I..., I am so surprised that I don't know what to say, Mother Duff!" I stammered in reply. "You Mothers have all been so good and kind to me during the nearly three years now that I've been a student here at Aurora Middle School, that to have you even think of an opportunity like that for me is almost beyond belief.

Thank you – so much," I continued, "but what did I ever do to deserve such consideration?"

"Reverend Mother Fitzgerald, our Mother Superior, Mother d'Huart your music teacher, Mother Bernard our chapel organist, Mother Thornton, Dean of Aurora College, Mother Loh, Principal of your Aurora Middle School and myself have long been aware of your natural vocal talent," she explained.

"We have all been observing you carefully since you first joined our choir in the spring of 1946, and have been impressed by your willingness to spend your Sunday mornings as a member of it, which you weren't obligated to do.

And, of course, we are all pleased that you are one of the relatively few students to have freely elected to take instruction from Mother d'Huart and be baptized in our Catholic faith.

Our conclusion is," she went on, "that you deserve the opportunity to develop your natural talent at a level beyond what is currently available in Shanghai, especially considering the terrible civil war that is about to engulf us here anytime now. We all hope that you will say 'yes' to this really splendid opportunity."

"You are all so kind," I said to her, "I will talk it over with my family, and will, of course, let you know by next Saturday."

As I looked down on the leafy Sycamore tree bordered intersection streets that lined the north and west sides of the one complete block in size Aurora College complex, I couldn't help thinking how much Shanghai had changed since the end of World War II, seemingly such a short time back.

"Just consider these two streets below me, " I mused to myself. "When I started school here in September, 1945 they had French names; Rue Bourgeat here on the north side, running east and west. And Rte Soeurs here on the west side, running north and south. Now, these streets and all others in the old French Concession that had French names now bear Chinese names! But I don't even know most of their new names!

The Nationalists did that; they changed all the old English and French street names in both the former International Settlement and the French Concession, and anywhere else they could find them in Shanghai, to Chinese names – back in early 1946. They retained the same names of those streets that bore Chinese names.

The problem is that they have put up so few new Chinese name street signs since that most people don't know the new names, and continue to call them by their old foreign names. Things used to be so orderly and well run in those two areas – but not any more. The confused street names scene here now is crazy!

"And street traffic now moves in right side lanes, as in America, rather than the old British style left lanes," I giggled to myself. That change, was brought about by the great number of accidents caused by left side drive wartime American-supplied trucks driven by traditionally right side drive oriented Chinese drivers on the Burma Road and in Chungking.

The British hated the idea of that change since they realized it would kill postwar sales to China of their manufacturer's right side drive automobiles. Their British Consulate-General here in Shanghai in late 1945 tried desperately to stop it from happening, by secretly leaking inflammatory stories to the Chinese language media that such a change would cause all of China's ancestral spirits to rise from their graves in anguished confusion! Chiang Kai-shek ignored that dire prediction and simply ordered the switch over as of midnight December 31, 1945.

"Unfortunately," I chuckled to myself as I looked at the two streets below "some Chinese still seem confused; when in doubt, seemingly, their solution often is – stay in the middle to be on the safe side! Look how some head right into each other from opposite directions!"

As my thoughts returned to my conversation with Mother Duff, I realized how she, Reverend Mother Fitzgerald and the other nuns had become so aware of my singing, although I had never realized that they had been paying such close attention to it.

I had joined the small twelve-person chapel choir during the spring term of my first year there, and enjoyed singing the Latin religious church music so much that I sang at Sunday mass as well as on special feast days during the week as choir soloist.

The organ, played by Mother Bernard; and our mixed choir of students and nuns, was placed at the back left side of the beautiful small convent chapel. The four highest ranking nuns of the order knelt on their individual priedieu just in front of and slightly to the right of our choir. There they constantly heard me singing – as part of the choir and my solos. Fortunately, I had both the wide range of pitch and good ear that always allowed me to hit high notes in tune. This enabled me to sing high soprano solo parts that no one else then in our choir could do. The nuns' favorite was my rendition of Bach/Gounod's "Ave Maria."

"All that is well and good," I thought to myself, "but this kind of singing is small time; something I've viewed only as a fun recreational activity, because I enjoy it. Am I really good enough to study singing seriously. Do I even want to study music seriously?"

Some sort of decision had to be made soon, I realized, because, at age 18, I would be graduating from Aurora's high school in just over four weeks.

This Ireland opportunity would now force that decision!

"Since I've promised to give Mother Duff an answer by next Saturday afternoon," I said aloud, to no one in particular, as I headed toward the stairwell leading to the ground level below, "I'd better seek the advice of some of my family members, without delay."

Fortunately, this was the Sunday of a long planned restaurant early afternoon "middle meal" (lunch) out with Suzie, Logan, Betty and her husband T.K., just married the previous year, and Ruth and Paul, recent February newlyweds.

"They will help me decide!"

As my rickshaw headed toward the restaurant for our 1:00 p.m. rendezvous, I couldn't help noticing that the streets and sidewalks were even more crowded than during the worst war years. I had heard that Shanghai was literally being swamped with refugees from the ever-widening civil war; today I could believe it!

The sidewalks this day seemed especially crowded with improvised stalls – most of them selling black market American relief goods – canned foodstuffs, medical and pharmaceutical supplies, U.S. military field rations, imported liquors and cigarettes and luxury goods of all types. I even saw American Red Cross blood plasma, donated to help save the lives of wounded Nationalist soldiers, being freely offered for sale.

The sidewalks in some cases were so crowded with these stalls and individual "hawkers" of black market items, many offering prices far cheaper than stores back in the United States itself, that pedestrians had to walk out in the street to get around them.

Street traffic was so packed with slow-moving masses of pedestrians and vehicles of every description that it sometimes slowly sputtered down into confused, congested motionless gridlock. Few police were in sight; those that were around appeared more interested in extracting "squeeze" from hapless passersby than in crowd or traffic control.

After all this traffic and confusion I was more than happy to disembark at the restaurant. There, however, I had to elbow my way through a thick entranceway crowd of pushing, shoving, loudly talking, without reservations would be diners. Finally, I reached our reserved table where Ruth and Paul were "holding the fort" for our group.

It was a happy "longtime no see" reunion with them, since we had not met following their recent wedding at American Community Church (Protestant) located on what was formerly Avenue Petain near the American School.

As Suzie and Logan and Betty and T.K. joined us, we all started trying to kid the newlyweds into telling us how they liked married life! Paul loved this type of repartee, and the fact that his quite religious Ruth found the subject so embarrassing that her smiling face frequently flushed a deep red. We, of course, complimented her on this "new fashion look," to her further embarrassment – and more flushes!

As we looked over the menus prior to ordering, Paul cheerfully announced: "You can't embarrass us – we are simply too happy today to be bothered by your jokes and comments about our new wedded bliss! We have just been given a nice place to live – and have already moved in – yesterday as a matter of fact. So there!"

"Where is your new residence? How did you get it? Will it be a permanent location?" The questions poured from the lips of all the rest of us, because this news came as a complete surprise!

As he and Ruth beamed, he told us that Daddy had just given them full use of his own ground level apartment at our family Peach Blossom Lane mansion.

"And more news!" he continued. "Ah Foo is retiring, to live with members of her family in the small town of Wujiang, near Soochow; and Mei Ling is leaving to marry a nice young employee of Dong Shing Cotton Mill here in Shanghai."

"My, my – so many changes all at once!" I gasped.

"That means that each Yang brother has your own apartment on a different level of the mansion with your own kitchen, and cook/maid!" commented Suzie.

"Yes, yes, that's correct," laughed Paul – "and we three sons plan to eventually fill the whole place with lots of Yang grandchildren for Daddy, and nieces and nephews for all of you!" Ruth's face once again flushed bright red!

"In the meantime, it seems that I will have a choice of bedrooms in which to stay during my free Saturday nights away from Aurora," I chimed in, as we all laughed and clapped over their good fortune, and at the very idea of a whole mansionful of yet to come nieces and nephews.

"But what about Dya-Dya and Auntie Silver Lotus? Where are they going to live?" questioned Betty. "They've already moved – last Thursday as a matter of fact," replied Paul, "into an apartment he owns over on Foo Chow Road, across the street from and a block west of Lester Hospital. That's within easy walking distance of his Standard Oil office and the Bund, which is only two blocks further east. It's really a convenient location for him.

Our second maid from home, Lu Fong, who has been trained by Ah Foo as a cook, moved there with them to serve as their combination maid/cook.

"What will happen to Grandmother? Will she continue to live at Peach Blossom Lane?" asked Suzie.

"She's already moved in with our Auntie Dr. Nyang Nyang, who has room for her now that her own recently married daughter Dorothy has moved to Taiwan with her husband. Grandmother seems very happy with her new living arrangement," he answered.

As we ordered our food, we continued to express both our surprise and pleasure at all this exciting news.

During our meal, I abruptly asked for their attention.

"I also have some unexpected news to impart," I then announced – "concerning which I need your immediate collective advice."

After describing Mother Duff's surprising Ireland music scholarship offer, I stressed that I had to give her my decision the following Saturday. I then asked for their individual opinions as to whether or not I should accept her offer.

Paul was the first to respond. "We know that Dya-Dya has always wanted each of us to become medical doctors. I attended Tung De medical college's premed course, but didn't like medicine. I prefer the business world. He probably will try to talk you into attending Tung De as well. But since you've always enjoyed music so much, I think you should grab this unique opportunity to study music in Ireland."

"I agree with Paul," said Betty, "I too stuck it out at Tung De for two years at Daddy's insistence, but just didn't like all the blood and gore, and being around sick or injured people. I really wanted to continue studying piano at the conservatory, but it's impossible to earn a good living here in Shanghai at that.

I solved my career problem by marrying this handsome young man," patting the arm of a grinning T.K., "because I fell in love with his big old blue Harley Davidson motorcycle!" she smiled broadly, as T.K. groaned in mock disgust. "You must go to Ireland!" she said firmly.

"Both Betty and I would love to be matchmakers and marry you off to some rich and handsome young local boy," said Suzie, "but I enjoyed travelling to Chungking, Kunming and New Delhi with Logan so much, that I think you should see Ireland and other parts of the world before simply getting married and hatching babies!"

Ruth, who had returned only a few months earlier from a year's study in America at Westmont College in Santa Barbara, California, also agreed that I should study abroad;" at least for awhile, before marrying and settling down."

"There is one other very important factor to consider," said Logan, the most mature among us, who had, up to this point, had said little while listening carefully.

"There is the very strong possibility that the Communists will soon seize control not only of Shanghai, but of our entire country! If so, who knows what will happen! You, alone among us, are being given a rare opportunity to get out of China before that happens. I say, go, go, go – tomorrow if possible!"

Totally surprised by his statement, as we peeled the skin from after dinner quartered fresh oranges, and ordered fresh hot refills of our table teapots, we anxiously asked him to elaborate.

"First of all, I must tell you that I have just sent in my letter of resignation from the army!" Logan began.

We all gasped in astonishment at this sudden move, for none of us except Suzie, of course, had any idea he was even contemplating such action.

"Why?" asked Paul, with a perplexed look on his face.

"First because my usefulness to the army in serving as an Interpreter/Liaison officer to the Americans has steadily lost real meaning," Logan replied. "That started back in April, 1946 when General Wedemeyer returned to America following disbanding of the China Theatre of Operations and the rapid demobilization and return to the states of most American army personnel in China. After that, I usefully assisted the Americans with their speedy repatriation back to Japan of nearly 3.5 million Japanese troops and civilians, and the repatriation overseas of remaining allied POWs and civilian internees, nearly all the Hongkew ghetto Jewish residents, and even many stateless White Russians.

"For the past several months however," he continued, "I've held only a routine liaison staff position with U.S. Navy headquarters at the Port of Shanghai. My job, as part of a logistical group, is to help speed turnover of incoming American and UNRRA (United Nations Relief and Rehabilitation Administration) relief supplies at the docks to the all Chinese CNRRA (Chinese National Relief and Rehabilitation Administration) organization. By agreement between China and the U.S., that is the only organization allowed to distribute the massive American and other international foreign aid within China."

"That sounds like a pretty good, relatively easy and secure position," laughed T.K. "Can't you stick it out until they promote you to General?"

"No chance of that," replied Logan "the corrupt generals and civilian bureaucrats, friends mostly of higher-ups in the Kuomintang Party, currently running CNRRA don't trust me. Remember, I've been an interpreter liaison officer to top American generals since April 1942. They probably think I'm a spy for the Americans. With the few remaining U.S. Navy and Army Air Corps personnel now in China, including the navy headquarters I mentioned, due to leave China completely within the next six months, the Chinese side has no further use for me.

I've seen such massive theft and corruption by the Kuomintang appointed crooks and constant pilferage at every downward level on the docks, that I simply can't take it any more. There's no room for an honest colonel in the army here in Shanghai any longer – I'm getting out! Besides, feeling that I know too much about their activities, some of these people might decide to imprison or even kill me at any time. The situation is that bad!"

He had said this with such a serious look on his face and bitterness in his voice that we collectively once again gasped with astonishment and disbelief!

"The continued rampant inflation in Shanghai has really gotten out of hand," angrily spoke T.K., chief accountant of a large cotton mill in the northern section of the city. "Ordinary salaried factory and white collar working people just can't keep up with the almost daily cost increases of food and rent. If the government doesn't get this situation under control soon, our mill workers may rise up in revolt. Many are already members of the Communist underground."

"How can the Kuomintang government control things when they simply keep printing new money in ever larger denominations?" interrupted Paul. "Do you realize that today's conversion rate in the street is one million Yuan to the U.S. dollar! It will take a huge wad of large denomination Yuan paper bills just to pay for our today's meal!

I made money when I sold my charcoal briquette manufacturing business last year," he added, but due to the constant rise in inflation have lost much of the profit since. My supposedly high pay salaried position, as Manager of Tien Dong Flour Mill on North Honan Road is barely enough to cover our personal cost of living these days.

It's been worth it," laughed Ruth, "since you come home much cleaner evenings than before! White flour beats black charcoal dust at the evening dinner table anytime!"

As everyone laughed at that, Betty asked Logan to update us on the current civil war political and military situation – "which you apparently think is pretty serious!"

"Do you remember that Christmas Eve of 1945 when I went out to the airport as part of General Wedemeyer's staff entourage to greet General George C. Marshall, America's top military officer, on his first visit to China?" asked Logan.

"Well, as you know, he was sent as special emissary to try and bring the Nationalists and Communists together in hopes of their finding a peaceful solution to China's political problems. For awhile, in early 1946, the two sides did seem to honestly be trying to work together, as they had during 1938-40, and the general went back to America to report this to his President.

But in Chungking, during his absence, negotiations quickly fell apart. Chiang Kai-shek, maintaining that the Kuomintang Party was China, insisted that his party handpick and appoint (not elect) all government officials throughout China, down to municipal magistrate level. He expected the Communists to disband and join in on that plan, in "hopes" that the Kuomintang would appoint a fair percent of Communists to these offices. That arrangement, of course, would have given him total military and political control of all China.

While that would have been a good deal for Chiang, the Communists reasoned that it would be a death-knell deal for them! Instead, claiming to represent a regular army of nearly one million, plus two million more militia troops, and firm control of long-held areas with a population of over 90 million, they insisted on equal participation in a new democratically elected government. Chiang decided that this wasn't a good deal for him!

General Marshall flew back to China in April to try and save the situation, but by that time it was too late. He was furious to learn that Chiang smugly felt that the Americans, who had helped rush his troops to North and Central China at war's end, and had freely supplied him, without any required accountability, with lavish amounts of war material and relief supplies ever since, had no choice except to continue fully backing him.

The Communists felt, as a result of all this aid that the U.S. was totally and unfairly in the Kuomintang's camp! Thus both Chinese sides ignoring Marshall, dug in their heels, and commenced trying to gain by war what they were not willing to try obtaining by peaceful negotiation."

"In August of 1946," Logan continued, "the U.S. imposed an arms embargo to try and force new negotiations. That didn't work either, so in January 1947 General Marshall, denouncing the intransigence on both sides, flew back to Washington to become the new Secretary of State. From then on, the United States basically washed its hands of China."

"What is the actual military situation in China's civil war right now?" asked Paul.

"The top American navy people left here in Shanghai tell me that the Communists, with an active army of around 1.2 million are now winning major battles nearly everywhere," answered Logan. "They now control Manchuria and most of North China, and large areas of Central and South China where their land reforms have met with great popular approval. Their army's morale is high, say the Americans, and in all the areas they occupy they enjoy active support of the peasants and even many landlords.

The Nationalists, on the other hand, they say, with a much larger force of 2.7 million, but widely spread and in defensive positions, are plagued by heavy desertions, low morale, often inefficient and corrupt leadership and lack of cooperation to outright hostility from the masses.

Since I don't trust anything local Nationalist army commanders say, I assume that the Americans are right, and that it will most likely only be a matter of time before the Communists are victorious everywhere.

What their victory, if it does come, will mean to us in Shanghai, I can't even begin to guess," concluded Logan, shaking his head sadly.

The following Saturday, after morning assembly, Mother Duff, the Vice-Reverend Mother of Sacred Heart Convent, and I met together privately as scheduled earlier in the week. After discussing my desire to accept the scholarship offer, she gave me a handwritten note to deliver to Daddy, inviting him to visit her at a given date and time the following week in the convent reception room. We agreed not to tell him the purpose of the meeting in advance.

When he and I arrived there together at the appointed time, we were greeted by Mother Duff, Mother d'Huart and Mother Loh (a Shanghai born nun), all quite impressive looking in their all black habits with black head veils.

They explained the scholarship offer, why they felt I deserved it and how its offer was a tribute to him as my father. They further made clear that my room, board and tuition for at least a three-year period of study in Ireland would be at their order's expense, with no strings attached.

"What we need from you, Mr. Yang," said Mother Duff, is your permission for her to go, a one-way prepaid airline ticket, and whatever personal expense money you wish to provide her."

I could almost hear the wheels turning in his head as he considered the financial pros and cons of the proposal! As he thought silently for several seconds, he nervously scratched the foot on his crossed leg. I chuckled inwardly at that since my Aurora school friends Inez and Agnes and I had just been talking the other day about the fact that Chinese men usually do just that when nervous or puzzled, whereas European or American men normally scratch their head.

Quickly concluding that it would be cheaper to buy me a one-time, one-way airline ticket to Ireland than having to possibly pay for two years Tung De premed school tuition, and risk my then quitting medicine like Paul and Betty, or having to pay unknown costs plus dowry to get me married off locally, he made an on-the-spot "yes, she can go," decision.

The nuns showed such elation that he swelled with pride at their profuse compliments, concerning him personally as well as his talented daughter!

He even got so puffed up with magnanimity during their (quite calculated) "Praise of Him" period that he promised to personally arrange all my ticket and passport formalities through "highly placed friends!"

The next four weeks, prior to my graduation passed so quickly that details seemed blurred. First came final exams, followed by long girl-type discussions about post-graduation plans and life in general with Inez, Agnes and other classmates.

Then, just a few days before graduation day came the sad message from Auntie Nyang Nyang that Grandmother, age 81, had unexpectedly just passed away quietly in her sleep the night before. This came as a surprise to everyone in our family since, considering her age, she had seemed healthy enough. We were delighted however, that her end had come so peacefully without any lingering, painful illness.

Her funeral service held the day before my high school graduation was a traditional Buddhist affair confined to family members and a handful of old friends. Twenty-four days later, as decreed by a Fung Sui Astrologer, she was laid to rest near Mother in the Yang family section of Wing On cemetery.

By most later accounts, the decisive turning point in China's civil war came during that summer of 1948 when, for the first time, large Communist forces starting defeating larger Nationalist forces in major battles.

In an effort to stem slumping civilian morale, the central government in August introduced a new currency, the "Gold Yuan" to replace the old Yuan notes, which by this time were selling at the massively inflated street rate of 12-million Yuan to the U.S. dollar.

Great efforts were made to force people to turn in any hidden gold or U.S. dollars in exchange for this new currency, which the government insisted was backed up by Central Bank held gold and U.S. dollar reserves. No receipts for the turned in gold or dollars were issued however, and a rumor soon spread that 12 tons of government gold and treasure had secretly been flown to Taiwan. Within three months the black market started up again full blast. Citizens who had cooperated and thus lost their savings now lost all trust in the central government.

Fortunately, Daddy had purchased my airline ticket to Ireland during the short time this currency reform held, so we were set there. All we needed now was my passport. The acceptance letter from Ireland had come, passport photos taken, and the application sent to the capital in Nanking. All we could do now was wait!

The cooler air of autumn brought with it increased social outings and activities with family, relatives and friends. Most of my social life the past three years as an Aurora boarder-student had been limited to Saturday night activities.

As it had been for much of my life, Auntie Nyang Nyang's home was the usual social gathering spot for cousins and friends of my age group. Daddy had always discouraged such gatherings at our mansion, due both to his concubines and his self-centered, basically inhospitable personality, while Mother had usually been too ill to protest. Fortunately, Auntie Nyang Nyang had always welcomed Betty, Paul and me. Now, even more than in the past years, knowing that I would soon be departing for Ireland, I enjoyed the social activities centered there.

Our usually good-sized gatherings of young people enjoyed mixed group card games, making hand-turned freezer ice cream, roller-skating and bicycle riding. There was never any dancing at these home gatherings. While we girls' sometimes joined to fold wontons or dumplings, we never did any cooking, or cleaned up after anything – the maids took care of all that! We frequently went out in groups to see the latest movies, especially American ones.

Our dancing and out in public socializing was largely confined to going out in mixed groups to one of the big close by night clubs or dance halls that catered to young people like us. There, as we drank tea or soft drinks, or ate ice cream, we would take turns on the dance floor, to the sound of live dance bands, learning and practicing the latest steps.

It was quite common in these clubs to invite people from the audience up to the stage to sing. I did this often, usually singing, to the accompaniment of the band, modern Chinese popular songs like "Yeh Lai Shan," which was about a sweetly smelling flower that blooms only at night. It, like many of the popular Chinese songs of the day, was played and sung in rumba time.

I also was often called upon to sing American or English dance songs, such as the waltz-step "One Day When We Were Young," a favorite of the famous at the time American singer Jeannette McDonald. And I was often cheered on by my friends, and the rest of the club crowd, to entertain them with non-dancing popular songs such as "Ah, Sweet Mystery of Life," and "Song of Songs." I loved to sing, and was not at all shy about performing before such groups – large or small.

It was at social gatherings like these that girls met boys, and boys met girls! Matchmaking was a popular female pastime, especially so among the younger recently married ones in our social group like Suzie, Betty and Ruth. They and other "matchmakers" were stimulated to action by the age-old Chinese saying: "for every marriage you bring together, you get a higher place in heaven." Based on this they each reasoned, the more matches I can make – the higher will be my standing in heaven! Most often, for me at least, their efforts to get me "matched up" were a pain in the neck!

January 1949 turned out to be a very busy month indeed, both for me personally and for China as a nation. With my new passport in hand and Pan-American Airways ticket purchased, I was firmly booked for departure to Ireland February 19. Things were moving smoothly for me.

The "ride" that month was much bumpier for China the nation – especially for the rapidly disintegrating Kuomintang government! Tientsin, the last Nationalist stronghold in North China fell January 15. Peking surrendered peacefully on my 19th birthday (January 23) to cheering Communist troops riding in on some 1,000 "hardly used" American-donated military trucks recently captured from fast-surrendering Nationalist forces. As Chiang Kai-shek "retiring temporarily" as President of the Republic of China, fled to Taiwan, the United States continued its policy of non-involvement.

It was Betty, Daddy's favorite among all his girls, who came up with the idea of combining a family farewell party for me with a Big 60th celebration for him. Since his 60th birthday was due to fall in late February, the idea made sense, provided that all the other siblings would agree.

The 21st and 60th birthdays of Chinese men are special milestone years in life; traditionally rating special celebration and homage. Unfortunately, while he had always "done his duty" toward us, such as providing a good education, everything he did was basically on his terms and timing. Our individual wishes were seldom invited or considered.

And his handouts were most often presented in such a begrudging, often verbally abusive manner, that we felt "unworthy" for causing him so much trouble and expense. When any of us had tried to do something nice or thoughtful for him, from our hearts and without ulterior motive, his reaction nearly always was a suspicious "why are you doing this? What do you want from me?" After repeated such rebuffs we had over time quit trying. We felt that he had the basic personality problem of being simply unable or unwilling to show or accept affection or kindness. Thus none of the rest of us had even thought of such a celebration for him.

Since each of us basically did appreciate all that he had done for us over the years however, we all said "yes" to Betty's idea – and looked forward to the pleasure we hoped he would feel as a result.

Two days prior to that planned event, I dropped by his apartment, where I had a Saturday night bedroom and storage space always at my disposal, to pack the two suitcases I would be taking to Ireland. He was at work, Lu Fong the maid was out shopping – only Concubine Silver Lotus was there. As she sat on the bed quietly helping me fold some clothing items for packing, she suddenly burst into tears.

"What on earth is the matter, Auntie Silver Lotus?" I asked, standing up and putting my hand on her shoulder to comfort her.

"Oh, Shiao Bei," she sobbed, "I can hardly bear to see you leave! Although you don't know it, you have always secretly been, in my heart, like a daughter to me – the daughter I could never have! I was just 19, like you now, when your father brought me into your family home. Just six months later you were born, and through the years, as you grew up, I pretended that you were partly mine!"

"What can I say to her?" I thought to myself! As a child I spent a lot of time with her and she played with me just like my own mother did. But I never thought of her in mother-like terms; she was simply "Auntie." As I grew older I realized that as a concubine, she was the cause of much of mother's unhappiness and started to keep more of an impersonal distance between us. "But I've got to say 'something' comforting now, so here goes:"

"Oh, Auntie," I whispered, "you know that Betty, Paul and me especially have always regarded you as an older sister and part of our family. I know you far better, for example, than my own older sister Nellie!"

"You have all been so kind to me over the years," she tearfully lamented, "but I am not, and never could be, a Yang family member. I'm just a lonely concubine – unable to attend your Grandmother's funeral, Betty and Paul's weddings – or even your upcoming farewell party. I just have to stay here, by myself and wait for your father to come home at his pleasure!"

That's true enough – up to a point, I reflected, but she shrewdly protected her own interests over the years, to the point that all us Yang children had to constantly be on guard against her. We had all learned early on that she was a potentially unfriendly spy in our midst who immediately reported everything that went on in the house to Daddy.

It was a simple matter of survival for all of us – so dependent were each of us on him! She had to compete with us for his attention, and we all tried to "use" one another to mutual advantage. She does have a point, though; she leads a very lonely life, and I do feel sorry for her.

"But, he's so fond of you," I answered soothingly.

"Yes, I can't complain about that; he's never beaten me or physically mistreated me, but he is not an affectionate person, and no matter how hard I try to please him, I always feel so empty in my heart.

He never takes me anywhere with him, and I am always alone in this new apartment, except for his company or that of the maid. When he is away, I am so blind that I can't read, do knitting or any kind of handicraft or ever go out alone except with Lu Fong. None of the children except you ever come to see me or pay any attention to me.

With no family or friends to go to, what will I do if he gets tired of me?" Tears streamed from her eyes and down her cheeks.

"Oh, he would never send you away!" I cried out in anguish.

"Maybe not, but what if he brings a another concubine home? He did it once before, with Second Concubine Ching!" She was now sobbing so hard that her whole body shook.

"What can I say to comfort her?" I thought sadly to myself.

While I had been somewhat skeptical up to this point during her lament, because we children had all somewhat distrusted her for so many years, I suddenly realized that with all of us now gone from her life, what a truly empty, possibly insecure future she now faced.

By tradition in China a concubine is a concubine forever! I knew that Daddy would never marry her, and could bring in a younger concubine at any time, as she feared. Like my mother, she too was a victim of custom and tradition in an age-old male dominated society. It was all so sad!

Just then we heard footsteps in the hallway outside the apartment entrance. Daddy was coming home!

Quickly she jumped to her feet and – frantically drying her eyes with a handkerchief, rushed to open the main door for him.

With a smile on her face, she greeted him: "Shiao Bei is here packing, we were hoping that you would come soon!"

Our family's "Big 60th for Daddy – Farewell for me" dinner went off without a hitch.

Everyone cooperated to make us both feel as appreciated as possible, and expressed their heartfelt best wishes for – "Long Life, Dya-Dya!"; "Bon Voyage, Shiao Bei!"

Early the next morning Betty, Ruth and Paul accompanied me to the airport; the other family members had to work or attend to their children. My ticket and passport checked, my two suitcases weighing in exactly at the 44-pound limit – we said our final good-byes at the departure gate.

"Will I ever see them again?" I tearfully thought to myself as I began the rather long open-air tarmac walk toward my waiting plane.

The February air was quite cold under the overcast sky, and a few snowflakes were drifting down – but I was suddenly starting to perspire under my body-covering padded chong sam; over which was a long, heavy woolen coat; and over it my new "going away present", a long fashionable with large shoulder pads, Chinese mink coat!

Ireland was cold, Mother Duff had told me, and since I couldn't pack them – I wore them all!

As I half-turned to wave a last goodbye to my two sisters and brother, I almost tipped over! Three years minimum stay in

Ireland was a long time, so I had stuffed everything unable to fit within my skimpy luggage limit, into my (now feeling like 100 pounds) one carry-on bag, heavily filled in part with my favorite personal music albums.

"I may 'evaporate' from wearing all this winter clothing and heavy coats during my plane's hot climate Bangkok, Calcutta and Karachi refueling stops," I muttered to myself – "but at last",

"IT'S OFF TO IRELAND!"

FINIS

EPILOGUE

I arrived in Ireland a week after my February 19, 1949 departure from Shanghai. Approximately three months later, on May 24, Communist troops occupied the city. The Peoples Republic of China was proclaimed in Peking by Mao Tse-tung (Mao Zedong) on October 1, of that year.

Three years later, I completed my studies at Royal Irish Academy of Music and National Academy of Art in Dublin, Ireland. I then went to Japan where for one year I taught as an elementary teacher in Seishin Gakuin (Sacred Heart School), Tokyo. Moving on to Hong Kong, I served for several years as head music teacher at Maryknoll Convent High School in Kowloon. In 1959, I immigrated to the United States as a Catholic refugee.

Having lost all his money and property during the Cultural Revolution, Daddy, who shared his final years in Shanghai with totally blind Concubine Silver Lotus in very distressed circumstances, passed away in 1968. Silver Lotus, assisted by a live-in niece, survived until 1989 when she passed on. My oldest sister Nellie and Suzie's husband Logan also died in Shanghai.

My brother Paul and his wife Ruth settled in the United States, my sister Suzie in Australia. My sister Betty and husband T.K., and my two older brothers Guo Liang and James remained in Shanghai.

Bessie Yang Reid

INDEX OF ROMANIZED CHINESE NAMES AND PLACES APPEARING IN THIS BOOK

Wade-Giles (up to 1/1/79)   Pinyin (after 1/1/79)

(List continued over)

265

Tsingtao	Quingdao
Yangtze	same
Yunnan	same
Whangpoo	Huangpu
Wuhan	same

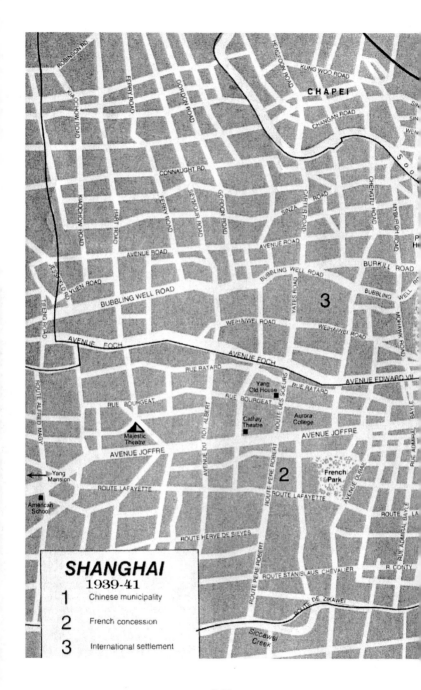

SHANGHAI
1939-41
1 Chinese municipality
2 French concession
3 International settlement

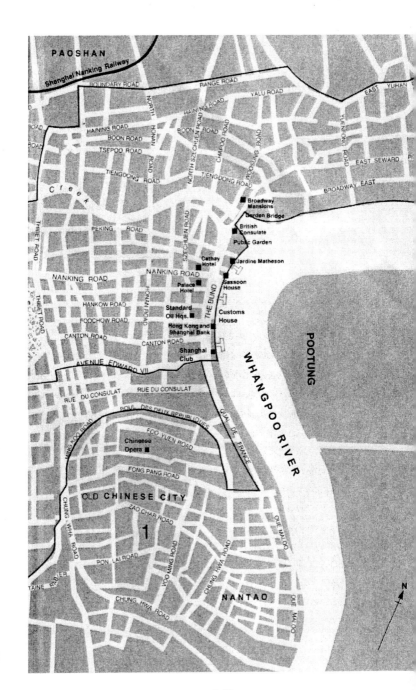